UNDER THE FRANCIS TREE

A Practical Theology for the
Church Grounds in the 21st Century

ERIC HOWELL

Advance Praise for *Under the Francis Tree*

Eric Howell is a remarkable pastor and a good human, and here I've discovered he's also a bold writer. It takes *chutzpah* to weave Baptist ecclesiology with Franciscan spirituality. But the idea of churches, and the few acres we inhabit, being a fulcrum for creation's healing—that's ludicrous. Unless it's true. Eric convinces me it's true, and he's offering us all good news.

—Winn Collier, author of *Love Big, Be Well* and *A Burning in My Bones* and Director of the Eugene Peterson Center for Christian Imagination

Eric Howell has reflected deeply on a Christian congregational response to our ecological crisis, both biblically and theologically. But he has also thought and acted practically, having led a congregation to engage in creation care practices that began on the "holy ground" of their church property and extended into their daily lives in their homes and community. *Under the Francis Tree* is a blessing to all congregations and their leaders who desire to respond authentically to caring for our common home.

—Robert Creech, Professor of Pastor Leadership (retd), Truett Seminary at Baylor University and Secretary-Treasurer of Creech Prairie Restoration

If creation declares the glory of God (and it does) and if creation is currently groaning for its redemption (and it is), then it matters greatly how Christians and the congregations of which they are a part live their creaturely lives in the time between times. *Under the Francis Tree* combines Franciscan spirituality, biblical and theological reflection, ecological awareness, and congregational rootedness to encourage readers to consider more fully the repercussions of Christ's incarnation as well as their personal and ecclesial responsibility to the Creator, creation, and other living creatures.

—Todd D. Still, Charles J. and Eleanor McLerran DeLancey Dean & William M. Hinson Professor of Christian Scriptures, Truett Seminary at Baylor University

Smyth & Helwys Publishing
6316 Peake Road
Macon, Georgia 31210-3960
1-800-747-3016
©2025 by Eric Howell
All rights reserved.

Library of Congress Cataloging-in-Publication Data

Names: Howell, Eric, author.
Title: Under the Francis tree : a practical theology for the church grounds in the 21st century / by Eric Howell.
Description: Macon, GA : Smyth & Helwys Publishing, 2025. | Includes bibliographical references.
Identifiers: LCCN 2024053800 | ISBN 9781641735841 (paperback)
Subjects: LCSH: Human ecology--Religious aspects--Christianity. | Creation. | Sacred space. | Francis, of Assisi, Saint, 1182-1226. | Clare, of Assisi, Saint, 1194-1253. | Moses (Biblical leader) | Burning bush.
Classification: LCC BT695.5 .H695 2025 | DDC 261.8/8--dc23/eng/20241206
LC record available at https://lccn.loc.gov/2024053800

Disclaimer of Liability: With respect to statements of opinion or fact available in this work of nonfiction, Smyth & Helwys Publishing, nor any of its employees, makes any warranty, express or implied, or assumes any legal liability or responsibility for the accuracy or completeness of any information disclosed, or represents that its use would not infringe privately-owned rights.

*For Jenny
and our children, Lara, Lily, and Jimmy,
and the beautiful life we share
with our friends*

Acknowledgments

I am grateful for many individuals and communities of faith for their support in this project. My brilliant and talented wife, Dr. Jennifer Howell, continues to teach me with her astute theological mind and her delight in beauty. The people of DaySpring Baptist Church, from whom this project developed and for whom it was conceived, consistently offer their support and encouragement. I want to acknowledge the many who have helped lead our Season of Creation observances: Brett Gibson, Tiffani Harris, Amy Everett, Kingsley Gibbs, Josh King, Emily Hills, Jeremy Everett, Scott and Andrea Moore, Sascha Usenko, and Butch Tindell. I am thankful for my teachers, Mike Beaty, who taught me to garden, and Barry Harvey, who points toward the sacramental life. I offer a special thanks to Rebecca Edwards, whose enduring patience and enthusiasm in the office brings all the ideas to life. Ron Rolheiser, Kingsley Gibbs, Troy Abell, and Bella Martinez generously gave valuable feedback and encouragement.

Special thanks to those who have traveled the journey with me: the Truett students in Creation Care as Spiritual Practice; Dr. Robert Creech and Dr. Melinda Creech, who host us each spring on their farm; and all who have gone in pilgrimage with us to Assisi. I wish to thank the professors and colleagues at Duke Divinity School, Truett Theological Seminary, and the Oblate School of Theology who have formed me as a pastor and theologian. Special thanks to Father John Markey, who directed my Doctor of Ministry project at OST.

Finally, I am thankful for my parents, who took us to the mountains, rivers, and forests.

Contents

Preface: Our Place in the World ... xi

Introduction: The Plan for this Book ... 1

1: The Francis Way ... 3
2: Church Grounds as a Site of Conscience ... 23
3: Church Grounds as an Ecology of Grace ... 53
4: Church Grounds as Holy Ground ... 89
5: Church Grounds as a Geography of Hope ... 115
6: Church Grounds as a Place of Conversion ... 137

Epilogue: Your Sacred Place ... 161

Bibliography ... 167

Preface

Our Place in the World

As far as I can tell, there is an unwritten rule that authors who write about environmental concerns should establish their *bona fides* through personal reflection on the loveliness of their home or the place they grew up. One author begins by telling childhood stories of playing among the redwoods on the Pacific Coast. Another describes his home in the lush beauty of the North Carolina mountains. I come from no such place. I was raised in Fort Worth, Texas, and I have lived in Waco for the last fifteen years. Fort Worth is a vibrant city in north Texas but is part of a population center known as "the Metroplex." Can you think of a less evocative description than the Metroplex? Since my upbringing in Fort Worth, I have lived in South Florida, in eastern North Carolina, and in Albemarle County, Virginia, in the shadow of the Shenandoah Mountains. Coming from Fort Worth, I am fortunate to have lived in some beautiful places. We cried when we left the beauty of Charlottesville, Virginia, to move to Waco. But here in Waco, we've learned deeper truths about creation and our place as creatures within it.

A friend says, "Waco is the saltine cracker of travel. You travel somewhere beautiful and then come back for a while to cleanse your palate before heading out somewhere else." From Waco, over the years, our family has taken long road trips to beautiful places. You have to go a long way if you begin in central Texas and are trying to get somewhere beautiful. All road trips are long from here. Each summer, my wife and I would load up our three kids in the car and drive for hours and hours to gawk at the Colorado mountains, play in the waves on a Florida Panhandle beach, or hike the trails of Acadia National Park in Maine (that was a long drive!). Waco is nice enough, with some parks and rivers, but we have to go a long way from home to find the great outdoors in a national park or wilderness area. When you're going from here, "getting to nature" can take a long time, especially if you think of "nature" primarily in terms of the famous places where other writers are from: Tinker Creek, Sand County, Walden Pond.

Living in Waco helps us remember that nature isn't just out there somewhere, a long way away. It's not always beautiful and not only for occasional recreation. Even if we're mostly unaware of it, no matter where we are, everything about our lives is connected to creation. Everything connects me, as a creature, with other creatures in the web of creation: my food and clothing, transportation and recreation, energy sources I use and where my waste goes, and even my church's grounds. While this connection is a pleasant thought, it also raises potentially uncomfortable questions:

- How regularly am I conscious of this deep connection with creation?
- How often am I genuinely conscientious about the impact of my actions on other creatures?
- How may I become more fully aware of Christ's incarnation in daily life?
- How can I live more redemptively in the ways I engage a creation in travail?
- Does creation have an important place in Christian faith? How? And where?

This book deals with such questions. The answers, I must admit, can be humbling. Speaking for myself, I am often too distracted to be conscious of any connection with creation or with the God of creation. I take for granted that the creatureliness of all that is around me exists to serve my interests. Especially when I eat distractedly and am less than grateful for what I consume, I don't nurture a contemplative spirit and am prodigious in my use and waste. Moreover, I am easily discouraged that my environmentally responsible actions make any difference.

But sometimes, in certain times and places, especially in ordinary daily life, I'm mindful and aware, prayerful and hopeful. Those are the times I am most alive. I want more of them. And I want them for all of us. The health of Earth and our place in it are at stake. For reasons we will explore, so is Christian faith and life in the twenty-first century. In "A Prayer After Eating," the Kentucky Baptist farmer-poet Wendell Berry offers a prayer that expresses such a spirit of interconnectedness and gratitude:

I have taken in the light
that quickened eye and leaf.
May my brain be bright with praise
of what I eat, in the brief blaze
of motion and of thought.
May I be worthy of my meat.[1]

I've come to know a path that can help us, a medieval prayer path recovered from a cloistered nun known as St. Clare of Assisi. This ancient path guides us to see the reality of the world around us more clearly, become mindful of our place in it, turn wanton use into grateful prayer, and learn to live redemptively in an age of ecological crises. I discovered the spiritual legacy of St. Clare when I was about forty years old. She has changed the lives of my wife and me. Simply put, in four interconnected steps, the prayer path of St. Clare of Assisi teaches us to *gaze upon, consider, contemplate*, and *imitate* Christ. The implications for creation care unlock a spiritual practice that goes far beyond stewardship, conservation, climate activism, or environmental justice. Creation care gathers these approaches toward the planet together in the life of Christ and in the practices of loving and following him. In this book, I follow St. Clare's model of prayer back to the wilderness with Moses at the burning bush, where we see a man whose life is about to be transformed through an encounter with God in creation that anticipates Clare's insights centuries later. Here, I apply Clare's prayer journey to our relationship with creation, specifically church grounds. Church grounds are not the only places that hold the transcendent significant; for some readers, they may not matter much at all, but I ask you to consider them on several levels. As spaces that are material, historical, communal, spiritual, and at least in some way non-capitalized, church grounds can be important places of spiritual and ecological renewal.

Our journey from here will range in various directions. We will engage Karl Barth, Maximus the Confessor, Karl Marx, Pope Francis's *Laudato Si'*, and Baptist ecclesiology. Along the way, we will consider the melting glaciers of northern Montana, the evolving narrative of Thomas Jefferson's Monticello, and Wallace Stegner's vision for preserving American wilderness. We will learn how an ordinary place like the grounds of your local church can offer a site of conscience, an ecology of grace, holy ground, a geography of hope, and a place for conversion. I hope and pray that this journey inspires you with fresh eyes to see the places that are both special to you and at risk. Seeing is the first step.

I have written this book for those who are part of a church congregation with their own piece of holy ground. They have a place to meet, some property around the buildings, and love for the place. I hope communities connected to and responsible for their church grounds find encouragement and direction in these pages. I hope this book offers new insight and direction for the care of their church's grounds in ecologically significant and spiritually enlivening ways. As a Baptist pastor, I will describe in some detail the church grounds I know best. I will explore the significance and potential that church grounds hold as community-oriented, consecrated, accessible spaces unbeholden to the limits of places that are individually owned, government-managed, or employed for industry. If we can learn to see some spaces differently, I hope that we will be able to see and relate to other spaces through a wider lens as well.

I also want to speak to the many for whom connection with a piece of land is not bound to church grounds. I hope what is written for church leaders allows others to discover and care for a place in their own lives. This book can only be a true search for meaning on church grounds when it is addressed to all grounds. I have fallen in love with the story in Exodus 3 as a point of departure for our encounter with God because Moses is in the wilderness, far from home and any consecrated sacred ground. Moses encounters God in a no-man's-land, which he believes is a no-god-land. After the burning bush, we can never limit the potential for sacred encounters. God ranges freely in the wild, even on church grounds where we have done all we can to tame the living God.

Like St. Clare of Assisi, St. Francis of Assisi will guide us. Even for people who are not Franciscan or even Catholic, Francis has a wide range of appeal to people from all backgrounds. It is said that he is the person in history most like Jesus Christ, and he may be just as popular![2] If we can see through his eyes, we can see the world, ourselves, and God in new ways and with renewed and true hope. This book rises from the place where Franciscan spirituality meets Baptist ecclesiology. In this place, critical lessons about divided modern life, sharpened by environmental sociology, clearly express the church's ministry of reconciliation.

Since Lynn White Jr.'s 1967 essay, "The Historical Roots of our Ecologic Crisis," Christian eco-theologians have largely followed his theory-to-practice approach either to refute or validate his argument.[3] Their approach is first to identify timeless truths or morals that must guide Christians and then apply them to environmental concerns. I believe, on the whole, that Christian theory-to-practice theological reflection has largely failed to rise to this challenge, much less to prompt actual ecological conversion. I take a different approach, using a method of practical theological interpretation to trace cultural and historical circumstances that necessarily and fundamentally shape our context and response. We will follow a hermeneutical spiral with four successive and interlocking tasks described by Richard Osmer: the descriptive-empirical, the interpretive, the normative, and the pragmatic.[4] This method is sophisticated simplicity, which is critical because the complexity of deconstructing spirituality *in* the twenty-first century and then reconstructing spirituality *for* the twenty-first century demands a methodology capable of holding together complex relationships between the various parts and the capacity to consider each part in isolation as clearly as possible. I utilize a practical theological methodology of practice-theory-practice as I describe the current context of DaySpring Baptist Church and our church grounds in Waco, Texas. My goal is to illuminate the possibilities for every congregation in their respective contexts.

Structurally, each chapter follows Osmer's four tasks. More explicitly, each chapter follows a step on St. Clare of Assisi's prayer journey and reframes Osmer's tasks as forms of prayer: gaze, consider, contemplate, imitate. Each chapter introduces a step on the prayer journey and its mirror in our primary biblical story of Moses at the burning bush. Then, I consider scriptural and theological resources within Christian teaching that enlighten our understanding as we seek a model for church grounds. Finally, I move toward congregational practices that can illuminate each model arising from the step of prayer and context. While St. Francis is beloved as the patron saint of ecology, his spiritual companion, St. Clare, articulates a journey of prayer that enables us to read Scripture, creation, and our actions christologically. For Clare, as for Francis, all creation could be seen as a vestige of the love of God most fully revealed in the incarnation of Christ and evident through all creatures. Francis and Clare loved creation because they first loved God and, therefore, could not help but encounter Christ in creation.

Introduction

The Plan for this Book

Chapter 1, "The Francis Way," maps the contributions of Franciscan spirituality and Baptist ecclesiology to a renewed vision of church grounds.

Chapter 2, "Church Grounds as a Site of Conscience," examines one place, the DaySpring Baptist Church grounds in Waco, Texas, in relation to our area's history, our denomination's theological tendencies, and our planet's climate crisis. As I introduce this place to you, I have two aspirations: one, that you join me in appreciating and caring for this place, and two, that you see in this exercise a path to take a penetrating gaze at a place you know well and desire to know more fully. Our first task, to *gaze*, involves learning to describe a particular place with penetrating insight. *How regularly am I conscious of this deep and abiding connection with creation?*

Chapter 3, "Church Grounds as an Ecology of Grace," examines the forces and forcings of modern, industrial life on relationships with the land and one another. Insights from environmental sociology will provide a critical lens through which to see the implications of our way of life as an ecological rift. *How often am I truly conscientious about the impact of my actions on other creatures?*

Chapter 4, "Church Grounds as Holy Ground," takes a closer look at the biblical story of Moses at the burning bush to ask what we may glean from that story for our place in a world increasingly entrapped in crisis. *How may I become fully aware of Christ's incarnation in daily life?*

Chapter 5, "Church Grounds as a Geography of Hope," moves us from communion with God to the ministry of reconciliation. In this chapter, I envision church grounds as a place of participation that complements and contrasts with "America's Best Idea," our national park system philosophy. *How can I live more redemptively in the ways I engage a creation in travail?*

Finally, chapter 6, "Church Grounds as a Place of Conversion," celebrates the church's life-in-place as a witness to the world of God's goodness and the gift of Jesus Christ's incarnation. *Does creation have a place in the Christian faith? How? And where?*

Life in the modern era awakens readiness for ecological conversion and everything it births: a renewed vision for relating with God in creation, a renewed vision for human relations in justice and truth, and a renewed vision for our participation with the creatures. One locus for such renewal is on the ground Christians occupy as congregations. For Baptists, like those at DaySpring, Christian community and the church's mission are at the heart of participatory Christian life. We each have a role in God's redemptive purposes in the world, including, and perhaps beginning with, care for the church's grounds. Though overlooked, church grounds, which were long considered specially set apart by congregations for the sacred life of the church, have the potential to inspire Christians to meaningful participation in the healing of Earth, the human community, and the community of all God's creatures. Our chief concern in the following pages will be to bring this claim to light and life.

Chapter 1

The Francis Way

To understand and confront the environmental challenges we face in this era, we need a place, a path, and a model. In this book, the *places* are the property of a Baptist church in central Texas and, by extension, other places special to us and on which we have some agency to act. The *path* is found in the Christian spiritual tradition that we travel with St. Francis and St. Clare of Assisi as our guides. Our *model* is the biblical story of Moses at the burning bush, as told in Exodus 3. An ancient biblical model helps us envision how a medieval contemplative path can guide our relationship with a contemporary place.

Admittedly, this approach is fraught with well-worn detours and cul-de-sacs. Franciscan-inspired spirituality can turn romantic when appropriated apart from its christological heart. A Baptist ecclesiology can eddy individualistic when isolated from its communal commitments. An ancient biblical model can seem out of touch or, worse, appropriated out of context when not approached hermeneutically. But these streams, when they flow together, can offer hope in the face of real challenges. Baptists offer a way of understanding Christian life as an exercise in communal discernment and practice in a local church. Franciscans offer a Christ-centered doctrine of creation. Moses removes his shoes on holy ground, meets God, and then changes the world. In this first chapter, I will map the Baptist and Franciscan streams and suggest how they interplay with Moses's story. But first, let us begin with our context and appreciate what a weird time we live in.

Global Weirding

Atmospheric Scientist Katharine Hayhoe knows all about hot Texas summers. Originally from Canada, Hayhoe is a Paul Whitfield Horn distinguished professor and endowed chair in public policy and public law at Texas Tech University in Lubbock, and she is also a Christian. Hayhoe is known for her hopeful spirit as she engages with sometimes skeptical Texans and others around the world about the need to confront the climate crisis. She says we shouldn't call what is happening "global warming" because what's happening with our climate has a broader range of implications. She says instead, it should be called "global weirding." We are getting heavier downpours and longer dry periods in between. When wildfires come, they're burning much larger areas than they would otherwise. When hurricanes come, as they always have, they've got a lot more rainfall associated with them, and they're bigger and stronger than they used to be. We also see that sea levels are rising, plants are blooming earlier in the year, our seasons are shifting, and sometimes we have unseasonably warm weather and then an extreme cold snap. Hayhoe writes, "What we see in the places where we live is global weirding. And, so, personally, if we're going to pick a term to kind of refer to it colloquially, I would call it that, but as a scientist I call it climate change because that really is the root cause of the problem."[1]

Weirdness isn't just measured in record-breaking heat, cold, rainfall, or drought. It's also how people respond to environmental crises, as I witnessed in Decatur, Georgia. A laminated, half-sheet sign of the times was taped to the top of a metal trashcan. It declared an all-caps warning about "THE CLIMATE CHANGE AGENDA." It's not apparent to me why a conspiracy theorist chose a trash can on the sidewalk of this otherwise pleasant street as a place to stand his ground. It seems incongruent here. There's not much weird here at all. A couple of chain hotels and restaurants flank a whitewater kayaking outfitter across the street. The headquarters of the Cooperative Baptist Fellowship are a block away. No one is screaming about climate change—or much of anything—here. Decatur is a quiet, upper-middle-class bedroom community outside sprawling metro Atlanta. Quaint shops, restaurants, pubs, and bookstores line its historic downtown district. Decatur is a place with a history and culture but also a placeless kind of place, a location of deeply rooted Deep South history but also where people of a wide variety of backgrounds, cultures, and politics blandly pass through on their way to a meeting or a new job in a big city. This road connects the historic downtown shopping district with tree-canopied neighborhood streets and suburban retail identifiers of twenty-first-century America. But someone decided to disrupt the placid scene with a scree:

> Like Communism, The Climate Change Agenda Will Kill Millions. Your government is playing you for a fool. CO_2 Carbon Dioxide is essential to life on this planet. Without it, we would all die, but that's what the globalists want.

It's a sign of the times to the extent that people, like the trash-can herald, are deeply anxious right now, awash in scientific misinformation and desperate to assign blame to vague entities like globalists. At the bottom of the message is a URL for a website predictably stacked with COVID-19 misinformation and links to videos by conspiracy theorist Alex Jones. Oddly, there is little mention of climate change or the nefarious "globalists" who, apparently, want everyone dead by eliminating carbon dioxide from the atmosphere. This sign was weird because of the truths its message invoked and twisted. Climate change is, as far as we can see, on track to bring about the deaths of untold numbers of people, animals, and plants.[2] Coral reefs are bleached, species face habitat loss, and humans are caught in the path of rapidly intensifying hurricanes.[3] We are in crisis—not from a climate change "agenda" but from the implications of a rapidly changing climate. I respect the urgency of the manifesto to disrupt a quiet city street. Climate change is the issue of this century, and it ought to wake us all up.

The manifesto twists another truth: life on Earth depends on a certain amount of carbon dioxide to survive, and its elimination from Earth's atmosphere would result in the loss of all life on the planet. Warnings from environmentalists about climate change can make it seem like CO_2 is to be treated as an enemy of life. Getting basic science right is essential. Standing on the sidewalk, I had to think about this for a moment to remember my high school science class. The existence of CO_2 in the atmosphere is not a problem in itself. CO_2 makes up about .004% of the atmosphere. Even in this small proportion, CO_2, with other similar heat-trapping gases, plays a vital role in the habitability of Earth. Over-saturation of CO_2 is like wrapping yourself in a thick blanket on a hot day. I don't mean to sound dramatic, but the truth is that an increase in just a few hundred parts per million (ppm) of CO_2 in the atmosphere could bring about something like a collapse of life on Earth as humans have experienced it throughout history. If that's the concern, then we need to appreciate and understand how life is made possible by delicate balances and processes that make Earth the only planet we know so far that can sustain life. We must understand what is happening to those balances and processes and how humans disrupt them. Anxiety in the face of climate change isn't irrational. In one sense, maybe a manifesto should be posted on every street corner in America.

But who's to blame for this? I'm not convinced scaring up either "communists" or "globalists who want everyone dead" provides a simple answer. But is a certain problem in society causing the crisis in the environment? If so, do we blame communists or capitalists, globalists or industrialists, dualistic Christians or God-denying atheists? Each of these groups has been put forward at one time or another as the source of environmental destruction. At the least, we can acknowledge that the way modern humans live in the industrial age is causing a rift in Earth's balances and processes. As a Christian, I believe that rift bears witness to disorder in our lives that goes against what the Creator intended: that humans live as creatures in the web of relationships comprising creation. Environmental destruction is critical evidence of fundamental structural problems in the relationship of humans with creation. All humans? Perhaps not. But enough humans wield enough power to make a difference, even if they don't realize what they are doing. Intertwined with atmospheric problems are the dislocations and disruptions manifest in our social and spiritual lives. We feel them in society and in ourselves.

This little story has all the important elements we need from here forward to begin to grasp the trouble we are in: climate change and misinformation or at least misunderstanding, dislocation from place and community and history, blame but not accountability, and urgency that leads to anxiety but not truth that leads to awareness and change. I wasn't surprised when, within a few months, the laminated half-sheet was scraped away as if it had never existed. The eyes of pedestrians on the sidewalk are no longer assailed by the "climate change agenda" warning. Life has gone back to normal, business as usual. Everyday life doesn't pay attention to these things. But business as usual isn't going so well, either.

In Search of Wholeness

I don't want to give the impression that there was a time, before the industrial revolution or in some ancient day when life was idyllic for everyone. We cannot just accept a spirituality that blandly romanticizes the past. Modernism isn't the first era to puncture the Edenic dream. Yet, for all its advances, comforts, and benefits (and there are many), fracturing forces blow through modern life as never before. We're being blown apart—from one another, from our inner selves, and from creation. We feel this, even if we don't know how to find words for it. Parker Palmer gives us an image of being lost in a story. In *A Hidden Wholeness*, Palmer presents a truly bleak but also apt picture of modern life in America. We live in a blizzard that

> swirls around us as economic injustice, ecological ruin, physical and spiritual violence, and their inevitable outcome, war. It swirls within us as fear and frenzy, greed and deceit, and indifference to the suffering of others. We all know stories of people who have wandered off into this madness and been separated from their souls, losing their moral bearings and even their mortal lives: they make headlines because they take so many innocents down with them.[4]

In the storm winds of modern life, Palmer guides us, like nineteenth-century pioneers on the Great Plains, to tie a rope from the back door out to the barn so we can find our way back home again and survive the whiteout blizzard. We survive the storm by catching sight of the soul, he says. Doing so, "we can become healers in a wounded world—in the family, in the neighborhood, in the workplace, and in political life—as we are called back to our 'hidden wholeness' amid the violence of the storm."[5]

I love this metaphor and Palmer's hope that we can reconnect with our souls to become healers. In the rest of his book, Palmer helps us recover the wholeness for which God created us. The paradox of this ecological era, though, only complicates Palmer's metaphor of the storm. In all modern parables of storm or soil, humans are unwitting victims of nature's force and contribute our own forces to nature's force back on us and all around us. To push the parable further, we are the homesteader lost in the storm, and we are fueling the storm.

This may sound impossibly convoluted, but dealing with complexity in our place(s) in the world may be the source of hope in an era of unprecedented crisis. Ultimately, the complexity of our examination makes the restoration of wholeness possible. Christians are said by St. Paul to have "the ministry of reconciliation" (2 Cor 5:18). We are likely to understand such ministry in two ways: as restoration of relationship between humans who are in conflict through peacemaking and forgiveness. And we are likely to understand reconciliation between humans and God through the church's witness to the saving ministry of Jesus Christ. To these, let us add a third dimension: we are ministers of reconciliation between humans and the Earth. The modern rifts and calls to repair this relationship are at the heart of my thesis. We who are searching for wholeness find it only at the place where our relationship with God, our relationships with others, and our relationship with the land are life-giving and fruitful. Our holistic ministry of reconciliation is refracted into these three dimensions to the extent that our brokenness is intertwined in all three. Unless we attend to all three, we do not get to the heart of our dislocations in modern life, so we fall short of reconciliation. It's a work in progress, to be sure, but every important relationship is multi-dimensional and worthy of our heartfelt attention.

I put forward my thesis, then: to fulfill our ministry of reconciliation, we need a path and a place. The path, I suggest, is the way of the Franciscan intellectual and spiritual tradition. Following the inspiration of thirteenth-century saints Francis and Clare, the Franciscan way is distinguished by christological priority, creation-affirming theology, and no small measure of hope and joy. We need all of this along the way. The place, I propose, is the simple place where a local congregation meets for weekly worship and gathering. "Church grounds," as I call them here, are often just the backdrop for church life. But if we give them a little attention, we can see them as places where Christians have had spiritual encounters with God and, often, meaningful friendships with others. Church grounds are communal in a way that personal homes and yards are not (at least in the US), and they invite participation in a way that public parks cannot. Every church's grounds are unique and offer various ways to engage them, but they are all, in one way or another, set apart for a higher purpose. The Baptist emphasis on individual participation in a local community-in-place gives us a framework for enfolding the church's grounds into church life. The remainder of this chapter introduces Baptist ecclesiology as a place for reconciliation and the Franciscan path as a guide.

A Place: Baptist Ecclesiology and Local Church Grounds

Baptists give us a place to begin. With Baptist emphasis on the priority of the local church, personal spiritual agency and responsibility, and lived theology in community, the makings are in place for an embodied ecology to fold into existing ecclesiological commitments. We all begin where we stand, and I stand within Baptist life in central Texas, where it is hot for months on end, farming is industrialized, and natural beauty is, shall we admit, primarily in the eye of the beholder. It's been said that there are more Baptists than people in Waco. I don't know if that's true, but there's a Baptist church or one like it on almost every corner. The beginnings of the Baptist movement are traced to the seventeenth century when a small group separated from the Church of England and formed a church in Amsterdam in 1609 based on the principle of regenerate membership following believer's baptism. A portion of its members returned to England in 1611, where, despite heavy persecution, the Baptist movement began to take root. From those beginnings, hundreds of Baptist groups have arisen worldwide.

Baptists in the United States

Though historically distinct as a descendant of the Protestant Reformation, Baptists are closely identified sociologically with "evangelicals," the ambiguous and fraught category of Protestants.[6] Throughout this book, I'll draw on sociological analysis of "evangelicals" as more or less representative of Baptists. So, when I say Baptist, most of the time I am invoking a broader cultural movement than that represented by churches with "Baptist" on their sign.[7] James McClendon deals with this in his systematic theology by coining the term "little-b baptists." I don't use the same lowercase designation in this book, but it's one helpful way of remembering that the particular Baptist identity is expansive sociologically, politically, and ecclesiologically and is relevant to matters relating to the church and the environment.

Surveys and census data establish two correlated observations about modern-day Baptists in the United States. First, unlike many parts of the world where Baptists are a tiny minority, there are many Baptists in the US. Approximately 15 percent of the US population identifies as Baptists, which means that Baptists are a larger group than the population of California.[8] As a result, Baptists embody a large carbon and electoral footprint and potential for social and political influence. Second, as a sociology and environmental studies professor, Laurel Kearns demonstrates that Baptists, like most large evangelical groups, are disengaged ecologically from environmental concerns. As Kearns describes it, Baptists tend to be absent from the interreligious dialogue and public conversation about the ecological crisis, deny climate change, or believe that environmental concerns are irrelevant to Christian life and witness.[9] In light of the ecological crisis, we are at a critical time for Christian congregations, specifically Baptist congregations that populate the American spiritual landscape, to robustly and redemptively engage all the vital relationships of creation care: relationship with God, with one another, and with the Earth.

Church Grounds

Like Moses at Sinai or Francis at Assisi, we start where we stand and first learn to see the place as holy ground. In the face of existential crises, it may seem of little consequence to suggest that any modest step is sufficiently revolutionary to begin to heal the world's rifts, but as Christian congregations in America take creative approaches to their church grounds, who knows what may result? The world shifts slightly when we move in a geography of hope, whether Sinai or central Texas. Let us begin to see how church grounds offer congregations a particular place to participate as a spiritual community, moving toward healing environmental, social, and spiritual rifts. It is just at this place that Baptist ecclesiology has essential contributions to make to a Christian practice and witness of creation care. I will suggest two such contributions and their respective correlation to care for creation. First, each Baptist congregation is autonomous, grounding the participation of its members in the doctrine of the priesthood of the believer. Second, for Baptists, each individual is responsible and has agency before God to determine their faith.

First, the autonomy of the local church is an expression of the priority of the local community characteristic of the anabaptist movement. When we say "church," we first mean the local, gathered body of believers within a particular congregation in a particular location. Only derivatively do we mean the church universal. This emphasis means that we understand the Christian faith to be lived in a specific community of Christians with whom we share life. The vision of Dietrich Bonhoeffer's *Life Together*[10] may exceed the practical expression of most of our congregations, but we share the intention. Translated ecologically, a Baptist spirituality of creation care begins on the ground where we are standing now. Like the relationship of the local church to the global church, we think of creation care first as concern for a particular place in time and only derivatively as care for all creation.

Second, the emphasis on the local church expresses that Christianity is lived as an individual within a community to whom we each have a responsibility to serve as ministers of the gospel. In Baptist spirituality, ordination designates specific individuals for particular leadership and service roles, but the participation of all its members fulfills the congregation's ministry. Baptists highlight the fundamental significance of each person's response to God's grace. Translated ecologically, we each have a role and responsibility to play within a community of creatures and creation caregivers. None of us are passive observers, but each is part of the whole.

Baptists, then, may be ecologically disengaged and may harbor dualistic tendencies along with much of modern America. Still, the resources for transformation are already with us on the church grounds of Baptist churches across the nation and the world. We need places like church grounds to be centers of an ecological-spiritual revolution. The ecological premise is familiar to Trinitarian theology and New Testament ecclesiology: relationship is everything. As Christians given the ministry of reconciliation, we have work to do that can and will make a difference, and we have a path and a place to do it. This work is spiritual, as our spirituality includes everything in the materiality of life. The spirituality of a congregation includes its relationship with its church's grounds.

All church grounds are different, for sure. Some congregations have vast expanses of lawn; others have shade trees and playground equipment, and others have patches of grass between sidewalks and parking lots. Every church's setting is different, but congregations generally love their grounds as the place where congregational life happens. I want to explore and deepen that affection and help congregations see their church grounds as a place to care for creation. Church grounds can be much more than a pretty place. They can be a habitat for life-giving, Christ-loving, gospel-witnessing, world-changing expressions of ecological and mindful spirituality. A maturing of this affection evokes at least three dimensions for our love: a contemplative-incarnational spiritual orientation, reconciliation of relationships within the human community, and care for the Earth through active participation in its healthy life. Throughout this book, we return to these three dimensions—*these vital relationships*—within a practical ecology of Christian life: Christ-centered relationship with God, cultivation of human community, and regenerative relationship with creation. Along the way I invite us to explore an interweaving of these vital relationships. The experience of my church, DaySpring Baptist Church in Waco, Texas, is a prime example I will draw on, among other Christian communities participating in creation care as a spiritual practice.

Hope needs a place to set its feet. The planetary environmental crisis continues to exceed our capacity, or at least our willingness, to address it adequately. Many feel hopeless and helpless, and the societal costs to address it are so significant that we turn away in despair or with superficial optimism that everything will somehow resolve. In either case, we neglect the place we are standing and the moment we are in. And we fail to see how such an impossible problem is also an unrivaled gospel opportunity. On our church grounds, we have not only the *how* but also the *where* and, most importantly, the *why*. It is time for a revitalized relationship with creation.

I am convinced we need places—*actual* places—that enfold individual efforts to care for creation within a communal whole and hope, by grace, in the redemptive ministry of God through the church. In much discourse about creation care, the spiritual dimension is absent. Dutiful reminders to "be good stewards" don't get there. When it's not tiresomely moralistic, "be a good steward" may prompt some framework of personal responsibility to reduce one's environmental impact, yet this managerial rhetorical framework offers little inspiration or direction for how humans can and are empowered to be transformed.

Transformation is what the gospel offers. People attempting to be good stewards may try to reduce their carbon footprint, recycle paper more often, or limit their use of plastic straws, for example, yet such stewarding activities tend to be morally adjacent to their Christian faith and life (their "spirituality"). We must work toward something beyond what can be quantified in pounds of paper recycled or similar metrics. A holistic, spiritually robust, ecological conversion or, put another way, an ecologically oriented Christian spirituality is needed. However, even where Christians are awakening to ecological responsibilities beyond the moral framework of duty, many still do not know where to begin or how to meaningfully connect the planetary crisis they fear with the personal faith they love.

Fortunately, Christian theology is primed for reanimation in and for an ecological age. This is particularly (though neither universally nor exclusively) evident among traditions that emphasize the centrality of the local congregation. Baptist ecclesiology, for one example, emphasizes the local congregation of gathered believers in a particular time and place as the prime locus of "church." We might say it is a grounded ecclesiology. A look at church grounds through a lens of congregational ecclesiology can enliven ecologically alert spirituality within a Christian community in a place already known and experienced as sacred. DaySpring, for example, offers one place to consider how care for church grounds is extended as a communal spiritual practice through care for a congregation's small slice of creation.

A Path: A Franciscan Spirituality of the Earth

The Baptists offer a place. The Franciscans provide a path. From his simple lifestyle and embrace of evangelical poverty to his affectionate relationship with animals and vulnerable humans to his *Canticle of the Sun*, St. Francis of Assisi has, in recent decades, become an icon of creation-oriented spirituality. Francis lived from 1181 to 1226 in and around the village of Assisi in modern-day Italy. Countless biographies have been written about his life, including Bonaventure's hagiography, *The Major Legend of Saint Francis* (1260); the well-known *St. Francis of Assisi* (1923) by G. K. Chesterton; and contemporary accounts by Donald Spoto, *Reluctant Saint* (2003), and Augustine Thompson, *Francis of Assisi: A New Biography* (2012). Yet Francis is elusive or, perhaps better said, expansive. I have seen Francis invoked as the exemplar of hermetic philosophy, a precursor of the hippie movement, as an exemplar of Christian piety, and as a heretic. Famously, for Lynn White Jr. in 1969, St. Francis was a radical (and welcome) patron-heretic of a new religion of ecology. In an article in the journal *Science* in 1967, White rocked the Christian theological world by calling Christian dualistic metaphysics and material utilitarianism to account for the environmental crisis. White was trying to shake Western Christians loose from the dualistic social and spiritual milieu they inhabit, so he anointed nature-loving Francis as the heretical patron saint of an ecology rejected by Christianity.

Historian Elspeth Whitney surveys how scholars countered White's claims on both historical and hermeneutical grounds as they pointed out that the modern secular world of capitalism is not the medieval world, nature is not a static entity to which humans "did things," and Christian attitudes toward nature are neither monolithic nor the only factor influencing human treatment of the natural environment.[11] White's historicity came under withering criticism, but the attention he drew to St. Francis held persuasively. Francis, though, in the account of Pope Francis, among others, is less of a heretic pointing us away from an anti-creation church and more of an exemplar, helping us rediscover dimensions of Christian faith we have been in danger of neglecting.

Paul Santmire's corrective is right and important for all who romanticize Francis as a nature lover: "Francis' nature mysticism is, in fact, more adequately thought of, if the term is to be used at all, as a Christ mysticism."[12] Francis's relationship with nature took on a cruciform character as he became a Christ-like servant of God's creatures—human and nonhuman. "Francis was not a romantic," Santmire adds. "He did not go directly to nature, at least at first. At first, he went directly to Christ. This meant that the only way to see nature as it truly is, as universally blessed and cared for by the Creator, was the way of humility, the way of Lady Poverty."[13] It may be disorienting for some readers to associate Christ with creation, as in Santmire's account of Francis's spirituality. For some, "God" would be a more easily recognizable theological invocation. "God" suggests a notion of a creator, whereas "Christ" is associated with a redemption that has little to do with creation. But this is the point Santmire is making of Francis's witness: we need to return Christology to its proper understanding within our doctrine of creation. For all these reasons, Francis is a faithful guide for us today, his ministry radiating outward through all the Earth and all time. It is particularly poignant for this time, when reconciliation with the Earth is paramount. For Pope Francis's *Laudato Si'*, St. Francis was an exemplar of Christian orthodox spirituality worthy of invoking in the twenty-first century as a faithful guide for "integral ecology."

The Early Franciscan Spiritual-Intellectual Tradition

The early generations of Franciscans paid close attention to the life and witness of their leader, Francis, and his closest female companion, Clare of Assisi. Inspired by Francis and Clare, the early Franciscans understood their vocation simply as loving Christ Incarnate as creatures in kinship with all creation in a harmony of praise. That love, made manifest in the lives of Francis and Clare, was then shaped in an ongoing way by Alexander of Hales, St. Bonaventure, and Duns Scotus, among others. The Franciscan intellectual tradition was never an effort to promote a Christian ecology or to develop an eco-hermeneutic, but perhaps nowhere else in Christian thought is found such a creation-affirming spirituality. Francis's love for nature grew from a deep theological conviction that God is truly present to us by Christ's incarnation and resurrection. Francis came to perceive Christ as present in all of material reality. All creation and each creature became the means to contemplate the wisdom and power of the Creator.[14] This intimate link between creation and Christ marks the distinctively positive view of creation in Francis's lyrical praise and in the Franciscan intellectual tradition. As Keith Warner writes in "Franciscan Environmental Ethics," "Against the backdrop of most medieval theology that conceived the purpose of the incarnation as satisfaction for human sin, the Franciscan school developed the 'primacy of Christ' as an alternative framework, drawing from patristic theologies."[15]

Inspired by St. Paul's vision of Christ as "the image of the invisible God, the firstborn of all creation," the primacy of Christ proposes a doctrine of creation that swings in the orbit of cosmic Christology. Drawing from Colossians 1:15-16, Ephesians 1:3-10, and the Gospel of John's prologue (John 1:1-4), the primacy of Christ asserts the incarnation as the highest, most perfect expression of God's love. It was not an afterthought or a remedial strategy. "Rather," Warner writes, "the Incarnation was conceived before the creation of the world as a means to unite humanity with God through love; it was not a discrete historical event, nor merely a precondition for the Word to be preached to us; it was not necessitated by sin."[16] Sin is not discounted or disregarded but is a subordinate concern relative to full communion with God through the incarnation.

Creation, therefore, is the cradle of Christ and is to be received with the significance of what was conceived by God before the beginning to be capable of bearing Christ in incarnate form. Warner summarizes, "The idea that all of material creation was made for Christ means that for Christ to come, there had to be a Creation, and Creation had to be capable of receiving, understanding, and freely responding to this manner of divine initiative. The act and process of creation was a prelude to a much fuller manifestation of divine love in the Incarnation."[17]

Francis, Conversion, and Burning Bushes

Ilia Delio, O.S.F., spells out the ecological implications of Franciscan spirituality when she characterizes Franciscan creation-oriented spirituality as embodying the Incarnate Word in creation, experiencing the kinship of creatures within creation, contemplating our crucified Earth, and practicing eco-penance as conversion in action.[18] This approach emphasizes love through communion with God and affirms the religious significance of creation. Creation is not merely a stage on which salvation history is played out, nor is it merely the materiality humans must manage as dutiful stewards. Care for creation is not just an activity adjacent to Christian ethics. Our relationship with creation becomes centralized as gratitude and devotion to Christ incarnate. Ilia Delio reflects on the humility of St. Francis:

> Francis was a brother to all creation; he was not a steward. He did not view elements or animals as something for which he was responsible but rather as brothers and sisters to which he related. . . . He wanted to be humble, to live in solidarity with creation just as Christ did through the Incarnation. Francis recognized Jesus as "brother" through his shared humanity with others and thus his shared corporeality. . . . He did not speak of stewardship, of being in charge, or being responsible, or of managing creation. . . . Life on Earth has intrinsic value because it is created

by God, not merely because of its economic worth. . . . it is a reflection of God.[19]

Consider how ecological conversion in the way of Francis may look something like Moses barefoot at the burning bush in Exodus. Exiled from his home and his people in the wilderness, Moses was no spiritual romantic and was stewarding nothing except a herd of sheep that did not belong to him. Lost and alone in the hot, dry Sinai, Moses is like an icon of humanity's dislocation from the life of creation in the modern, industrial era. From the depths of dislocation, rifted from the home and life he knew, Moses encounters God and discovers a vocation of renewal for himself and his suffering people trapped in a system of domination and dehumanization. Israel willingly chose to relocate to the Egyptian theater but did not, nor possibly could have, anticipated the disastrous consequences of their decision, which would affect the lives of generations of Jewish people to come. In a dramatic spiritual epiphany, a burning bush becomes the material means by which God transforms the future of a people through the hope and courage of Moses, who redeems God's people from their long-suffering enslavement.[20]

Biblical scholar Ellen Davis has declared that everything before Exodus leads to Exodus, and everything after Exodus is just commentary. The more I spend time with Exodus 3, the more I wonder if everything in the canon after the story of Moses at the burning bush is commentary on that divine-human encounter. Among the other texts I regularly consult for ecological insights, I turn to this text for several reasons. First, Moses responds to God in a pattern that remarkably anticipates what St. Clare describes as prayer: gaze, consider, contemplate, imitate. I have not discovered any source that suggests that Clare drew on this connection, but I think it is worth exploring. Second, the story is a narrative of an encounter with the transcendent God through creation (even a modest scrub bush), and, in a rifted world, we need any prompt we can find that renews our sacramental imagination for connection with the divine through material means. Third, few eco-theological scholars treat this story in their teachings because, I assume, this is not a text explicitly about creation care despite the evocative declaration of "holy ground."[21] As I explore the meaning of church grounds for our community in the Anthropocene, I wonder what the image of holy ground evokes for congregations. Fourth, insights from historical-critical scholarship on this pericope complement and enrich contemplative insights from prayerful reading. I will demonstrate how Clare's model, reflective of Franciscan spirituality, gives space for both. As Christians living in an era of climate change, we are searching for models to understand how science and theology complement one another. Finally, this is a call narrative from isolated despair to sacrificial, redemptive courage set in the wilderness of human experience. We need powerful narratives for the Anthropocene—stories that reframe our place in the world and lead to conversion.[22] What story could be more potent than this one for these purposes? With her four-fold prayer path, Clare will guide our reading of this story as it also fits the order of Moses's response to God's intervention. Our conversion, like that of Moses, must be as transformative and impactful as it is unexpected.

Praying with the Saints

St. Francis is more well-known, but St. Clare, his contemporary and first female follower, articulates the model and spirit of Franciscan prayer. To one of her students, Clare outlines a path of devotion to God, who is revealed fully in the crucified Lord and mirrored in every creature in all creation. Her work revolutionized the monastic *lectio divina* prayer of spiritual ascent. "O most noble Queen," Clare advised,

> Gaze,
> Consider,
> Contemplate,
> As you desire to imitate Your Spouse [Jesus].[23]

These four verbs—gaze, consider, contemplate, imitate—became, for Franciscans, a simple, profound path of prayer. In Clare's prayer journey, *gaze* leads to *consider* as we experience an impulse to study, investigate, examine what has captured our attention. Franciscan spirituality is comfortable with scientific rigor, and some argue the Franciscans gave birth to it in the modern era.[24] Seeking understanding, we desire to know a thing as fully as possible, whether it is the biochemical inner workings of a field of wildflowers or the effects of climate change. This desire is a form of love. As a place-reading strategy, we consider the meaning behind what we have gazed upon.

Thoughtful focus gives way to the phase of contemplation, which marks a definite shift in the journey. In the first two steps, *gaze* and *consider*, we are taught to read the object of our attention with patience and humility. In the third step, we are prepared for the possibility of God's presence with us. God's presence at the burning bush is not just reassuring but transformative. God, with the promise of divine help, tasks Moses with the seemingly insurmountable challenge of delivering God's suffering people from the social, political, and ecological degradations of captivity. God becomes the central character of a story that, until now, seemed to be empty of divine presence and redemption. Although Moses is still in the wilderness by the end of the burning bush episode, the whole Earth does not seem as barren and hopeless as it did before his encounter with God. If the task ahead of us seems insurmountable, the passage offers encouragement to trust in God's call and provision for the way forward.

Clare's prayer ends with the fourth and final step: *Imitate*. When Clare used the term "imitate," she meant to embody as fully as possible the image of God on whom she gazed.

> What God has wanted me to be from all eternity, who I am to be in my inmost self, is imaged in God's Son hanging on a cross. When I gaze at the cross, I am looking into a mirror. I see my true self. . . . Imitation is transformation insofar as Christ comes alive in my life.[25]

To imitate is to become who *we* are called to be in Christ in and for this place and time. We desire Christ to come alive in our lives. This four-fold journey of prayer guides the chapters to follow. We begin with visual attention, a penetrating gaze into everything that reveals the crucified Christ. This gaze leads to meditation (consideration) of Christ, then to contemplation, and then to its fruit, imitation. In the end, we do not simply arrive at union with God; we pray that we may become what we love.[26]

From her monastic cell at San Damiano in the thirteenth century, St. Clare lights the path that theologian Philip Sheldrake insists we need to take in the twenty-first century. If one theme comes to dominate Christian spirituality in the next fifty years, he writes, it is the development of ecologically alert spiritualities: "Rather bland or romantic creation-centered spiritualities will need to give way to more robust and challenging versions of eco-spirituality that counter the irresponsibility of extreme consumerist lifestyles."[27] Averting the pitfalls of superficial optimism, apathy, despair, and bland romanticism, Franciscan spiritual ecology preserves a sharp mystical edge and clear-eyed dedication to both truth and hope.

Chapter 2

Church Grounds as a Site of Conscience

Over the next several chapters, we will follow St. Clare's four-fold prayer path to engage church grounds. We will *see*, *consider*, *contemplate*, and *imitate*. Each step in our prayer will accompany Moses as he traverses the same spiritual path at the burning bush. Each step will generate an approach to church grounds that can stand on its own but can also develop from one step to the next. We begin simply by learning to *see* and, by doing so, learning to be conscious of the place where we are standing.

In Exodus 3, the scene opens with Moses alone in the wilderness. In the Scripture, "wilderness" is a term for desecrated, abandoned geography beyond any national claim to territory. It is a no-man's and no-god's-land. In the wild, Moses is alone in the world and appears destined to remain so, tending sheep not his own until forgotten in his death. But then, one day, his world changes. He doesn't know it yet. All he knows at first is that he sees something for which he has no preparation: a bush burning but not consumed. Moses *sees* the bush. Let us not underestimate the significance of this simple act. The burning bush becomes a site that opens Moses's consciousness of God's presence with him even in the wilderness and stirs his conscience to respond, even over his protests, to God's call to return to Egypt and set the captives free. Everything begins with "turning aside to see."

In this chapter, we will develop a rich practice for the discipline of seeing so that our consciousness may be opened and our conscience stoked. To see is to begin to pray because truly seeing depends on paying attention, and paying attention is prayer. Someone says, "I saw something for the first time," by which they mean they "see it with new eyes." We all know the experience of becoming conscious of something for the first time or becoming conscious of it in a more profound way than before. Some lovers describe their experience of falling in love this way. They saw something in the other that they had not noticed before. Was this not Belle's experience of the Beast? A day came when Belle realized she saw something in him she had not seen before. She came to a new consciousness, and her heart began to change toward him. "Beast" was turned from a term of derision to a term of endearment and then, eventually, released altogether.

Seeing what is right in front of us is not always so simple. In many ways, the truth of the thing or person in front of us may be masked or obfuscated. We don't always have ready access to the truth. Perhaps more often, we are not truly prepared to see. I've been nearly legally blind in my right eye since birth, but the physical function of our eyes is not even the problem. Constant distraction generates fleeting attention. Seeing-as-prayer involves more than acknowledging the presence of a thing. It suggests a penetrating vision of the truth of what is before you. To see is to be conscious, awake, and alive to where you are standing and whom you are standing with. If we are to care for creation, our first task is to learn to see creation where we are standing and to see with clear eyes whom we are standing with.

The Stewardship Option

It's helpful to explore how and why this is a different starting point than the "Christian stewardship" model familiar to American Protestants. Rather than seeing it as a spiritual act, a stewardship ethic is oriented to fulfilling a duty, drawing on an evangelical interpretation of the biblical mandate for humans to take care of the Earth. Stewardship interprets the Genesis commandment (Gen 1:26-28) as a divine charge to take care of God's creation.[1] While I am convinced this approach does not lead very far into a genuinely renewed relationship with creation that is both possible and needed, stewardship has some basic advantages that deserve reckoning.[2] Stewardship typically gains traction by encouraging Christians toward environment-affirming choices they can manage without significant sacrifice, such as recycling paper or reducing electricity use, and linking those activities to dutiful faithfulness. Further, by focusing on individual actions and specific problems from a human-centric point of view, stewardship can sidestep the politically prickly dialectical challenges of dealing with climate change. So, if our aim is to provoke modest environmentally conscious behavioral changes and find common ground among Christians on environmental concerns, stewardship provides a certain popularized framework. Soil health, clean water, or conservation of wilderness land are all areas in which partisans of diverse political and theological persuasions find common cause.

In practice, a stewardship ethic alone is limited at best because it only addresses human activities without examining fundamentals in the relationship between humans and the rest of creation. In an ecological vision, at stake is who we are, not just what activities we do or restrict. Unfortunately, stewardship's primary focus on individuated action disregards our contexts, which consequently allows us to conveniently obfuscate the reality of our situation and avoid critical assessment of our activities that both derive from and contribute to the context. In other words, we are so enmeshed in the current reality that we can hardly know what proper stewarding would entail. In practice, the stewardship ethic functions like a governor on some environmentally destructive activities but not as a holistic, hermeneutic reframing of our place in the world characteristic of the transformation that may best be described as christological-ecological conversion. For this reason, a stewardship ethic is not ultimately helpful just to the extent that it is not meaningfully hopeful.

Gaze: Seeing Differently

Here's a story that will help illustrate the dynamics at stake. In 2017, my father and I backpacked in Glacier National Park in northwest Montana. Dad had introduced me to love of the outdoors in several national parks when I was a child. Returning as an adult to a national park with my dad was a special gift. As it turned out, this would be our last outdoor adventure together and one of our favorites. I will remember the experience for these personal reasons and because of the intersection between the marvelous beauty and troubling problems we observed at Glacier. The park is stunning and surely one of America's finest protected landscapes, but seeing firsthand evidence of dramatic and rapid reduction in the size of the glaciers still haunts me, as it does for many visitors to Glacier. The glaciers are disappearing. In the mid-1800s, more than 150 glaciers were known to exist in the park area. By 2017, only 25 remained.[3] Officials project that by the end of the twenty-first century, no glaciers will remain in the park named for them. Over long spans of time, the volume of a glacier expands and contracts, but the rate of change of the glaciers in the last century is unprecedented, unnatural, and undoubtedly a consequence of a warming climate. Visitors to Glacier National Park have a front-row view of the shrinking size of these massive bellwethers of climate change. It is a real "uh-oh" moment for many. It was for me and for Dad. Though we don't see eye to eye on many political issues, our love for the outdoors and concern for its future unite our politics and our desire for its protection. I have found this phenomenon to be true in other relationships as well. Individuals can have widely divergent political and social views, but the circles of their convictions overlap in concern, one way or the other, for the state of the environment.

How would a stewardship ethic function in our lives concerning the diminishing glaciers of the national park? We were there as temporary visitors and had no agency in the management of the park. Even those who do are equally helpless in arresting the rate of glacier melt. The glaciers are responding to atmospheric, cultural, industrial, and economic forces wildly beyond park management. So on one hand, seeing the rugged beauty of Glacier is delighting in the aesthetics of the park. On the other hand, seeing with a more penetrating vision is noticing the changes in the glaciers and recognizing the effects of climate change. Stewardship supports the designation of certain landscapes for federal protection but does not begin to address the planetary issues affecting even protected landscapes. And I experienced another layer of seeing beyond stewardship at Glacier. Led on a guided hike by a park ranger, a group of us set out for an exciting afternoon walk. As Dad and I enjoyed the day, I noticed that another father and son in the group were having a different kind of experience. I overheard the father furtively commenting on the surrounding mountains. As the US Park Ranger pointed to Mt. Rockwell, the father would tell his son, "The name of this mountain is Rising Bull." They were of the Blackfoot tribe, and this father was teaching his son the true place names. I inched closer to listen. As the walk continued, the father re-narrated key features of the landscape for his son, and I had the sense that he saw and was teaching his son to experience everything around us in a different way. This was catechesis, learning how to see by learning what to say about what you see.[4]

My father and I were experiencing an adventure in one of our country's most beautiful national parks. The other father and son were on a spiritual pilgrimage through a place that makes them who they are. The Blackfeet have an ancient and tragic history in northwest Montana.[5] In 1895, the US Government, having nearly destroyed the Blackfeet through a pogrom of buffalo eradication, forced them to sell the land that became Glacier National Park. Effectively, the eastern half of the national park remains contested as stolen land. Blackfeet tribal members are granted free admission to the park but do not have the right to gather food or hunt on the land. To see Glacier today requires conscious attention to the story of the park—its environmental story and its social and political story. The *Wellian Magazine* at Duke University attempts to foster this consciousness and "to explore what makes us human from a contemporary and historical perspective." In a recent issue, the *Wellian* published an article that included an interview with Ernie Heavy Runner, who was raised on Blackfeet land in northwestern Montana. Reflecting on the relationship of Native Americans to Glacier, the author, a Chickasaw native, observes,

> Land has been used for millennia by humans and much longer by other species. "Untouched" land is a concept that humans have invented. This idea can be useful for fighting climate change and species extinction, but it is extremely harmful when applied to silence Native American claims. The National Park Service should

adopt the idea that Native American culture is part of the environment that they are preserving. They must also consider how a conserved space can be used to sustainably uplift the surrounding community.[6]

These are not easy issues to adjudicate, but we begin to cultivate consciousness where we become attuned to the relationship and the story and begin to knit ourselves, our communities, and our relationship with the world and God back together.

A Penetrating Vision of Reality

St. Clare of Assisi described the spiritual act of paying attention as a "gaze." We begin by simply paying attention (which is not so simple, it turns out), "being open to the wonderful presence of God with no words, no thoughts, just being there."[7] Soren Kierkegaard drew on similar wisdom in writing about Jesus's blessing of the "pure in heart" who "will one thing." Simone Weil echoes Clare's insights for distracted and overwhelmed modern twentieth-century students: "Absolutely unmixed attention is prayer."[8] For Weil, "attention" is a negative effort that requires us to stand still rather than lean in. It is not a muscular focus but a passive, open, expectant waiting, and Clare's gaze has some of the same overtones. The aim of this prayer is a penetrating gaze into the ordinariness of life through what is directly in front of us.[9]

St. Clare's medieval-era prayer anticipates the first task of modern practical theology methodology as developing a thick description of any context under consideration. In Richard Osmer's *Practical Theology*, for example, the descriptive-empirical task sets out to simply yet thoroughly answer the question, "What is happening?" Before analyzing why something is happening or devising a strategy for what to do in response, practical theologians observe by gathering information that helps discern patterns and dynamics in play. This task is more than simply aggregating facts about an event or situation. Rooted in a spirituality of presence described as "priestly listening," this approach foregrounds the "quality of attentiveness congregational leaders give to people and events in their daily lives."[10]

Exodus 3 is an ideal passage to demonstrate how this method can be applied to Scripture reading, as Moses, the character in the story, practices the art of seeing before understanding or acting.[11] As a reading strategy, gaze is a posture of expectant humility by the reader before the text-in-itself.[12] We give attention to the speaker and the story, mindful that we, too, are an intended audience of the text, standing in a long line of those before us who have looked upon and dwelt with this text. Gaze teaches us to slow down and view the object of our attention as a gift to be received on its own terms rather than an object to be used or exploited for our own ends. This has implications both methodological and ecological. Moses did not rush to extinguish or use the burning bush for any reason; first, he instinctively turned to see what was happening in front of him.

Similarly, to look with a penetrating gaze at the Exodus 3:1-6 pericope is to observe how the passage is presented. The narrator handles the details carefully. Until this theophany scene in chapter 3, readers of Exodus may ask, "Where is God?" since no mystical dimension of the narrative is apparent thus far. From Israel's bondage in Egypt (Exod 1:8-14) to the midwives' creative subversion of Pharoah's edict (1:15-21) to the rescue of the baby Moses from the Nile (2:1-10), all action is human action. With subtle sophistication, the beginning of Exodus is narrated as if to convince the reader this will be nearly completely an anthropocentric story.[13] As an adult, Moses operates within a world created by this divine vacuum, confronting injustice through violence and then fleeing his actions alone into the wilderness (2:11-22). The exclusive anthropocentrism of the story only dramatically shifts once the narrator arrives at the central issue of the book: Israel's deliverance from Egypt by God. This is foreshadowed at the conclusion of chapter 2: "Their cry for rescue from slavery came up to God. And God heard their groaning, and God remembered his covenant with Abraham, with Isaac, and with Jacob. God saw the people of Israel—and God knew" (2:23-25).

As Exodus 3 opens, the sparse details are offset by the intensity of the unfolding story. Moses is far from home. In the wake of Israel's suffering and God's hearing and seeing their suffering, the dimensions of the story now are meager—at the heart of the text, there is merely one person and a shrub. By this time in his life, Moses has become an ordinary person doing ordinary things (tending sheep) in an desperately desolate place (the west side of the wilderness). The narrator's use of grammatical form presents the action as continuous and ongoing: Moses is *shepherding*, as if that is what he is always doing. In the absence of disruption, Moses's mundane and lonely work would presumably continue.

Then, fatefully, Moses goes beyond his familiar range into an area unknown to him: wilderness—a land belonging to no man, claimed geopolitically by no tribal deity. There, Moses seemingly stumbles upon the holy mountain without knowing it when he comes "to Horeb, the mountain of God" (Exod 3:1). While Moses does not seem to know he is in an important place, in a bit of foreshadowing of later events in Exodus, readers are told that this is already God's Mountain. It is there, at the mountain of God, that a strange sight captures Moses's attention: a bush burning but not consumed (3:2). Standing before the burning bush, Moses *gazes*. He lets all other concerns fall away and looks with penetrating, focused attention at the mystery now before him. In St. Clare's terms, Moses has begun to pray and will soon learn that the prayer ground under his feet is holy, and he is not alone, even beyond wilderness.

We will return to the story of Moses in the next chapter. For now, by seeing differently and paying close attention, we, like Moses, will discover we live in a world we didn't see before. To put it another way, we are re-placed in the Earth. Seeing the place and seeing ourselves as inhabitants of a place is an art all but lost in the wilderness of the modern world that "rests on a deception, a willful turning away from context . . . . It is a conception that renders a picture of human beings as fundamentally disembodied and disearthed, floating apart from Earth and never really within it."[14] In the next chapter, we will explore more fully why such disembodiment and dualism are inherent to modern life. For now, we simply want to "turn aside and see" that in doing so we may see a different world than the one we have seen before, and, as we will see, been conditioned to see.[15]

On Church Grounds

A Franciscan spirituality of seeing echoed in the story of Moses gives us a path; we will take a close look at the church grounds of DaySpring Baptist Church in Waco, Texas. By looking at one church and its context, I mean to invite a similar look at all other churches and even all places. Church grounds have certain unique characteristics, but what we do there can model our approach to other places as well.

As a briefly told history, for more than fifteen years, I have served as pastor of DaySpring Baptist Church, self-described as "a Baptist church in the contemplative tradition meeting in central Texas." In 1993, seven families established the congregation. From the beginning, DaySpring prioritized worship, rest, and spiritual renewal. Soon after its founding, the church adopted the slogan "sacred and simple" as an expression of its aspiration and later "a Baptist church in the contemplative tradition" as an expression of its identity. In 2001, the congregation acquired four acres on the outskirts of Waco and, over the next decade, constructed a 300-seat sanctuary, a prayer chapel, offices, children's education spaces, and a playground. In 2020, the congregation acquired an additional two acres, including a small grove of live oak trees whose origins are estimated to date to the mid-eighteenth century. In addition to the six acres we own, we have primary responsibility for an adjacent tract of eight acres that includes trails, a small stream, old oaks, and countless invasive species. We will look at this church and these fourteen acres on the outskirts of Waco from three angles of vision: physical environment, social history, and Baptist theological-cultural perspective.

TallGrass: DaySpring's Physical Environment

An environment is the context—the circumstances and conditions—in which a person, animal, or plant operates. In a congregational sense, the DaySpring environment directly includes the fourteen acres at the church site and, by extension, the climate and conditions of central Texas, which itself is part of the planetary climate and conditions of the early twenty-first century.

The aesthetics of the land on which the church worships and meets has been a meaningful part of our congregation's identity and the shape of our spirituality. The sanctuary is designed with large, open windows overlooking the trees and hillside. A longtime member said, "We wanted to blur the distinction between inside and outside as much as possible. We wanted to bring the outside . . . inside." In the trees and trails behind the church property, our "forest" stretches to a small creek and is scattered with implements of the farm that used to encompass this piece of land. Like many congregations, this church feels a close connection to its land and place.

We have been the proprietors of this place for twenty years. Before human intervention, this property, like vast areas from south Texas to the northern great plains, was tallgrass prairie, broken only by riparian zones along creeks and rivers. The prairies here are gone, as in most of the central United States, since by the mid-twentieth century, 98 percent of native grasses were plowed under or paved over.[16] Humans destroyed one of the world's great carbon and water sequestration biodiverse ecologies.

A few remnants of clumps of native grasses are visible on the property, but the trees garner the most attention and affection. An old live oak, dubbed our St. Francis Tree, is the iconic image of the DaySpring grounds. The health of the old live oaks is a concern for central Texans who watch for signs of oak wilt and other invasive diseases that threaten these slow-growing, beloved giants.[17] All life in Texas faces all kinds of environmental challenges, such as hurricanes, tornados, and extended extreme droughts. Underfoot and above our heads, Texans live at the intersections of some of America's most inhospitable conditions. In every case, a warming climate amplifies weather conditions. The changing climate will affect us and every church's grounds everywhere, one way or another. To fully see the state of our local environment, we need to grasp the situation we're in as affected by planetary climate change.

Texas Tech University atmospheric scientist Kathryn Hayhoe insists the most important thing we can do to address climate change is "Talk about it!" Yet talking about climate change is one of the last things most of us want to do compared with the happy respites of life on church grounds, like dog-walking, picnics, games, or even less controversial environmentally friendly actions like recycling.[18] Despite possible aversion to the subject, during DaySpring's Season of Creation in fall 2021, I decided to talk about climate change as clearly and carefully as possible. In a discussion on science and faith, I presented these two graphs and asked the congregation to interpret what they saw:[19]

Graph 1.

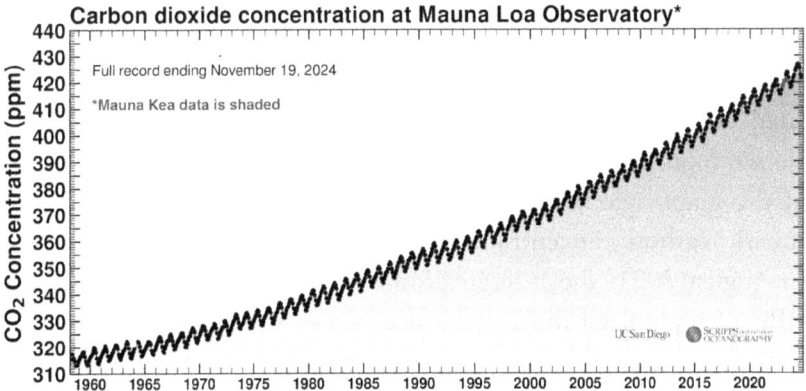

(Credit: Scripps Institution of Oceanography at UC San Diego, CCA 4.0)

Graph 2.

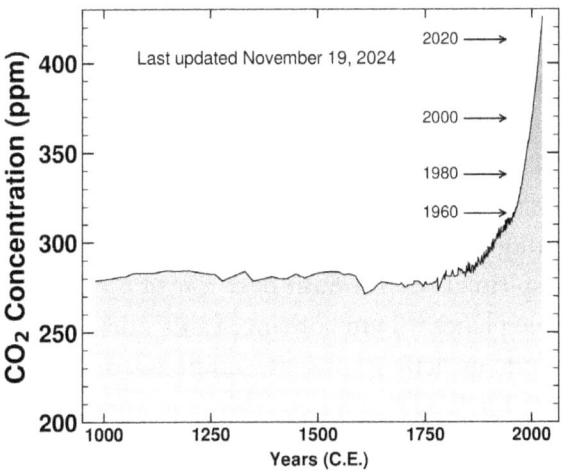

(Credit: Scripps Institution of Oceanography at UC San Diego, CCA 4.0)

At first glance, most of them were unsure what to make of the graphs, though they noted the dramatic upsweep on the right side of the line. They understood that something unusual and important was happening here. I explained that the first graph shows the Keeling Curve, described as "The Most Important Graph in the World." What it tells you is going to shape your whole life, no matter your field of study or your career. One way or another, this chart tells the story of the present generation and those to come.

I had their attention. The Keeling Curve plots the change in concentration of carbon dioxide in the Earth's atmosphere over the last six decades, from 1958 levels of 280 parts per million until current readings of more than 420 ppm.[20] The second graph is populated with data before 1958, estimated from ice core samples. As we see represented in the sharp upward trajectory at the right side of the graph, global data demonstrates a remarkable rise in atmospheric carbon concentration from the late 1800s through today. In August 2021, the Intergovernmental Panel On Climate Change (IPCC) recognized the significance of the Keeling Curve: "There is a near-linear relationship between cumulative CO_2 emissions and the increase in global mean surface air temperature caused by CO_2 over the course of this century for global warming levels up to at least 2°C relative to pre-industrial."[21] In less technical terms, Earth's atmosphere is warming at a rate mirroring the rise in CO_2 concentration—clearly mapped on the Keeling Curve.

The Most Important Graph in the World begins to tell a story, but it does not alone interpret what kind of story it is telling. Science is always an exercise in interpretation. Climate-change deniers insist that this story is a natural global phenomena cycle misinterpreted by a conspiracy of scientists with an agenda to propagate a myth of global warming to gain power.[22] Some Christians assert that climate science is a spiritual test for faith over fear or a reminder that Earth is a disposable planet.[23] I am convinced this story is about the implications of human activity and its unintended, though very real, consequences for God's creation. This is a story about us and our place in the world. Creation is a mirror, said St. Bonaventure. If we have the courage to look in the mirror, we may see something we don't like, but that doesn't mean it's not true. The Earth is telling us something about its life and about ourselves. We should listen.

Kathryn Hayhoe is blunt: "The Earth's climate is complex. Understanding what we humans are doing to it isn't."[24] For starters, the atmosphere is like a natural blanket of heat-trapping gases. Energy from the sun pours through the blanket like light through a window, heating the Earth. The Earth in turn absorbs the sun's energy, warms up, and gives off heat energy. The atmospheric blanket traps heat energy. Without it, Earth would be a frozen, lifeless planet. This natural, delicate balance creates conditions for life on Earth and keeps it sustainable for life. The problem, as Hayhoe explains,

> is that whenever we dig coal, oil, or natural gas out of the ground and burn it, we release carbon dioxide or CO_2 into the atmosphere—carbon that would not naturally reach the atmosphere for millions of years. And CO_2 is one of the main gases that make up our heat-trapping blanket . . . .. Hundreds of years' worth of carbon dioxide, methane, and nitrous oxide emissions have artificially increased the thickness of the natural blanket. You'd overheat if someone replaced your perfect blanket with a thicker one you didn't need. In the same way, the Earth is also heating up.[25]

This science is not new information.[26] Scientists have known since the 1850s that carbon dioxide traps heat and has been building up in the atmosphere from the coal, oil, and natural gas humans have burned since the start of the industrial revolution.[27] The IPCC report flatly states, "It is unequivocal that human influence has warmed the atmosphere, ocean and land. Widespread and rapid changes in the atmosphere, ocean, cryosphere and biosphere have occurred."[28] For all the attention climate change has generated in media and international conventions in the last half century, we are not turning the trend around yet. Not even close. The IPCC details with varying degrees of confidence what is likely to happen in the future because of continued warming of the climate. In one of many dire forecasts, the report predicts, "Many changes due to past and future greenhouse gas emissions are irreversible for centuries to millennia, especially changes in the ocean, ice sheets and global sea level."[29] Humans have unwittingly ushered in a new epoch in planetary history. The implications are staggering and will affect every place on Earth, including our church's grounds.

The absence of tall prairie grass on our property bears witness to the legacy of a much larger story of human intervention on the Earth. In America, the systematic conversion of the prairies to agriculture and concrete indicates our incapacity or unwillingness to relate to the land sustainably. Attention to deep history can connect our consciousness of how planetary issues affect and are affected by local contexts.

Cathedral of Oaks: Waco's Social History

The beloved live oaks, while we have no intention to cut them down, are just as vulnerable to conditions in a warming climate. They also have a symbolic and tragic role in the social history of central Texas. During the Covid-19 pandemic, DaySpring worship services were held outdoors in the grove of live oak trees. Under the shade of their canopies, we found one of the few places in a pandemic era where we could gather to sing and simply be together. The "Cathedral of Oaks" was a place of respite for all of us in the spring of 2020. For the first time, some congregants were brought into closer proximity with vestiges of the land's prior use as a working farm from the 1920s to 1960s for the Methodist Children's Home (MCH). The MCH cares for children living in foster care, experiencing homelessness, or enduring other similar crises. For decades, MCH brought children to the land that is now DaySpring property to tend to cows, pigs, and chickens; pick peaches; work in gardens; and play. Still today, there are implements of this era throughout the DaySpring property: an old farm truck, an old chicken coop, and, most iconically, a water storage pump and water tower flanking the oak grove. For the first time in DaySpring's two-decade history, our worship was in the shadow of this special era in the history of the place.

Not all historical awareness is so pleasant. Spring 2020 was also the period of the murders of George Floyd in Minneapolis, Breonna Taylor in Louisville, and Ahmaud Arbery in Georgia. Against the backdrop of the pandemic, the nation faced a wrenching racial violence epidemic resulting from the trauma of these killings. In Waco, Texas, racial violence is mapped against central Texas's violent history. One congregant worshiping under the live oaks was thinking about this legacy. "As we began worshiping on the first Sunday outdoors," he said, "I looked at the tree behind the pulpit and thought about the low-hanging branches. And I couldn't help but wonder if anyone had been lynched from any of these trees." That he would consider such a possibility is part of the consciousness of central Texas's history, particularly the racial violence that characterizes this part of the state. Taking account of the land under our feet is, at least in part, taking account of its social history and the history of the land around us.

Our relationship with the land is always bound with human relationships, sometimes for the flourishing of both land and human community but often with tragic consequences. To worship under, revere, and care for the trees is to bear the weight of their history and ours. The Huaco and Tonkawa tribes walked the central Texas land that is now our church grounds. They rested under the ancient live oaks, hunted the ancestors of local animals, and grew food to eat. Through violent interactions that characterized life here in the nineteenth century, white settlers colonized the area. Some of them enslaved Black and Brown people. We have no record of our church grounds from that era, but we are connected to the whole area's history—its triumphs and tragedies. Like many places in the South, the soil of central Texas is stained with the blood of its suffering Black and Brown communities.

To be sure, even those motivated to care for creation habitually treat the world of grass and trees as ahistorical. "Nature," in the American naturalist tradition, describes places supposedly beyond human impact. In this framing of the world, human civilization and wild nature stand in contrast to one another.[30] Henry David Thoreau, for example, famously traded the bourgeois society of Concord, Massachusetts, for wild Walden, where he wanted to live deliberately. Though it would surely make Thoreau cringe, his Walden years have been glossed as "the most famous vacation in American history."[31] Americans have sought vacation in nature ever since and sought to conserve places where they vacation. Pulitzer Prize–winning

Western writer Wallace Stegner draws on this tradition in his influential "Wilderness Letter" as he argues for protecting wilderness areas where humans have no permanent presence. For Stegner, the sweeping landscape of the American West is a "geography of hope" to be quarantined from the destructive commodification intrinsic to American industry and enterprise. He concludes, "We simply need that wild country available to us, even if we never do more than drive to its edge and look in."[32]

In the "Wilderness Letter" and characteristically throughout his novels, Stegner seems to harbor little constructive awareness of the humans who lived on the land. Constructing the idea of wilderness as a place untouched by human activity, he is either unaware or uninterested in the history of Native American presence on the land, nor is he interested in learning from their practices for its care and preservation. Thoreau's nineteenth-century experiment in living in nature and Stegner's twentieth-century advocacy for preserving the last of it tend to ignore the lived history of human habitation on and with the land.[33] Today, we realize that even "wild country" has a human history. We recognize the limits of a pervasive logic in American culture that romanticizes land while using it to devalue the lives of racial minorities. James Cone puts it bluntly:

> The logic that led to slavery and segregation in the Americas, colonization and apartheid in Africa, and the rule of white supremacy throughout the world is the same one that leads to the exploitation of animals and the ravaging of nature. It is a mechanistic and instrumental logic that defines everything and everybody in terms of contribution to the development and defense of white supremacy.[34]

If we are to conceive a practical theology of church grounds that avoids the trap of bland, romantic spirituality and the dark pitfalls that plague white environmentalism,[35] we must account for the real relationship between humans and the land in "relation to capital and also to carbon, in postmodernities and in parts per million, in dates and in degrees Celsius."[36] We in McLennan County, like hundreds of counties around the country, must include one more haunting metric: in bodies burned. Throughout the history of McLennan County, trees were used for lynching. No historical evidence suggests that DaySpring's live oak trees were used for this horrific crime, but they are the sort of available scaffolding that was used not far from our church grounds.

We have become mindful of this history and our place in it and try to be redemptive. Today, Waco has racial diversity. According to the 2021 census, Waco's population is 142,000. The white population is 43 percent, Black population is 20 percent, and Hispanic population is 32 percent. However, DaySpring, like many local congregations, is predominantly white. Mindful of this, we have partnered with several local African American congregations on ministry projects. Race relations have been an abiding theological concern for the congregation, amplified during the racism-fueled murders in the summer of 2020. In the aftermath of George Floyd's murder, about twenty DaySpring members participated in a march for justice in downtown Waco. Dozens of congregants participated in an eight-week study on race and racism using Jamar Tisby's *The Color of Compromise: The Truth about the American Church's Complicity in Racism*. Beginning in the summer of 2021, we have commemorated the Sundays between Juneteenth and July Fourth as a "Season of Justice and Peace," with study and sermons specifically on God's call to racial justice and reconciliation. Prompted in no small part by the story told by low-hanging live oak branches in central Texas, congregants have held the social trauma and tragedy of racial violence at the forefront of their minds.

In central Texas, the historic symbol of the logic of white supremacy is the lynching tree, specifically the now-long-gone tree near downtown Waco, from which Jesse Washington was hung and his body tortured on May 15, 1916.[37] James Cone describes the psychological effects of a lynching culture on Black communities:

> The lynching tree was the most horrifying symbol of white supremacy in black life. It was a shameful and painful way to die. The fear of lynching was so deep and widespread that most blacks were too scared even to publicly talk about it. When they heard of a person being lynched in their vicinity, they often ran home, pulled

down shades, and turned out lights—hoping the terror moment would pass without taking the lives of their relatives and friends.[38]

The Jesse Washington lynching was unique because of its scale and location. An estimated ten thousand observers in the heart of a larger city watched with excitement.[39] The story and, unusually, photos from Washington's particularly violent lynching spread nationally.[40] W. E. B. Du Bois was particularly incensed by the "Waco Horror," as he coined it, writing, "Any talk of the triumph of Christianity, or the spread of human culture, is idle twaddle as long as the Waco lynching is possible in the United States."[41] In 1920, Du Bois rereleased his 1911 poem-story "Jesus Christ in Georgia," updated to "Jesus Christ in Texas" to include a divine visitation to Waco at the time of the lynching. Throughout his visit, Jesus remains unrecognized, except to children and the downtrodden. A rector thinks he recognizes Jesus as someone he once knew, but Jesus denies their acquaintance.[42] Washington's lynching and Du Bois's subsequent advocacy were turning points in efforts to end the practice of lynching.

To be sure, the Waco Horror was far from an isolated occurrence around the nation or in central Texas.[43] At the National Memorial for Peace and Justice in Montgomery, Alabama, eight hundred steel monuments are suspended, one for each county in the United States where a racial terror lynching took place. Central Texas was a particularly violent breeding ground for racial terror. At the National Memorial, the monument for McLennan County lists the names of fifteen African Americans lynched there from 1885 to 1922. Historian William Carrigan describes the culture of central Texas as a cauldron of violence used as a means of maintaining social order and terrorizing those perceived to threaten it. White vigilantes who committed violence were lauded as "community heroes" and "defenders of justice" in a connective historical tissue that linked and shaped central Texas as a robust culture of violence.[44] All the ingredients were in central Texas, whose western border follows the Texas prairies to meet the Great Plains and whose eastern border follows the Trinity River. This was the westernmost point of profitable cotton agriculture and the attendant enslaved labor to produce it.

Geographically, agriculturally, and culturally, "central Texas can thus be said to lie on the edge of the South and the brim of the West."⁴⁵

At the intersection of South and West, a cauldron brewed from the violence of combined cultural histories and power struggles. The diversity of historical actors is simply not found in many other locales. As Carrigan writes,

> In particular, the region found itself contested by a slaveholding and mercantile elite, small landholders, poor farmers, African Americans, Native Americans, and Mexicans. Many people came together in the cultural borderlands of central Texas. It is unfortunate but hardly surprising that they did not always come in peace.⁴⁶

In his magisterial assessment of modern sensibilities, Charles Taylor reminds us, "Our past is sedimented in our present, and we are doomed to misidentify ourselves, as long as we can't do justice to where we come from."⁴⁷ The lynchings of Jesse Washington and fourteen other Black people travel in the geographical and historical orbit of enslavement, segregation, and violence that accompanied the establishment and maintenance of white supremacy in central Texas. The live oak trees on our church grounds have stood from the eighteenth century as silent observers or, as we tremble to imagine, scaffolding in the tragic history of central Texas. A predominantly white congregation bathed in dappled sunlight flickering through the branches of tall trees might ooze a warm, sentimental, ahistorical nature-spirituality for a while, but the history of this place ultimately disallows it. To account for our place and participation on land in central Texas is to understand its environmental and social dimensions and to know ourselves in relationship with the history of the place. Linking concern for the environment with concern for racial justice, Cone maintains that to address one issue is to address both:

> People who struggle against environmental degradation but do not incorporate in it a disciplined and sustained fight against white supremacy are racists—whether they acknowledge it or not. The fight for justice cannot be segregated but must be integrated with the fight for life in all its forms.⁴⁸

God and Culture in a Baptist Church

If Norman Wirzba worries about humans who live as if they are disembodied from the Earth, Franciscan theologian Ilia Delio worries likewise about Christians whose faith places God so distant from the Earth that their spirituality becomes otherworldly. Our inability to see is so severe that we live with what she calls a "Christian unconsciousness." Delio laments, "We pray to the God of heaven and earth yet we relate to God as if God has nothing to do with earth."[49] I must say that in my experience, this isn't precisely true, at least in certain contexts. Ask a room of middle-class, white, churchgoing American Protestant Christians to describe when they have experienced God, and they will eagerly describe standing on the rim of the Grand Canyon or a favorite quiet place on the seaside. They will describe places where the world seems big and they seem small in comparison. For many people, the superlative places of the natural world are experienced as mystical sites of encounter, even for people who are thoroughly entrenched in a religious culture of materialistic dualism. Contra Delio, it seems that most people intuit that God may have something to do with at least some places on the Earth, or they have something to do with God in places where they feel small and God seems big.

In some spiritual traditions, these are described as "thin places." The preacher Barbara Brown Taylor describes a thin place as an area where "the veil between heaven and earth is pulled back" and that "makes you work to be more aware of the thin veil between the apparent reality and the deeper reality."[50] Sainthood must be the condition of living in the world in such a way that every place is a thin place. Nevertheless, we can see the challenge of translating an occasional personal experience into a holistic, ecologically mindful spirituality. Though I am folding in spiritual wisdom from the Franciscan tradition, DaySpring is a Baptist Church in central Texas, and we must admit that Baptists, as a group, have rarely been overly enthusiastic about social justice issues or environmental concerns.

This was made clear to me in the early 1990s when, as a student at Texas A&M University, I regularly joined a mid-week noontime prayer service at the Baptist Student Union (BSU). On one occasion, our speaker talked about our need to trust God's providence and care. As an example, he referenced well-publicized international efforts to address the problem of the hole in the ozone layer of Earth's atmosphere. In the 1980s, atmospheric scientists had raised an alarm that the ozone layer was being depleted due to the release of chlorofluorocarbons widely used in hairsprays and refrigerants. An international consensus successfully emerged to regulate CFCs, and within a few years, the ozone layer began to repair. It is a rare success story of science-based, international, multi-agency cooperation to solve an environmental catastrophe.[51] Today, it is a hopeful reminder that such cooperation and healing are possible. However, our speaker made it clear that he was unimpressed with the scientific consensus on the ozone layer, the need to address the issue, and environmental matters in general. He said, "You don't need to worry about the hole in the ozone. You don't need to worry about global warming. God is in control. The Earth's going to burn one day anyway, so it doesn't matter what we do or don't do. It's all in God's hands." No one else in the room blinked or seemed to be bothered by this at all.

I suppose this was typical fare for Baptist preaching, and it still is in many pulpits: God is sovereign; the eschaton is coming soon, at which time Earth will be destroyed; Christians will be delivered to their heavenly, non-bodily reward. And Christ will reign. From this perspective, creation is the stage on which Christ's creation drama plays out in individual human hearts. Leaving the BSU that day, a fellow student parroted what he had just heard: "See, we don't need to worry about the Earth at all." At the time, I had no way of unpacking the deeply layered dualistic theological-cultural context from which that sermon had sprung. Fortunately, many Baptist and evangelical leaders have successfully counteracted this common dualistic theology. But is anyone listening? Even today, despite near-unanimous consent within the scientific community on human-induced climate change,[52] public opinion remains polarized, and so-called Christian messaging is winning.[53]

The Evangelical Climate Initiative

Today, many influential Christian leaders are trying to change minds on the subject. In February 2006, readers of the *New York Times* and *Christianity Today* were confronted with a full-page ad announcing the Evangelical Climate Initiative (ECI), a four-part statement signed by some of the world's most well-known and influential evangelical Christian leaders.[54] The ECI Call to Action was not the first Christian statement on the environment, yet it represented a significant public move by conservative evangelicals to call the American church to attention and action on climate change. Until Pope Francis's encyclical *Laudato Si'* in 2015, the ECI was arguably the most significant Christian statement on environmental concerns in a generation or more. The ECI was a notable attempt to rebuff the claim, made infamous by Lynn White Jr. in 1967, that Western Christian tradition was largely to blame for the world's ecological crisis.[55] White argued that Christian belief in a transcendent deity who proffers otherworldly spiritual rewards promoted an anthropocentric "dominion over nature" worldview and said environmental degradation would continue as long as this theology persisted.[56]

Lynn White's theory that Western Christian dualism created the conditions for Western abuse of creation ran straight through that sermon I heard at the BSU. As is well documented, the politically and denominationally conservative end of the partisan spectrum in the US correlates significantly with skepticism about the human role in climate change.[57] The ECI made claims that, while familiar to the scientific community, were then considered scandalous in theologically conservative denominations:

1. Human-induced climate change is real.
2. Consequences will be significant and will hit [economically vulnerable groups] the hardest.
3. Christian moral convictions demand our response to the climate change problem.
4. The need to act now is urgent. Governments, businesses, churches, and individuals all have a role to play in addressing climate change—starting now.[58]

The ECI was signed by leading Christian personalities of the day, among whom were Rick Warren (pastor, Saddleback Church), Duane Litfin (president, Wheaton College), David Neff (editor, *Christianity Today*), and Todd Bassett (national commander, Salvation Army). Despite objections from fellow conservatives, hopeful allies heralded the ECI as a landmark moment for the Christian environmental movement, representing a crowning achievement of the "Greening of Christianity." The headwinds then were undoubtedly strong. More than fifteen years after the ECI statement, we would like to know whether it made a difference to Christian perspectives on the environment.[59]

The "Greening" of Christianity?

According to the Greening of Christianity theory, Christians, persuaded by the Evangelical Climate Initiative and other similar public statements, have now awakened to a new environmentalism in which they are increasingly active personally and systemically to effect change on behalf of the environment. The old notion of biblically authorized *dominion* over the Earth is being recast as a call to careful and loving *stewardship* of Earth's resources. Christians are listening and changing their ways. However, the Greening of Christianity, while an attractive thesis encouraged by reams of anecdotal evidence, remains unverified when examined through sociological analysis. According to surveys and focus groups among laity in evangelical churches, institutional environmental consciousness demonstrated by ECI and others at the "grasstops" has not trickled down to the grassroots.[60]

Katharine Wilkinson's research among laity in Protestant congregations throughout the southern United States reveals a framework of Christian skepticism, even antagonism, to environmental concerns largely based on scientific skepticism, conservative political ideology, individualism, and antistructuralism.[61] Indeed, sorting out the specific role of religion and religiosity in determining environmental concern is an inconclusive process though some general trends can be identified. For example, Arbuckle and Konisky find that evangelical Protestant denominations tend to express the lowest levels of environmental concern among Christian groups and that a negative correlation exists between religious commitment and ecological concern.[62] Studies like these demonstrate scant evidence that Christians as a whole have expressed more environmental concern over time. Konisky somberly concludes that the "now considerable body of research collectively points to a conclusion more consistent with White's thesis and the notion that Christians tend to express less worry about environmental quality."[63]

This is my theory: environmental concern cannot be shaped or assessed purely from a theory-to-practice methodology; it is better understood as a practice-theory-practice hermeneutical spiral. We do not simply need a new cosmology per White or a bold statement from religious leaders per the ECI.[64] *A new imaginary comes only through critical integration of our practices with our theology that births new practices and in turn reshapes our theology.*

By only framing our relationship with creation as environmental crisis and climate change policy, we fail to access and activate the many ways Christians care deeply about creation, particularly the places they know and love. In missing the importance of personal points of connection, we overlook key elements in understanding the population, and we are ill-equipped to help individuals and communities connect the dots between their love of a place and how that place is affected by planetary issues such as climate change. We are also incapable of helping people recognize the ways they have agency in the face of daunting, super-scaled problems. In the abstract, Christians may indicate that they do not have spiritual or theological concerns for the environment or support climate change mitigation efforts, but in the material reality of the places they love, they tell a different story. Even among Baptists in Texas, it is in those stories of connection with place that hope for "greening" may truly reside.

Church Grounds as a Site of Conscience

It is to this end that I propose in this book four conceptual framings for church grounds specifically and all grounds by extension: church grounds as a site of conscience (ch. 2), an ecology of grace (ch. 3), holy ground (ch. 4), and a geography of hope (ch. 5). Each framing responds to a step in the Franciscan prayer journey.

Church grounds as a site of conscience responds to the step in prayer known as *gaze*. I am borrowing the designation "site of conscience" from the United Nations Educational, Scientific, and Cultural Organization (UNESCO) designation and the International Sites of Conscience group though I'm not suggesting that any given congregation's grounds, nor DaySpring's in particular, should apply for formal UNESCO designation. Rather, I am invoking the idea of the designation as a conceptual framework for places that are seen with an environmental, historical, and theological gaze.

The concept of a UNESCO Site of Conscience developed in the 1990s at the crossroads of human rights advocacy and heritage conservation in recognition of places that interpret history, engage the public in programs that stimulate dialogue on pressing social issues, share opportunities for public involvement and positive action on the issues raised at the site, and promote justice and universal cultures of human rights.[65] Sites of conscience "often deal with events in recent living memory and are focused on confronting the history of what happened at that place and spurring visitors to reflect on history's contemporary implications."[66]

Truly seeing a place involves recognizing the ways our lives are bound up in relationship with the world and others around us. At Glacier National Park, it is seeing the effects of climate change on the glaciers and the history of the dislocation of the Blackfeet Nation from their tribal lands. At DaySpring, it means seeing the peace and tranquility of the space, not just as a retreat from the world's violence but as a place for healing. This is what it means to be a site that sparks the Christian consciousness. At the site of one famous American icon, it means learning to tell the truth.

One of the highlights of Charlottesville, Virginia, is a tour of Thomas Jefferson's famed mansion and farm, Monticello. While living in Charlottesville in the early 2000s, I accompanied visiting friends on their tours until I could have given the tour myself. While I admired the house and the grounds, I found it somewhat curious that tour guides made little mention of the roles of enslaved people on Jefferson's plantation and no mention, as I recall, of the "relationship" between Thomas and his enslaved housemaid Sally or the children he fathered by her. The fact that Jefferson held many enslaved persons, up to 130 at a time, was public knowledge but hardly registered on the official tour. That Jefferson fathered multiple children with one of his slaves was unmentioned. The official Monticello tour was curated to prevent visitors from confronting the difficult social questions inherent to the history and legacy of Jefferson's Monticello.

But something changed over time. In 2019, we took our children to Monticello and immediately noticed a change in the approach to dealing with Jefferson's duplicitous history: the lives of enslaved people were featured prominently in the presentation. There is now a dedicated tour of slave quarters offered throughout the day. In one room of the mansion, the tour guide spoke candidly about Sally Hemings and her relationship with Jefferson. The guide answered any question asked of her with knowledge and candor.[67] I wondered about this change. What prompted this? Who at the Thomas Jefferson Foundation decided to acknowledge the dark side of Jefferson's legacy and to explain that Monticello is as much an achievement of enslaved persons' labor and creative ingenuity as Thomas Jefferson's creativity—that it is a plantation, not just an estate? Who wrote Black people back into their story on the grounds from which they had been whitewashed?

I tell this story of our history and place in the world to help frame the historical and social dimension of our relationship with the land, particularly the context of the DaySpring grounds. Monticello, the home of Thomas Jefferson, author of the Declaration of Independence, is a UNESCO heritage site; now, the site bears witness to enslavement and to the plight and contribution of enslaved workers. It's an International Site of Conscience, a designation recognizing "historic sites, museums, and memory initiatives—that activate the power of places of memory to engage the public with a deeper understanding of the past and inspire action to shape a just future."[68]

Like Monticello, church grounds can function as sites of conscience when seen with penetrating insight. In a culture like ours in central Texas, in the southern United States, ignoring the racial history of a place is an act of white privilege. To know a place is to account for its history, even its tragic history. This dark thread of American history ties Jefferson's early nineteenth-century slave-keeping on top of the mountain with Charlottesville's 2017 Unite the Right rally through the city streets. Perhaps this was the moment that prompted the transformation of the Monticello narrative, forcing its keepers to abandon the animated suspension of its past and finally bring it to light and to life. Monticello's tour in 2019 felt honest in a way that a previous generation failed to realize.[69] Because it felt honest, the tour engaged visitors personally; since we were not just visiting a historical site frozen in time, we related to our past and thus learned our place in its unfolding story. This kind of dialectical engagement with history is paramount for seeing with a penetrating vision.

Sites of conscience are not entrenched in the past but are forward-looking. They "are distinct in their steadfast commitment to the future. Their exhibition content, public programming, and mission are resolutely forward-thinking. They are connected with the past only insofar as it can teach and inspire communities to act upon related issues today."[70] Sites that spark our consciousness may be marked formally by historical markers. In downtown Waco, city leaders recently unveiled a Texas historical marker commemorating the lynching of Jesse Washington.[71] A monument may be raised to honor individuals in the past. The University of Virginia recently erected such a monument for enslaved laborers who constructed the university.[72] Or signage may help tell a deeper story when done well. At Glacier National Park, signs mark the location of glaciers at points in history, though the signs had to be replaced after incorrectly forecasting the demise of glaciers by 2020.[73] Any of these approaches may be appropriate for some church grounds. For the church, the question is, *how do our past and our context inspire or inform our future ministry and witness? How is our witness to the gospel re-placed as we see the world in a new way?*

For DaySpring, the signs are already all around us. The absence of native grasses prompts us to ask how our campus may become carbon-neutral and a habitat for diverse creatures. The live oak trees pose the challenge of racial justice and racial reconciliation. And the water tower, a vestige of the children's home era, challenges us to create a church environment in which vulnerable children are received and healed through their engagement on the grounds in both play and participation.

For a church's grounds to function as a site of conscience, the congregation must cultivate relational awareness of the place, the people, and the spirituality. What is this place? What has been the relationship between the people and the place and the people to one another in this place? What do we believe about God in and through this place? How may this be a site of spiritual encounter?

The oldest churches in Europe were always sites of conscience. Churches in Rome like St. Peter's Basilica on Vatican Hill or St. Paul-Outside-the-Walls Basilica were founded over the burial tombs of the saints. From the earliest centuries, Christians gathered for remembrance at the tombs of their beloveds and the saints. The Basilica St. Agnes-Outside-the-Walls, for example, was established in the fourth century at the tomb of a thirteen-year-old girl, Agnes, who was martyred for refusing to worship Roman gods. Worship took place around the living memory of her witness to faith. As Margaret Visser details in *Geometry of Love*, for more than 1,700 years, the church has not forgotten the courage of that little girl. St. Agnes Basilica, then, is not merely a place of remembrance of the past. It is an embodied site of conscience, in stone and wood, of the faithfulness of one of God's saints, and it bears witness to the courage of faith all Christians may be called to demonstrate. Visser glosses St. Agnes Basilica as "an ordinary church," though most of us would dispute that a church so beautiful dating to the fourth century is hardly ordinary. But Visser's point suggests that the experience of one church is reflective of churches everywhere.[74]

Few churches in America are built on ground that is anything of similar historic significance. But aren't they? Aren't all ordinary places, once seen with a penetrating gaze, also places of consciousness? Anywhere in the world the altar is set and the Eucharist is shared is a place of embodied memory. The question is simply, *what holy ground is this on which we stand?*

Conclusion

We ought to worry about the retreating glaciers in northwest Montana and elsewhere, but if we talk about our relationship with creation only as environmental crisis and climate change policy, we will continue to fall short of accessing and activating the many ways Christians care deeply about creation, particularly the places they know and love, such as their church grounds. When we miss the importance of personal points of connection, we not only miss key elements in understanding the population but are also ill-equipped to help individuals and communities connect the dots between their love of a place and how that place is affected by planetary issues such as climate change. We are also incapable of helping people recognize the ways they have agency in the face of daunting, super-scaled problems. In the abstract, Christians may indicate that they do not have spiritual or theological concerns for the environment or support climate change mitigation efforts, but in the material reality of the places they love, they tell a different story. It is in those stories of connection with place that hope for "greening" may truly reside. Places have environmental, social, theological, and historical meaning. No place is bereft of meaning; it is a matter of paying attention to it in every way possible.

In this chapter, I have sought to establish the starting place for an ecological consciousness as "turning aside" to see clearly and thoroughly the place where you are standing. While there are lovely things here, both to our eyes and in our past, our history in central Texas mirrors the environmental degradations characteristic of American westward expansion, the racial injustice and violence that accompanied it, and the dualistic spirituality that flows in its wake and distances those concerns from contemporary individualized spirituality. Yet God's creative act, mirrored in the covenant with Israel, interweaves relationship between God, others, and the world. That we see brokenness from all three angles testifies to our need for places that provoke our consciousness of the reality of the situation. It is necessary to address these three angles if we are to be made whole. Church grounds are well situated in our affections and cultural landscape to serve as such sites of conscience.

A site of conscience helps us understand how each relational angle contributes to and is shaped by the other angles. We have not considered yet how dualistic spirituality, the degradation of land, and racial violence are connected, but we begin to see the totality of our need for reconciliation. There is no simple solution to our myriad troubles; everything is connected. This is the good news, ultimately. At this point in our journey, it is important to see clearly, with penetrating vision, that we may be re-earthed. At a site of conscience, memory is turned into action. In the next chapter, we begin to consider how each of these three dimensions is linked to the others in the past and linked to Christian witness in the world we have brought into being.

Chapter 3

Church Grounds as an Ecology of Grace

We live most of our lives among our neighbors in relatively ordinary landscapes, like those of my home, neighborhood, and church grounds in central Texas. Absent the sweeping panoramas of Yosemite or Redwoods, ordinary places are neither escapes nor vacations, unworthy of federal protection. But these places are the habitats of our lives and where we live out our allegiances and affections. They are the places where we work out our deepest commitments with those of our neighbors. In ordinary space and time, we confront our limitations—both of materiality and of our imaginations. We cultivate our love for God and neighbor in the ordinary places, not the fierce landscapes. The question is how such ordinary habitats can include creation and our neighbors in an ecology of grace.

Paul Brockelman, in "With New Eyes," tells the story of famous conservationist John Muir, who "went through a period of profound turmoil and disorientation in which he struggled to find himself and his role in life. Pulled this way and that, he couldn't seem to discover who he was or was to become."[1] And then, in March 1867, at the height of his melancholy, Muir suffered an eye injury at his mechanic's shop, rendering him essentially without sight. He was devastated: "I would have gladly died . . . my eyes closed forever on all God's beauty! . . . I am lost!" A specialist wrapped Muir's eyes in bandages and confined him to a darkened room for a month. On an April day, a month after his accident, the bandages were removed, the shades raised, and Muir discovered he was able to see again! The experience transformed him. That he "might be true to himself," Muir reoriented his life to exploring nature and advocating for its conservation.[2] From this point forward, Muir lived his life in and among astonishing landscapes that would become national parks in no small part due to his advocacy.

Consider: Taking a Critical Look

St. Clare's path of prayer helps us take a critical look at our attitudes, actions, and relationships with the world. It may be a flash of focus or a long journey of starts and stops, but one way or another, in Clare's terms of prayer, *gaze* leads us to *consider* when we experience an impulse to study, investigate, and examine what has gripped our attention. Franciscan spirituality is comfortable with scientific rigor, and some argue that the Franciscan tradition gave birth to the scientific method in the modern era.[3] There are times when we are so captivated by the object of our attention that we desire to know the thing as fully as possible, whether it is the biochemical inner workings of a field of wildflowers or an ancient text. This is often initiated when, as Richard Osmer describes it, an experience "brings us up short," an experience that has the potential of evoking new interpretive activity. These experiences "puncture taken-for-granted interpretations of God, morality, and what it means to live as a faithful Christian," such as losing a job at midlife, going through a divorce, discovering your government is practicing torture, or witnessing changes in the congregation's neighborhood.[4] In Muir's case, the accident that almost cost him his eyesight changed his life. For the remainder of his life, Muir helped Americans see the vast Western landscapes with new eyes. He became the patron saint of American wilderness, advocating for delight in and preservation of the American landscape. Muir translated his personal experience of delight and transcendence in the mountains of California into a mission to "save the American soul from total surrender to materialism."[5] Yet for all of this, Muir could see the land with clear eyes but could not see his neighbors with any grace, describing "Native Americans and Black people as dirty, lazy and uncivilized." In an essay collection published in 1901 to promote national parks, he assured prospective tourists that "As to Indians, most of them are dead or civilized into useless innocence."⁶ His vision of his fellow humans was uncritically accepted by those who followed him in the Sierra Club and other wilderness conservation advocacy efforts. It was only in 2020 that the Sierra Club critically assessed the racist legacies of the organization's founders.⁷

In the Old Testament, Moses, like Muir, had an experience that gave him new eyes to see the world. Liberated from Pharoah's house, exiled from Egypt, and alone in the wilderness, Moses was brought up short and given new eyes at the sight of a bush burning but not consumed. And like Muir, Moses translated a transcendent experience in the wilderness into a life- and culture-saving mission that changed the world. Unlike Muir, Moses's experience led him to an ecology of grace in the wilderness of God's redemptive purposes. Let us now take close consideration of the centrality of this story in the exodus experience. In doing so, we have two aims: to discover the fruit of close, focused consideration as a step of prayer and to see what this particular story—which has already captivated our attention—will reveal to us.

Consider Moses Considering the Burning Bush

A bush is burning but not consumed. Moses says, "I must turn aside and look at this great sight, and see why the bush is not burned up" (Exod 3:3). His other concerns—for his animals and his personal safety—fall away as he "turns aside" from them to examine the mystery that has captivated his attention. As a Scripture-reading strategy, penetrating attention to what is before us creates a desire to understand fully what we encounter. This desire is a form of love and, when enacted, is a form of prayer. Tools of study such as form criticism, typological analysis, and structural analysis can deepen our grasp of the meaning of the text and sharpen our attention on the central message it holds for us. What may we learn from Exodus 3:1-6 by considering it as attentively as Moses attends to the bush? Despite its relatively smooth narrative flow, certain difficulties in the passage have prompted students to carve up Exodus 3:1-6 into various source threads. By employing historical-critical methods, they found seams of redaction glaring through the three designations of the deity appearing in unusually rapid succession.[8]

> (2) There the *angel of the* LORD (*mal'ak YHWH*) appeared to him in a flame of fire out of a bush; he looked, and the bush was blazing, yet it was not consumed. (3) Then Moses said, "I must turn aside and look at this great sight and see why the bush is not burned up." (4) When *the* LORD (*YHWH*) saw that he had turned aside to see, *God* (*Elohim*) called to him out of the bush, "Moses, Moses!" And he said, "Here I am."

One way to examine the story is to deduce the contributions of J, E, and P sources. But there is another way: to read the revelation of the names of the deity. Moving beyond the examination of potential clumsy redaction seams, read the passage as an experience of prayer and experience how the names of God in succession invite the reader into the phenomenology of the mysterious presence in the burning bush. Each name (*mal'ak YHWH . . . YHWH . . . Elohim*) represents a stage in the human-divine interaction of theophany. From this perspective, the various names of God reveal Moses' perspective as he tries to make sense of the situation in which he finds himself. It is as if the spiritual light of understanding is slowly beginning to dawn.

Like Moses, we need time and space to process what we are experiencing. Nothing particularly mythical or mystical has happened to this point to prepare Moses or the reader of Exodus for the burning bush. The theophany is a sharp break from the earthbound narrative up to now, so the narrator handles it carefully, taking the reader with Moses to see what this sight is.[9] All of our focus is demanded of us, and the payoff is worth it all.

Let us go back now and read it again carefully, entering the experience of the story with Moses. As he considers the scene before him, Moses sees in the burning bush a divine phenomenon, *mal'ak YHWH*, the angel of the Lord. The circumlocution suggests Moses's uncertainty as he approaches the strange sight before him. We know that this angel of the Lord is some kind of messenger of God present at the burning bush, but we are left pondering who this is and what this means.

While Moses ponders this from within the limits of his knowledge, *YHWH* (the Lord) sees Moses. Note that *YHWH* sees him, but Moses does not yet see *YHWH*. To this point, seen by *YHWH*, Moses's only possible categorical understanding of the deity calling to him is *elohim*, the generic name for "god." However, "god" will be self-defined soon by relationship with the patriarchs—"I am the *Elohim* of your father, the *Elohim* of Abraham, the *Elohim* of Isaac, and the *Elohim* of Jacob"—and by relationship with the people God is sending Moses to deliver: "my people, the children of Israel, out of Egypt" (Exod 3:10). Rewarding readers who give close attention, multiple rhetorical tools communicate how Moses's call, a radical break with the past, is initiated by God. Brevard Childs writes, "Neither previous faith nor any other personal endowment had the slightest part to play in preparing a man who was called to stand before *YHWH* for his vocation."[10]

As significant as the personal spiritual experience of the bush may have been for Moses, the purpose of the encounter from God's perspective was to initiate freedom for the slaves of Egypt. (In an echo, after his accident and healing, Muir understood his vocation to be to liberate Americans from the tyranny of consumption.) In terms of semiotician Roland Barthes, the burning bush is a particularly dramatic example of a "distributive function,"[11] a narrative feature that serves as a hinge, a place where the story pivots decisively. For Moses, the experience at the bush encounter is the beginning of a call to return to a world—Pharoah's Egypt—that he once fled in fear, where he will confront an insurmountable challenge to secure the freedom of God's enslaved people. Not only is Moses changed at the burning bush, but every major character and relationship in the wider narrative of Israel's bondage and deliverance is changed by Exodus 3:1-6. Consider the permanent shifts in characters and relationships in the Exodus narrative before and after the burning bush:

Exodus 1–2		Exodus 3f
Pharaoh is savior, then oppressor		Pharaoh is enemy
Hebrew slave, singular		Hebrew slaves: "the people"
Egyptian soldier, killed	**Burning Bush**	Egyptian army, drowned
Moses mocked		Moses followed
God unknown/ hidden/ silent		God revealed and active

By closely considering the text, we see how the deep structure of the narrative reinforces its phenomenological drama. God's calling presence in the burning bush takes center stage in this pericope, and, one may argue, the entire arc of Israel's history is distributed from this encounter. This encounter with God is the means by which the coming transformation begins. Through careful consideration of the text at hand, we have discovered a remarkable paradigm: the place where God is met in creation can be a transcendent personal experience—the beginning of our personal transformation *and* the beginning of our ability to hear and respond to God's call for deliverance of a suffering world. "Consider this!" the narrator of Exodus asks of us: God speaks through creation's travails, even a bush burning in the wilderness.

Brought Up Short

This extended consideration of the burning bush story both reflects Moses's curious examination of the bush ("What is this? I must turn aside to see.") and demonstrates the attention we give to what registers with significance in our consciousness. Richard Osmer describes these moments as those that "bring us up short." When we turn, as we do now, to consider our environmental context, we may be brought up short by a burning flame such as this that diagnoses our effects on the Earth as "Anthropocene." It may be that terms such as "ecological crisis" or "environmental degradation" are far too tame for the world we discover we are bringing about when we pay attention to what it is: a world on fire and also being consumed.

> It is of the utmost importance to understand that the "Anthropocene" is not a term coined to describe the continued spread of human impacts on the landscape or further modification to ecosystems; it is instead a term describing a rupture in the functioning of the Earth system as a whole, so much so that the Earth has now entered a new geological epoch.[12]

Clive Hamilton's description of "rupture in the functioning of the Earth" is intended to be startling and demands a response. Considering the consequences of recent human history, it is not, however, without merit. Let us consider this astonishing claim. Something is breaking, and collectively, we are somehow breaking it. How did we get ourselves, and all creation, into this mess? And how do we get out of it? In this chapter, I explore (as if there were a burning bush right in front of us) the implications of the idea of "Anthropocene" as a description of and warning about the impacts of modern human life within the (dys-functioning) Earth system. By understanding the ecological rupture, we may begin to see more clearly how Christians can lead humanity's ecological reformation.

In the last chapter, I looked closely at the *what*: What is happening in the world as seen through the prism of the grounds of DaySpring Baptist Church? In this chapter, I consider the exceedingly complex challenge of *why*: Why are humans causing widespread environmental destruction? Even beginning to come to an answer to that sort of question will help us get clear on another *what* and another *why*: *What* ought we to do now, and *why* ought we to do it? To help in this task, I first consider the science of metabolism and its usefulness as a metaphor for the functioning of the Earth system. Key to metabolism—as science and metaphor—is the idea of process. Each creature, humans included, participates in the ongoing processes by which life is given and shared. When the soundtrack of *The Lion King* croons about "the circle of life," there is truth about the way the Earth system functions in the air we breathe, the soil beneath our feet, the food we eat, and the waste we produce. Metabolism, as a description of biochemical processes and as a metaphor for healthy processes, names the circle of life as the basic level of food and energy, waste and soil, carbon and oxygen.

Second, I introduce the discipline of environmental sociology, which studies how environmental and social phenomena can be understood as the consequences of rifts in metabolic cycles. The development of "The Theory of Metabolic Rift" helps us understand how the human relationship with Earth is complex, ordinary, interrelated, and broken. My aim here is to give an account of the context of life in the Anthropocene as thorough as the account of Moses at the burning bush. Anthropocene is a complex social and ecological designation that most of us inhabit for seemingly ordinary reasons even while the collective, interrelated consequences of such are breaking people and causing the travail of creation.

Welcome to the Anthropocene[13]

In the newsletter of the International Geosphere-Biosphere Programme, atmospheric chemist and Nobel laureate Paul Crutzen and his colleague Eugene Stoermer first proposed in 2000 the term *Anthropocene* to identify a new epoch in geological time in which human activity has been the dominant influence on the Earth's climate.

> To assign a more specific date to the onset of the "Anthropocene" seems somewhat arbitrary, but we propose the latter part of the 18th century, although we are aware that alternative proposals can be made . . . . However, we choose this date because, during the past two centuries, the global effects of human activities have become clearly noticeable. This is the period when data retrieved from glacial ice cores show the beginning of a growth in the atmospheric concentrations of several "greenhouse gases" in particular CO_2 and CH_4 [methane]. Such a starting date also coincides with James Watt's invention of the steam engine in 1784.[14]

Taking seriously the implications of human-caused climate change, humanities scholars are deconstructing the distinction between human history and natural history. Ian Baucom at the University of Virginia proposes that "our understanding of the *force* of human politics, history, and culture must be held in interpretive tension and dialectical exchange with what we are discovering of the *forcings* of climate change as we address the fully planetary condition of the Anthropocene."[15] Baucom asks, what is this new world of the Anthropocene? What planetary conjecture does it describe? In other words, if we set out to care for creation, what are the conditions of creation for which we are to care, and what is our role in creating those conditions? It is baffling to think of our context in terms of geological epochs, yet to give a full account of the context now requires such categorical assessment. A changing climate on Earth is the ecological context of all life, including every human life, whether we are fully conscious of our situation. The effects of climate change, soil degradation, and pollution are embedded in every place on Earth.[16]

This new reality is directly linked to historic and ongoing human activity. In countless quotidian ways, we modern Westerners inherit and extend a way of life by which the planetary conditions for life are being altered.[17] The far-reaching consequences of the Anthropocene hollow out antiquated notions of sanctuary, wilderness, or nature as places beyond human influence. No place on Earth is untouched by human activity. We should at least pause over this statement. It was not always so, but due to rapid population growth and voracious consumption over the last two centuries, there is no "nature" in the world separated and distinct from human life, and there is no natural history set apart from human history. Anthropocene offers a critical framework for understanding the condition of the world and for any self-aware attempts to be caretakers of any particular piece of creation. It may be possible, with some short-term political gains, to avoid a discussion of climate change when discussing Christian responsibility with creation. By now, we can see that we are avoiding the truth of our existence and the implications of our way of life in doing so. In denying or disregarding the conditions described by Anthropocene, we, perhaps willfully, neglect to account for the vast implications of our activities so thoroughly normalized in modern daily life.[18] In doing that, we forestall true, meaningful participation in the work of renewing our relationship with creation. For Christians, the inability or lack of desire to do so is a matter both practical and theological, both real and critical, both imminent and eschatological.

Anthropocene Rift: "Metabolism" as Root Metaphor

Metabolism is the ultimate "process" theology of creation. The term *metabolism*, introduced as early as 1815, was adopted in the 1830s and 1840s by physiologists to refer to material exchanges within the body related primarily to respiration. Over the following decades, the idea became a key concept applied to the cellular level and in the analysis of entire systems of organisms.[19] Today, the concept of metabolism "constitutes the basis on which life is sustained and grown and reproduction becomes possible."[20] In common usage (especially among middle-aged folks lamenting their expanding waistlines!), the root metaphor of "metabolism" describes the process by which a human body turns food into energy.[21] The metabolic function of a body is its capacity to process food inputs, generate energy, and manage its internal system. In the systems-theory approach to the relationship of organisms to their environments, metabolism refers both to the complex process of exchange by which an organism draws on materials and energies to convert these into resources necessary for growth, as well as the regulatory process that governs these complex interactions. Thus, metabolism as a concept can refer to "all biological levels, beginning with the single cell and ending with the ecosystem."[22] In a well-functioning system, an effective metabolism governs inputs and outputs, creating and reflecting good health. So metabolism describes the process of life, whether of the human body, the healthy soil of a farm, or the oxygen-carbon cycle in the atmosphere.[23]

Consider the usefulness of metabolism as a way to understand climate change. Today, sixty years after the debut of the Keeling Curve, we understand that CO_2 is a significant contributor to the warming of Earth's atmosphere. Yet, amid the flood of information, climate change alarm, and trash-can manifestos, we forget the lessons basic to grade school science class. Carbon dioxide is not our unnatural enemy but occupies a natural and necessary function in the metabolic process of life on Earth. Understanding this seeming paradox can help us demystify the phenomenon of climate change and clarify the causes and solutions to the problem. All animals, including humans, exhale CO_2 as we breathe. Volcanic eruptions produce concentrated levels of CO_2, as do decomposing vegetation, wildfires, and the slow decay of carbonate rocks.

When regulated in balanced exchange with oxygen-producing organisms and carbon-capturing ecosystems, CO_2 makes up a natural part of the metabolic cycle of life on Earth. Trees and grassland absorb CO_2 from the atmosphere and move it through their root systems into the soil, where it nurtures subterranean organisms. In metabolic exchange, trees and grasses, in turn, release oxygen into the atmosphere, which humans and other animals inhale, and the cycle continues. In a sustainable, regulated oxygen-carbon cycle, plants and animals depend on one another for life. This is the beauty of the metabolic design of creation as an ecological system, i.e., a community of creation giving and receiving life from one another.

The current state of the atmospheric metabolic cycle has become neither sustainable nor regulated. Since the industrial revolution of the mid-1800s, humans have burned massive quantities of fossil fuels, releasing vast and increasing levels of CO_2 into the atmosphere. In the same era, humans have also cut forests and plowed up prairie grasses that function as the world's most effective carbon absorbers, carbon "sinks." Predictably, through this release of excessive carbon into the atmosphere and the diminishment of Earth's capacity to absorb it, the metabolic oxygen-carbon cycle historically regulating the climate's temperature has ruptured. We have understood both the implications of this metabolic disruption and its human cause since the streets of Manchester were first blackened with soot.[24]

Similar insights became instructive to soil science in the late nineteenth century. Soil, it was discovered, is not merely an inert supporting structure to hold plants and trees in the ground; rather, like the atmosphere, it functions as a complex metabolic cycle of life. Briefly put, the vitality of soil depends on key nutrients such as nitrogen, potassium, and phosphorous (popularly referred to by gardeners as the NPK ratio). In a regulated environment, a diversity of plants both contribute to the soil and require varying amounts of these nutrients from the soil in their growth cycles.[25] Human activity, however, as with the oxygen-carbon cycle, has disrupted the natural cycles of soil life. Monoculture industrial agriculture, a vast field of corn, for example, uses key nutrients from the soil to grow the plants but does not replace these nutrients in the soil in a natural cycle. Growers have the option to address nutrient depletion by promoting a diversity of plants or by composting organic matter, but most rely on now-commonplace synthetic fertilizers, the production of which heavily depends on the burning of fossil fuels.[26] The disruption of soil metabolism and atmospheric metabolism go hand in hand.

Though atmospheric science is center stage in public discourse in the era of climate change, the health of soil is a more accessible idea to ordinary people. Waco area farmer Butch Tindell, who spoke with our congregation about the spiritual significance of the life of soil,[27] helped us see that the soil is already alive when it is healthy. Meeting outside on a beautiful fall evening, church members who heard Butch's words looked at the ground in a new way. Butch helped us become more alive by expanding our awareness of the complex, intricate, and desecrated life of the soil under our feet. Reaching down and scooping soil into his hands before us, Butch said, "There are billions of microorganisms in this scoop of soil . . . if the soil is healthy. If it is desecrated by fertilizers, pesticides, invasive grass species, and pollution, the soil dies. The soil is our origin and our destiny. We must care for its life as if it were our own."[28]

I suppose once upon a time, people enamored with industrial-era logic would have dismissed Butch's comments as mystical and impractical, but we see more and more clearly how this basic soil science is a neglected key to food systems. And, if it is mystical, then why not delight in the integration of mystical vision with environmental science? With a simple introduction to the rich life of often-overlooked soil beneath our feet, we became more aware of the tangible role our activities have in either nurturing or diminishing the vitality of the soil. The metabolic cycles inherent to healthy air and soil, while sophisticated at the technical level, are quite understandable to us, and they are spiritually delight-filled when we are mindful of our place in the richness of life all around and within us.

Humans and the Earth: Complex and Ordinary

A basic introduction to the science of metabolism describing life on Earth prepares us to reengage the question posed in this chapter: how did we get into this mess? To help us grasp the reasons that we are in the mess we are in and the implications of it for humans and the rest of creation, we can draw on insights from environmental sociologists who study the relationship of humans to our environments. The remainder of this section will be a dialogue between environmental sociology and Christian theology because we want to understand not only what is happening but why it is happening. And as it happens, both sociology and theology have experienced a significant environmental awakening in the last several decades.

Until the late twentieth century, the discipline of sociology exhibited the same ecological disinterest that characterized evangelical Protestant theologies and human exceptionalist philosophies. In the early 1970s, however, at about the same time Christians were responding to the accusations pressed on them by critics such as Lynn White Jr., environmental sociology as a subdiscipline began to develop as a response to the emergence of widespread societal attention to environmental problems. The field's formal debut came in 1976 with the founding of the Section of Environmental Sociology of the American Sociological Association. Two years later, William Catton and Riley Dunlap put forward the field's defining argument challenging the larger discipline's anthropocentric orientation by recognizing that "all societies are fundamentally embedded in and dependent on the natural environment."[29] While this may seem obvious in retrospect, it is a counterclaim to the promise of the technological age that aims to liberate humans from their embeddedness and dependence on the natural environment—food, labor, and waste, among other examples. It was a revolution within sociology that heretofore had focused exclusively on human communities without formal consideration of the relevance of their environments.

Environmental sociologists argue that environmental problems are social problems—humans both cause these problems and are affected by them. While the natural sciences (biology, chemistry, physics) are essential for understanding what is happening in the world (the science of metabolic exchange, for example), they have limited utility in explaining or changing social factors that lead to environmental problems. Even if we understand that burning fossil fuels disrupts the atmosphere's metabolic exchange cycle, we still do not yet understand *why* humans burn fossil fuels at the rate they do, why they continue to do so, who benefits, who suffers, and how to effect change. Measuring carbon in the atmosphere gives climate scientists the tools to assess the implications of greenhouse gases and forecast implications for seawater rise, glacier melt, and other effects of climate change. Yet even the data presented in the Keeling Curve graph is not as self-interpretive as human moral guidance. In a discussion about climate change with the Keeling Curve posted on a screen in front of us, one church member observed that CO_2 had only risen a small proportion in the last century. He asked, "So perhaps it's not as bad as it seems, if it's only risen from 275 to 420 parts per million?" Philosopher of science Bruno Latour empathizes with such uncertainty, perceiving that humans are typically ill-equipped to interpret data about increasing levels of CO_2 in the atmosphere. Latour asked how people are supposed to react to a piece of news in a headline screaming that CO_2 levels crossed another warning threshold.

> I think that it is easy for us to agree that, in modernism, people are not equipped with the mental and emotional repertoire to deal with such a vast scale of events; that they have difficulty submitting to such a rapid acceleration for which, in addition, they are supposed to feel responsible while, in the meantime, this call for action has none of the traits of their older revolutionary dreams. How can we simultaneously be part of such a long history, have such an important influence, and yet be so late in realizing what has happened and so utterly impotent in our attempts to fix it?[30]

Environmental sociology is the discipline of social science most directly engaging the challenge Latour describes. Three complementary perspectives dominate the field: the human ecological perspective, the Marxian political economy perspective, and the Theory of Metabolic Rift. In the human ecological perspective, biological, physical, and social aspects of life are considered together in the context of environment. The relationship between humans and their environments comprises a *system* of biological organisms and social beings in which the person and the environment are interconnected in an active relationship of mutual influence and change. From this perspective, we see the relationship between environmental problems (pollution, clean water, etc.) and basic conditions of society (population size and growth, scale of production and consumption, and technology).[31] Researchers commonly analyze a variety of environmental impacts of human activity, including ecological footprints, carbon dioxide outputs, and other greenhouse gas emissions.[32] The fundamental argument of human ecologists is reinforced through study after study: population and affluence are the primary driving forces behind environmental degradation.[33]

The development of the human ecology perspective in the 1970s coincided with the development of ecologically alert spiritualities at the margins of Western Christianity.[34] As a starting point, both fields—sociology and theology—were beginning to give attention to complex social dynamics and consequent environmental degradations. Environmental sociologists and Christian environmental activists, though both exceptions to the mainstream of their contemporaries, were beginning to raise awareness of the impacts of human activity on the environment. They began to note, with increasing urgency, the impact of environmental degradation on human communities, particularly people experiencing economic and social hardship.

Marxian Political Economics: Complex and Ordinary Forces

Any alliance between environmentally conscious sociologists and Western Christian theologians would be strained by environmental sociology's turn to Marxism in the 1980s.[35] Complementing the human ecological perspective with a sharp historical critique of industry and urbanization in Western Europe and America, students of Marxian political economy, such as John Bellamy Foster, blamed environmental and social degradation squarely on Western capitalism. If, per the human ecology perspective, population and affluence are the dominant causes of environmental degradation, then capitalism is the logic that drives population concentration in urban centers and creates the conditions for affluence and the relentless pursuit of it. "Treadmills" of production and consumption fuel the machine of capitalism through the insatiable consumption of natural resources. The machine trades (metabolizes) community, good work, and care for the land in exchange for profit (for a few), individualism, loneliness, and environmental degradation. And there is no end to it. Western society runs faster and faster and simply cannot find a way or a will to stop. Environmental degradation becomes an unfortunate and largely unseen by-product of ordinary activity in a relentless growth machine.

On the treadmill of production, modern industrial economies endlessly expand production to generate more profits for producers. The profit-seeking actions of producers who employ technological innovations result in job losses for laborers. Mechanization not only means fewer workers are needed per unit of production, thus straining the social fabric of labor, but it also requires higher levels of resource consumption and pollution.[36] The treadmill of production generates an accelerating cycle of profit, production, and environmental degradation.

Linked to the production side of the machine is the consumption side, which is also an accelerating treadmill of environmental and social degradation. For Americans who associate increased happiness primarily with increased material consumption, the pursuit of the "good life" is bound inextricably to material possessions and closely correlates with an emphasis on individuality and the loss of community. Paul Watchel observes the social psychology constitutive of the modern pursuit of affluence:

> Faced with the loneliness and vulnerability that come with the deprivation of a securely encompassing community, we have sought to quell the vulnerability through our possessions. When we can buy nice things, we can look around and see our homes well stocked and well equipped, we feel strong and expensive rather than small and endangered.[37]

Paradoxically, despite all the effort put into wealth accumulation, even as the cycle of competitive and individualized consumption accelerates, personal satisfaction does not increase, yet we continue to consume more than we need and consume more than we actually want.[38] On the treadmill of consumption, we accelerate the cycle of loss of community, increase of envy, and empty pursuit of happiness through material consumption.

The interconnected treadmills of production and consumption comprise "The Growth Machine" of economic and social life in Western cultures.[39] John Bellamy Foster identifies six key elements to its logic:

> 1. Increasing accumulation of wealth by a relatively small section of the population at the top of the social pyramid;
> 2. A long-term movement of workers away from self-employment into wage jobs contingent on the continual expansion of production;
> 3. New, revolutionary technologies to serve expansion are necessary for businesses to avoid extinction;
> 4. Wants are manufactured in a manner that creates insatiable hunger for more;
> 5. Government becomes increasingly responsible for promoting national economic development while ensuring some degree of "social security" for at least a portion of its citizens;
> 6. The dominant means of communication and education are part of the treadmill, serving to reinforce its priorities and values.[40]

American culture ubiquitously and uncritically inhabits the growth machine. We know that an economy is "thriving" when it is growing (running faster), and it is "failing" when it is not growing (grinding slower). Regarded as a good worthy of national political priority and individual relentless pursuit, growth is calculated officially as gross domestic product (GDP) and judged anecdotally by individuals as perceived purchasing power. The cost of the growth machine is measured by the loss of social bonds in community, forests harvested, racial inequalities, and CO_2 levels in the atmosphere. The cost is further experienced through the unseen force determining the lives of ordinary citizens.

A defining trait of the system is that it is kind of a giant squirrel cage. Everyone, or nearly everyone, is part of this treadmill and is unable or unwilling to get off. Investors and managers are driven by the need to accumulate wealth and expand the scale of their operations to prosper within a globally competitive milieu. For the vast majority, the commitment to the treadmill is more limited and indirect: they simply need to obtain jobs at livable wages. But to retain those jobs and to maintain a given standard of living in these circumstances, it is necessary, like the Red Queen in *Through the Looking Glass*, to run faster and faster to stay in the same place.[41]

"Running faster and faster" extends the metaphor of the treadmills of consumption and production and their social and environmental consequences: erosion of community fueled by individualism and envy without increases in personal satisfaction in exchange for increased, and increasingly dirty, extrapolation of resources from the Earth.[42] However darkly portrayed, individuals running on this "treadmill," operating as a cog in this "machine," or spinning in this "squirrel cage," have little agency to choose an alternative world if they even have the imagination for it. For the vast majority, participation is the necessary state of finding and keeping a job and satisfying the personal desires contrived by an increasingly invasive and sophisticated desire-making advertising industry. When we return to Bruno Latour's question, "What are we to do with this information [about climate change]?" we find ourselves bound as participants within a system in which we are both marginal agents of environmental destruction and virtually required to continue environmentally destructive practices just to stay in place. It's exhausting in every sense of the word, psychologically and environmentally. How do we get out of this mess we are making?

In Woodway, Texas

A debate in the small community of Woodway, Texas, illustrates the challenge of ordinary life. Woodway is a small, middle-class residential community on the outskirts of Waco. Most of the drinking water for the city of Woodway is drawn from six municipally owned wells supplemented by water from Lake Waco. The supplemental water is purchased through an agreement with the city of Waco, which controls the lake's water. In early fall 2023, the entire central Texas region was withering through an extended drought. The water level in Lake Waco had dropped eleven feet below normal to 55 percent of its usual capacity. Stage 2 water restrictions had been in place in Waco and surrounding areas since July 2023, and the triggering of Stage 3 restrictions had been staved off only by a few passing rain clouds in August. Meanwhile, several large neighborhood developments were in the final planning stages for Woodway. The city was growing. Out of concern for lake water levels and sustainable development and water use, a newly elected Woodway city council member, David Russell, proposed a temporary moratorium on new building permits that would require installing a water meter. Russell brought his recommendation to the Woodway City Council in a public meeting on September 26, 2023. The proposal suffered a resounding defeat and was mocked as being radical.

To be clear, I am not going to deride the decision made by the Woodway City Council to deny Russell's recommendation. These are difficult decisions with no clear winners, and other more modest conservation efforts, which had not been tried, probably should be enforced before taking such a step. I tell the story here to demonstrate how arguments put forward to oppose this proposal in one small municipality show how real-life concerns, particularly economic interests, methodically forestall conservation efforts and similar environmentally mindful municipal and corporate initiatives. Resistance is impractical. We must keep growing. The treadmill must continue.

At the open Woodway City Council meeting, fourteen Woodway residents spoke against the proposal, which, they argued, stifled future growth in Woodway and would hurt the city's tax base. An attorney for the Heart of Texas Builders Association suggested a number of legal obstacles to the proposal. One council member stated that residents, not developers, are responsible for conserving water. Builders do not use the water, he pointed out. Another council member said he would vote against the moratorium because he does not want to stop economic progress in Woodway: "I'm not going to stop the progress that's needed in Woodway to benefit our residents . . . . If you're asking me to stop Woodway residents from making a living, it's not happening."[43]

Consider the arguments put forward amid a drought against a water-conservation measure: it would hurt growth, diminish the tax base, stop progress, and prevent residents from making a living. Undoubtedly, these are all concerns that any civic leader needs to consider carefully. Is this all, though? There was no discussion about what a sustainable water usage rate might be, how the municipality or its residents could care for their water sources more responsibly, or whether unlimited growth is a good thing for the residents, the Earth system, or the relationship between the two. No one has made an unreasonable argument, but collectively, Woodway has set a course for their shared life together that looks a lot like a giant squirrel cage: a system designed to serve one purpose above all—economic growth. Such is the force of the logic of capitalism when it confronts environmental constraints.

Less obvious but also true is how the economic system, by design, is morally and culturally degrading. Recent sociological research demonstrates how "the (objectively) uneventful and (subjectively) irrelevant" contributions of individual actors produce environmental changes through the nominal workings of industrial societies.[44] Individuals within the system, with varying degrees of unawareness, contribute to environmental degradation with each revolution of the treadmill. The reasoning of economic growth contains little capacity to substantively address the environmental or social impacts of its logic. Within the consumptive-productive logic of capitalism, we become lonely individuals disconnected from societal bonds and environmental actors dislodged, in our daily awareness and decisions, from the Earth system in which and by which we have life.[45] That system, encompassing entities as diverse as the city council of

Woodway, Texas, and global multinational industries, is environmentally unsustainable by *design*. In this chapter, we will examine this design. St. Clare assures us this investigative consideration is an important step in the journey of prayer.

Metabolic Rift: Humans, Water, Soil, Air

In the natural rhythms of Earth's life, creatures function together in a carefully balanced regenerative cycle to sustain life. By contrast, in the growth machine of a capitalist economy, the twin treadmills of production and consumption conspire to metabolize the Earth's life into affluence and loneliness. In the judgment of environmental sociologists, humans, particularly those living within the logic of modern Western capitalism, have denigrated the environment through ordinary, subjectively irrelevant actions that collectively do great damage. We have caused and increasingly will suffer from, a fatal severance in the essential relationships inherent to life on Earth. The effects of human activity since the industrial revolution, whatever their benefits to the quality of life for some humans, have opened a devastating "rift" in the metabolic system of the Earth. Within the Marxist economic critique of Western industrial capitalism, the Theory of Metabolic Rift takes square aim at a system inherently designed to foster the degradation of the environment as the cost of capital via production and consumption.

In the same era that the concept of metabolism was developed, the second agricultural revolution (1830–1880) in the newly industrialized West supercharged the growth of the fertilizer industry and sparked a revolution in soil chemistry.[46] I briefly introduce this period in history and this particular issue because soil fertility depletion in mid-nineteenth-century Britain and North America serves as context for the development of the metaphor of metabolism and, just as surely, the alarm about metabolic rift. Marx, among others, concluded that the issue was not just an accident of history nor a necessary but unfortunate consequence of growing hungry human populations, but was the direct outcome of the relentless growth philosophies of capitalist economies that valued all things only for their temporal financial worth.

Rapid developments in agriculture took place during the lifetime of Karl Marx (1818–1883), the infamous critic of capitalism. Marx's critique of capitalism and capitalistic agriculture, as well as his contributions to ecological thought, must be seen against the disordered agricultural practices he observed in his lifetime. He was not alone in his concern. Depletion of soil fertility through the loss of soil nutrients became an overriding concern to societies in Britain and North America. Soil, as a living, complex ecosystem, depends on additions of organic matter for the primary nutrients—nitrogen, potassium, and phosphorous. With these nutrients and healthy microbial life, soil is a vital life source for plants of all kinds, including food for human consumption. Seen from this perspective, the health of soil is one step in a cycle of life and death. Life above ground draws nutrients from the soil in life and returns nutrients to the soil upon death. The soil in a forest, for example, provides nutrients to trees and, in exchange, receives carbon from falling leaves and nitrogen from decomposing plants. Humans historically participate in this cycle in many ways, namely through consuming food in sustainable moderation, rotating crops, letting land lie fallow when appropriate, and composting organic waste, scraps of food, and plant matter. When humans, in pursuit of quick profits, over-farm in monocultures and do not attend to the long-term health of the soil through composting organic waste, soil loses fertility. By the late 1800s, the metabolic cycle of the life of soil in Britain and North America was "rifted," and an agricultural crisis unfolded in fields of worn-out soils. A hunt for soil amendments went worldwide. In America, the soil of vast agricultural fields in southern California was amended by bat guano from the newly discovered Carlsbad Caverns in New Mexico. In Britain, the need to re-enliven soils worn out in capitalistic agricultural schemes led to an expansive, global search for nutrient-rich soil amendments. Imported Peruvian bat guano, already exhausted by 1860, gave way first to imported Chilean nitrates and then to the quest for new synthetic sources of potassium and nitrogen fertilizers. This was a period of intense contradictions between innovations in industrial-style agriculture and the realization that those innovations were leading to increasingly wicked problems. Foster observes,

The decline in the natural fertility of the soil due to the disruption of the soil nutrient cycle, the expanding scientific knowledge of the need for specific soil nutrients, and the simultaneous limitations in the supply of both natural and synthetic fertilizers, all served to generate serious concerns about present and future soil fertility under capitalist agriculture.[47]

In *Capital*, Marx takes aim at Western societies and economies by tying together three concerns: the rise of urbanization, the depletion of soil, and the plight of the impoverished worker. In "Large-scale Industry and Agriculture," Marx highlights the effects of the growth of large cities and their physical (and existential) separation from fields and gardens, which "disturbs the *metabolic interaction* between man and the Earth, i.e., it prevents the return to the soil of its constituent elements consumed by man in the form of food and clothing; hence it hinders the operation of the eternal natural condition for the lasting fertility of the soil."[48] Marx saw the failure of the Western project as both social and environmental: "All progress in capitalist agriculture is a progress in the art, not only of robbing the worker, but of robbing the soil; all progress in increasing the fertility of the soil for a given time is a progress toward ruining the more long-lasting sources of that fertility."[49] The achievement of Marx is his ecological vision—he understood intuitively that our complex economic, political, social, and environmental relationships weave together.

For Marx, the concept of metabolism had a socioecological nature.[50] Capitalistic societies, through urbanization and industrial-scale agriculture, opened a rift in the symbiotic relationship between humans and the soil. The metabolic cycle was disrupted, resulting in cities polluted with human and animal waste and soils depleted of those waste products necessary to restore vital nutrients through organic recycling.[51] A nineteenth-century rift in the soil-compost cycle was emblematic of an expansive, holistic rift in the complex, interdependent relationship between humans and nature. In 1844, Marx wrote, "Man *lives* from nature, i.e., nature is his *body*, and he must maintain a continuing dialogue with it if he is not to die. To say that man's physical and mental life is linked to nature simply means that nature is linked to itself, for man is a part of nature."[52] With this holistic perspective, the concept of metabolism and its rift grew from its limited biochemical application to a wider ecological significance and then to an even wider social and spiritual meaning.

The description of nineteenth-century soil depletion as a metabolic rift is an early industrial-age example of rifts seen widely by the mid-twentieth century in other life cycles on Earth, namely the oxygen-CO_2 atmospheric cycle. The metaphor of metabolic rift helps us come to terms with the seriousness of the effects of human activity on the health of the biotic system and suggests pathways toward restoration through responsible participation. While I do not suggest that Marx had a spiritual vision per se, Marx's holistic vision of society stimulates Christian spirituality to remember that it, too, must embrace sociological and environmental dimensions if its vision of the good life is going to be truly good in an age of rift.

Going Beyond Marxism

To be sure, Marxism has limitations as a source for interdisciplinary dialogue toward healing the rifts Marx identified.[53] His analysis proved to be more salient than his solutions. Peter Dickens notes two critiques from the outset that should temper enthusiasm for Marx's analysis. First is his basic philosophical posture. Marx's assertion that human freedom lies in subjugating and governing nature seems at least to be in tension with the anti-anthropocentrism of modern environmentalism. Human domination of nature is widely considered to have been at the heart of creating the very ecological problems with which we now must deal. Second is the lack of historical witness to the environmental benefits of societies ostensibly founded in Marxist thought. The environmental record of twentieth-century communist societies is hardly a counterexample to the record of capitalistic economies. Additionally, "collective control" of nature produced social interactions arguably even worse than those experienced under capitalism.[54] Marx leaves a complicated legacy for modern-day environmental sociologists to sift through.[55]

After this altogether brief survey of the strengths and weaknesses of Marxism, we now leave behind Karl Marx *per se* in order to focus on the Theory of Metabolic Rift as it has developed within environmental sociology and as a dialogue partner with evangelical Christianity. The soundness of the Theory of Metabolic Rift is rooted in its correlation with multiple fields of inquiry, from the physical sciences to the social sciences, and its strength for our purposes is its capacity to bind together the three dimensions of our situation outlined in chapter two—environmental, social, theological—and the trait they have in common: alienation.

Rift and Reconciliation

When we begin talking about alienation, rift, or division between what should be and what exists, the vocabulary becomes familiar to a Christian theological consciousness mindful of the fall from grace associated with the third chapter of Genesis. The possibilities for meaningful interdisciplinary dialogue between Christian discourse and environmental sociological concerns, strained by the sociological turn to Marxism and evangelical devotion to Western-style capitalism, can begin to reestablish common ground.

Moving Christians toward robust ecological spirituality necessitates engaging them in their language because the language we use is determined by and shapes how we see and apprehend the world. Here, I focus on rhetoric within American evangelical communities because Baptists are loosely folded into evangelicalism as a cultural description, and evangelical Christian culture, in particular, has strong theological and biblical rhetorical fields operating within it. In 2009, Prelli and Winters studied emerging evangelical discourse about climate change such as the Evangelical Climate Initiative. With the goal "to disclose the salient terminological features that together constitute green evangelical discourse, and then explore whether those terminological features open or foreclose opportunities for establishing identification, or grounds in common, with other evangelical discourses,"[56] Prelli and Winters determined that significant distinctions exist between green evangelical discourse and other environmental discourses in religious and secular spheres. Unlike other types of environmental actors, evangelicals situate environmental issues within biblically derived rhetoric of humans stewarding and restoring God's creation.[57]

While I challenge the limits of a stewardship ethic to bring about transformation, this research offers insight into why evangelical Christians often recoil from discourse patterns common to other environmental advocacy communities. They are coming to the conversation, if they come at all, with a commitment to a language grounded in *sin, redemption, God's sovereignty, salvation by grace, and faithful responsibility*. Mapped through the lens of this matrix of rhetorical features, discourse from other perspectives falls flat with evangelicals. Consider, for example, the "Green Romantic Environmentalists"—idealists seeking "to *change consciousness* so that material changes in industrial society presumably will follow."[58] Green Romantic Environmentalists understand humans as part of, rather than superior to, nature, which itself has agency and is alive with meaning and purpose. Green Romantics appeal to human intuition, passion, and empathy arising from a renewed animalistic connection with the Earth.[59] Evangelicals, even those who are ecologically alert, suspect Green Romantics of nature worship and inevitably clash with them or disregard them. Moreover, Green Romantics reject the political and economic institutions that evangelicals assume as the backdrop for political action, liberal democracy, and capitalism.

This is important because the dialogue around the metabolic rift in human-earth interaction and the discourse of Green Romanticism share traits, principally the pointed critique of industrial society, a feature not currently prominent in evangelical discourse. In evangelical Christian culture, care for creation advocacy seems to need discourse other than metabolic rift to find any traction. Yet, with some caveats, I do not believe a rejection by evangelicals of metabolic rift is inevitable. Indeed, I believe a deeper convergence is present that can sharpen evangelical Christians' instincts, which adds Christian sensibility to the concerns environmental sociologists articulate.

The idea of metabolic rift, with its seriousness about brokenness and restoration, sharpens and deepens the critical commitments that already animate evangelical Christians in a way that Green Romantic Environmentalism does not, and the metabolic rift theory can strengthen evangelicalism's standard rhetoric of stewardship while also functioning as a corrective to the uncritical embrace of Western political economics. American evangelicals may not be ready to adopt Marx's sharp critiques of capitalism or industrial agriculture, but they know there is something deeply fractured in human life and that radical individuality and consumptive excesses are near the heart of the fractured human condition. Let us offer, then, four connections between the theological rhetoric of evangelical Christianity and the sociological rhetoric of metabolic rift, fields that have more in common than might be assumed, especially when we intersect the commonalities through church grounds. Consider this an outline for how church grounds can serve as an ecology of grace.

Church Grounds as an Ecology of Grace

Church grounds as an ecology of grace demonstrates practical strategies by which congregations inhabit their ecclesial environment, contextualizing environmental crises and theologically interpreting Christian responses.[60] As with church grounds as a site of conscience, the particular expression of grace in each location will be contextualized in space and time, yet several principles will animate each local expression. These are integral to fulfilling the challenge George Kehm poses to practical environmental theologies: they must "demonstrate that indispensability to the Christian story of an idea or theological claim: that this idea or claim must be in the story or else the story would not be that story."[61] As Willis Jenkins describes, "a practical Christian ethic should show how the environmental crisis amounts to a crisis in the intimacies of God's salvation."[62] Environmental sociology assists this effort not by attempting to fundamentally change the Christian story but by expanding our consciousness of just what the Christian story entails and how the "intimacies of God's salvation" are inherently interwoven with environmental concerns. Underlying principles of an ecology of grace manifest on church grounds bring this awareness and subsequent commitments to life.

Mutually Embedded Relationships

First, the world is constituted fundamentally as a web of mutually embedded relationships. Therefore, our church grounds bear witness against radical individualism and for shared life together. Both Christianity and Metabolic Rift Theory affirm the relational ontology of being over against the radical individualism of liberal democracy. Christian discourse approaches relationship from the conviction that humans are created in the image of the triune God and called into the community named church with one another. Rift theory approaches relationship on a metabolic level, identifying the human place within the biotic community necessary for sustaining life. Both approaches offer corrective to Western-style individualism.

In *Moses in Pharoah's House*, John Markey insightfully traces how radical individualism in American culture creates moral obliviousness. Drawing on the work of sociologist Robert Bellah, Markey demonstrates how, in the American context, individualism

> is premised on the belief that each individual is a personal moral universe. Each person is responsible for determining what is best for him or her, and then working for self-fulfillment. What is best for each person depends on that person: no other reality can dictate or even shape the needs and possibilities of each. The good is basically defined as one's personal preference.[63]

Metabolic rift theorists reject this premise on biochemical grounds. Each individual is hardly a personal moral universe and is indeed more deeply embedded in the metabolic cycles of the Earth System than they may recognize or realize. Christianity rejects the individualistic premise on Trinitarian grounds. Created in the image of God, each individual is not a personal moral universe but lives in a creation constituted by relationship. Environmental sociology, likewise, critiques American radical individualism by recognizing the biotic community and social systems to which they ontologically belong. Completing a Christian vision of *koinonia*, environmental sociology expands the notion of human community to include symbiotic relationships with the land, air, water, and food sources. Environmental sociology also critically examines how human-to-human relationships are mediated through and often determined by our place within the biotic world. It is simply not possible to be individuals who gain freedom *from* human relationships or intrinsic relationships with the material world. We are members of the community of creatures who depend on one another for health and life and who suffer and cause suffering by our neglect of these relationships.

An ecological vision is fully energized, if not predicated on, awareness that each of us is connected—biochemically, socially, spiritually—with one another and with the other creatures. John Donne was right: "No man is an island." Yet, as Markey demonstrates, the cultural forces toward individualism are strong. In modern life, the function of society is to give each individual as much freedom as possible from constraints that govern personal destiny. Rather than freedom *for something*, such as love, service to others, and long-term bonds of community in the Spirit of God, America's individualistic culture understands freedom as *freedom from*. In practical experience, this *freedom from* implies freedom from bonds that create and sustain communal life, from a just social order that might limit the relentless pursuit of financial gain, and from "the religious vision of a final judgment that will hold people individually accountable for their actions either for or against God's plan for creation."[64]

We live in this culture and perhaps take for granted its assumptions, but we also live in the tension between the radical individualism of our cultural moment and the underlying claims of Christian faith. An audacious claim, perhaps: Evangelical Christian faith, particularly in the Baptist expression when practiced with intention, serves as a counter-witness to the radical individualism that predominates American culture.[65] Baptist ecclesiology emphasizes the priority of the local congregation as a church community. For Baptists, Christian life is expressed through participation in the local assembly in worship, theological and spiritual formation, celebration of the sacraments (often called "ordinances"), and the church's witness of faith in the world. Drawing on anabaptist roots, "community" is a key word for the Baptist expression of faith. Other Christian denominations, naturally, hold the same values. A church's grounds are an ecology of grace, by extension, to the extent that they nurse increasing biodiversity in whatever ways possible. Baby steps can be accomplished through creative landscaping with native plant species and through habitat preservation and thoughtful site planning. The site itself bears witness to God's creative diversity as celebrated in Psalms 104, 148, 150, and in the heavenly throne room scene of Revelation 4–5. DaySpring's campus, for example, is recognized by the National Wildlife Federation as a Certified Wildlife Habitat "for its commitment to sustainably provide essential elements of wildlife habitat: food, water, cover, and places to raise young."[66] Appreciating the diversity of creation present on a church's campus can be a delightful experience for all generations. Apps such as iNaturalist, Seek, and Merlin provide excellent information about the variety of flowers, plants, birds, and insects in a certain space.

Fractured Core Relationships

The second conviction of an ecology of grace is that the core relationships that define the world are fractured, and that fracture cuts deep. We all need grace. Therefore, we bear witness against superficial optimism and toward hope. Both Christianity and Metabolic Rift Theory are determined to diagnose and respond to the world's troubles. Metabolic Rift Theory emphasizes our collective environmental dislocation in the industrial age, and Christianity prioritizes one's spiritual fall from relationship with God.

Environmental sociology, particularly Metabolic Rift Theory, emphasizes sharp judgment on human activity for the condition of the world's environments and communities. Historian John McNeil describes the daunting future awaiting life in the Anthropocene: "Human activities have become so pervasive and profound that they rival the great forces of Nature and are pushing the Earth into planetary *terra incognita*. The Earth is rapidly moving into a less biologically diverse, less forested, much warmer, and probably wetter and stormier state."[67]

Christians, one might think, would name such fracturing activity as "sin" and harbor little optimism for the capacity of humans to redeem themselves or overcome sin apart from God's grace. All creation groans in travail, according to Romans 8. Christian spirituality holds close confession as a proper response to the groaning we both cause and suffer from in creation. Psalm 51 confesses, "I know my transgressions and my sin is ever before me" (NRSV), and the Apostle Paul in Romans 7 laments that he cannot break free from his own moral compromises. Monastic evening prayer expresses communal Christian confession in acknowledgment not just of what we have done but also of what we have failed to do.[68] Sin, which names the separation of an individual from God and names the state of the "fallen" world, is understood to be pervasive and the consequences to be persistent in suffering individually and communally.

In recent generations, Christians in America have been forced to confront communal sin manifested through participation in and acquiescence to unjust and oppressive human economic and social systems. Christians, however, do not seamlessly connect their tradition of sin-confession-repentance-salvation with their collective responsibility for environmental degradation. Even while maintaining a rather dim view of human capacity for righteousness, they tend to maintain a kind of optimism about the environmental situation. In "The Faithful Skeptics," researchers interviewed evangelical Christians active in their congregations in North Texas. One-third of the interviewees stated belief that God alone is in control of the Earth's climate. For example,

> I think that we've had warming and cooling, and the earth is going to do whatever God wants, and I don't think that human beings are going to make a big difference. I do think that we must be conservative of the earth, and we can't just run roughshod, but I don't think as far as the emissions of the gases [that we're] going to change the climate.[69]

What looks like climate skepticism is actually "climate optimism" because it is a version of an incipient assurance of desirable outcomes that bedevils American religious life. Superficial optimism confuses hope with wishful thinking. While Christian hope shares a conviction that God has a plan for the universe and the power to carry it out, authentic hope is not passive in the way that often results from Christian affirmations of the sovereignty of God and human exceptionalism, particularly as they relate to environmental concerns.[70] Both Christian discourse and environmental sociology discourse insist, over against superficial optimism, that our core relationships are fractured. Addressing the rift will require more than minor tweaks to our habits; it will require a holistic spirituality born of conversion to a new way of understanding our relationships with one another and the Earth.

Church grounds as an ecology of grace prompts hope as a counter-witness to superficial optimism. In response to what St. Paul diagnoses as the travail of creation, we are assured that nothing can separate us from the love of Christ (Rom 8:31-39). An ecology of grace embraces its role as a place of spiritual healing and environmental restoration. A congregation choosing to use renewable sources of electricity, for example, is enfolding human activity on their campus as a small participation in the healing of the world.

Suffering of the Vulnerable

Third, economically unstable and other vulnerable communities suffer most acutely from our collective failure to address the rift. We bear witness to compassionate action for those who are suffering. Both Christianity and Metabolic Rift Theory recognize the particular vulnerability of some due to the inaction of others. Metabolic Rift Theory, especially in its Marxian expression, implicates capitalism in a way that amplifies historic concerns of Christianity for vulnerable people—those experiencing poverty or other hardship. While capitalism, in theory, promotes the belief in self-regulating markets in which all of society's assets become commodities to be bought and sold at will, in practice, capitalistic societies have taken steps to mitigate the free market's inequitable burden on the most vulnerable. Social safety nets assist people experiencing poverty; religious institutions and other nonprofit organizations regularly organize ministries of compassion in their communities. According to Markey,

> The result has been a "double-movement" in which each society has simultaneously attempted to advance laissez-faire markets while

developing social-mechanisms to limit the cultural damage that has inevitably resulted from laissez-faire economics. Most Western societies, however, have never seemed to question the underlying economic ideology, and instead go to great lengths to maintain the illusion of the self-regulating market and to subordinate broader social needs to economic ones.[71]

The proximate implications of the human-earth rift are most dramatically suffered by the poor and vulnerable—as noted in Metabolic Rift Theory—who are also embedded squarely within the compassion of God—as insists Christian theology. Israel and the church answer the call to care for the widow, orphan, and sojourner in the land. These three represent those made vulnerable by life's unfortunate ordinary circumstances and willful injustices of political economy disjointed from communal justice and righteousness. Care for the environment is directly correlated to care for the vulnerable and marginalized. Consider James Cone's assertion of the irreducibility of the connection between racial and environmental justice:

> People who fight against white racism but fail to connect it to the degradation of the earth are anti-ecological—whether they know it or not. People who struggle against environmental degradation but do not incorporate in it a disciplined and sustained fight against white supremacy are racists—whether they acknowledge it or not. The fight for justice cannot be segregated but must be integrated with the fight for life in all its forms.[72]

Implicating human activity, social critics use the term "Anthropocene" for this era, but some are even more precise in their assessment, dubbing this not Anthropocene but "Capitalocene." Though ultimately deciding in favor of the term Anthropocene, theologian Norman Wirzba appreciates the precision of Capitalocene, which "draws our attention to the financial institutions and government policies that had to be argued for and enforced to install an economy that would be so damaging."[73] We are aware that not all humans are equally responsible for the geologic epoch brought about by the industrial revolution and its beneficiaries. As Jason

Moore points out, "Capitalism was built on excluding most *humans* from Humanity—indigenous peoples, enslaved Africans, nearly all women, and even many white-skinned men (Slavs, Jews, the Irish).... They were regarded as part of Nature, along with trees and soil and rivers—and treated accordingly."[74] Though I earlier signaled a move away from Marxist critique of the ideology of Western capitalism as a means to address existing evangelical sensibilities, there is simply no escaping the effects of Western capitalism *as it has been practiced* on the most vulnerable among us. This is not to argue historically that societies differently organized have markedly better outcomes; it is to recognize the problems inherent to the system we inhabit in North America.

One might expect that Christians, with their ostensible priority on care for economically or socially vulnerable people, would be outspoken in critique of the inherent dangers of the capitalist system, but Christians in the West take for granted that the dominant economic system aligns with an authentic Christian vision. It seems clear that we need to hold a more critical and holistic view of human economy and its environmental relations to be faithful to a holistic Christian vision. Care for the Earth by reengaging our place as creatures within the community of creation is an integral part of healing environmental and social wounds, including racist injustices. Randy Woodley, a Christian and recognized Cherokee descendant of the United Keetoowah Band of Cherokee Indians, put forward a vision for such reengagement that he describes as "An Indigenous Vision" of shalom:

> Justice and equality, provision and freedom, salvation and healing of all creation are found in Christ. As those who have answered the call to represent Christ by living in the community of creation, Christians, above everyone else, must realize that Jesus' shalom community will only manifest itself wherever we act in accordance with shalom. As Jesus' shalom-keepers we are to exhibit a new order—a Sabbath way, a Jubilee lifestyle, and a shalom way of being in, with, and for the community of creation.[75]

Consider the Calvary Reformed Church in Cleveland, Ohio, which planted twenty-five trees in their neighborhood, a low-income area suffering from rising heat. Members of Calvary walked from their church during a Sunday service to plant the trees. "It was such a joyful day," said Pastor Dean Van Farowe. "And now we walk down that street and see them getting strong."[76]

Human Agency and Responsibility for Healing

Fourth, humans have agency and responsibility to heal the rifts. We bear witness to hope by cultivating an ecology of grace. Both Christianity and Metabolic Rift Theory affirm this point, but both bring significant skepticism to the ability of individuals to make changes needed in the face of crisis. I will say more about our agency and responsibility in the next chapters. The distinction I want to insist on here is between (1) the discourse of "stewardship" activities that aim to govern our destructive habits with pragmatic moderation and (2) a vision of participatory creation care in which humans have a constructive participation in reordering their lives and communities to the *shalom*-like goodness of all creation.

Christians are oriented to a participatory vision of themselves in relation to their communities. Environmental sociology's Metabolic Rift Theory helps Christians more fully understand and lament the ruptures in every level of community life in the modern era.[77] We who are made by and for community live in a moment when the constitutive community binding life on Earth is rifted by human activity. We will all suffer, though those who suffer most acutely are the most vulnerable. Motivated by love of God and compassion for others, we recommit ourselves to a new way of being in the world as ministers of reconciliation. Reconciling societal and environmental ruptures requires a holistic vision that includes bearing witness against radical individualism and superficial optimism with which we have made too-easy alliance. In an expansive vision of beloved community, with hope born of resurrection and grace, Christians are particularly equipped to be the agents of reconciliation needed for the Earth's life in the Anthropocene.[78]

Toward Ecologies of Grace

The Canticle of St. Francis is well-known for the images in its opening stanzas, calling upon Brother Sun and Sister Moon to the praise of God emanating from their intrinsic characters. Brother Sun, the day through whom God gives us light, is joined by Sister Moon, who is precious and fair; stars, wind, air, cloud, fire, and earth are all called together to praise God. Less well known are the following two stanzas:

> Praised be you, my Lord,
> through those who forgive
> for your love
> and who bear sickness and trial.
>
> Blessed are those
> who endure in peace,
> for by you, Most High,
> they will be crowned.

Legend says that Francis added these lines to the original canticle to encourage two leaders in Assisi to reconcile a conflict that had divided them and possibly the town. So, in a hymn that calls creatures to praise God, the praise of humans joins the chorus through their forgiveness of one another, bearing with one another in sickness and trial, and enduring in peace together. Ecology is integrated with grace when we knit together that which is broken, practicing a ministry of reconciliation.

Chapter 4

Church Grounds as Holy Ground

In chapter 3, we undertook the task of a critical assessment of our contemporary situation. Modeled on Moses's "turning aside to see," we "turned aside" to consider the world's reality carefully. The Theory of Metabolic Rift interprets the forces and forcings on planetary health consequent of human activity, and the designation of the Anthropocene takes into account a full assessment of our situation. In the end, we highlighted four principles that critically correlate Christian theologies with the insights of environmental sociologies.

In this chapter, we go a step further but also take a step back because, at this point, confronted with the seemingly insurmountable crises gripping our planet, we need to recognize that our relationship with creation isn't reducible to problem-solving. The Earth and its material life are not merely problems to solve or challenges to overcome. The ground of our being is holy ground. By cultivating a contemplative-incarnational orientation to creation, we become attuned to and participate in the mystery of the divine life around us. For a world beset by ecological challenges, this is good news to which Christian life bears witness.

In the first section, we move from the questions of chapters 2 and 3, "What is happening and why is it happening?" to the question of this chapter and the next, "What ought to be happening and how shall it happen?" This step emerges from a hermeneutical exercise of prophetic discernment. In the second section, I practice such discernment by considering two well-known, contrasting approaches to Christian environmental concern: a Barthian stewardship ethic and a Franciscan kinship spirituality.[1] In the third section, I return to the story of Moses at the burning bush in Exodus 3 for a model of a contemplative-incarnational transformative encounter that, in the end, brings the two strands together. Organized by St. Clare of Assisi's contemplative prayer, I describe Moses's experience at the bush as an ecologically rich direct encounter with the living God. Building on this, in the fourth section, the mystical theology of Maximus the Confessor roots our personal experiences of holy ground in Chalcedonian Christology.

Prophetic Discernment for the Anthropocene

Our journey moves from the descriptive and interpretive tasks, "What is going on and why?" to the normative task of practical theology: "What *ought* to be going on?" The question is not merely the reductive, "What, if anything, does the Bible say we should do to care for creation?" That question has value within theological reflection but does not account for how context shapes readers of Scripture. Rather, we ought to ask the context-laden question, "What is God's word for us when environmental degradation reveals our collective failure to care for creation either as faithful stewards or participants? And how can we be equipped to hear such a word?" Such contextual framing includes informed acknowledgment of our situation, confession of our collective failures, and space for a Christocentric spirituality of grace and calling. Only then are we possibly prepared to discern how Jesus Christ is present to us and a guide for us as we receive and participate in the Word's (Jesus Christ's) redemptive mission in the world.[2]

Christians have responded to ecological crises in the last five decades with a wide variety of accounts of our theological struggle to care for creation. In 1985, Paul Santmire, who compiled a comprehensive survey of biblical themes and theological movements in Christian history related to ecological theology, concluded that the church's theological tradition is neither morally bankrupt nor romantically certain but constitutes an "ambiguous ecological promise."[3] More hopefully, in 2008, Willis Jenkins explored how ecological theologies function within doctrines of redemption in Orthodox spirituality (via Maximus the Confessor), Catholic spirituality (via Thomas Aquinas), and Protestant spirituality (via Karl Barth).[4] Over the last decade, a number of other authors have surveyed ecological themes from various biblical and theological perspectives.[5]

In *Creation Care: A Biblical Theology of the Natural World*, Douglas Moo and Jonathan Moo offer a thoughtful, biblically oriented approach to creation care. I draw on it here as a good example of how evangelical theologians are navigating the hermeneutical intersection where biblical method engages ecological concern. To help navigate what they dub the "traffic pattern of biblical theology," Moo and Moo suggest the image of a roundabout where interpretation moves from ancient text to contemporary application and from our world back to the text. Navigating this roundabout, practical theologians call upon historical and systematic theology, culture, and science to help guide traffic smoothly while at every turn emphasizing the authority of Scripture.[6] Four signposts for biblical interpretation guide travelers:

To be *biblical*, biblical theology must be descriptive; theologians summarize and synthesize the teaching of the Bible using its own categories and with attention to its redemptive-historical movement.

To be *theological*, biblical theology should also be prescriptive: "Our focus will be on the horizon of the text. But that focus must not become tunnel vision that leads us to ignore entirely the horizon of the contemporary reader or listener."

Biblical theology must be *inclusive*. The theologian "operates as a Christian who assumes that, for all their diversity, the books of the Bible are ultimately one book." The authors note that "this inclusive principle poses particular challenges for our study of creation care."

Biblical theology must be *canonical*, which is especially critical in addressing the issue of creation care since Scripture's direct witness concerning the human-earth relationship is uneven.[7]

While the evangelical Protestant Moos stops short of calling for an eco-conversion of the sort prescribed by Franciscan theologian Ilia Delio[8] and resist the Marxist-inspired deconstruction of Western society found in strains of environmental sociology, they pointedly remind readers enmeshed in "Western culture" to be self-aware of the contribution that modern, industrial-era, consumptive practices make to environmental degradation. The Moos criticize evangelical theologians who claim that biblical texts simply function to affirm a special and unique place for humans in the created order and, therefore, give license to domination theologies in which humans are ordained to use nature in any way they see fit. In light of our present historic, social, ecological location, we must be intensely self-aware of how strategies for biblical interpretation are rooted in the ecological failures of this era. Delio adds,

> Shifts in culture can illuminate assumptions that we have unconsciously adopted and that do not, in fact, align with a genuinely biblical worldview.... In this case we think there is clear evidence that modern Western culture has tended toward an unbiblical understanding of human dominion over the created world. Admittedly, theologians and biblical scholars are themselves enmeshed in culture, and we think that some have tended to read our anthropocentric Western culture into their interpretations of Scripture.[9]

The Moos' project to centralize Christian theology and the church's spirituality within our ecologically tenuous context is right on. As Joseph Sittler said in a message to the World Council of Churches in the early 1960s, we need a theology *of* ecology rather than a theology *for* ecology.[10] Too often, ecological matters are about *I* or *they*: What can *I* do to make a difference? What are *they* (nations, multinational corporations) doing to cause such harm? But ecology, which is fundamentally about relationship, is about *us*: mutuality and participation. We are seeking to (re)discover the ecological heart of Christian faith and life in an era and context of ecological crisis. As essentially ecological, Christianity is rooted in relationships, in recognition of brokenness and in hope of restoration, holding together the complex social, economic, and cultural realities that inform our social and biotic relationships.[11] This approach, rooted in a theory of *ecology* in its broadest sense, restores humans to a life-giving place in the web of creaturely relationships. Given the intrinsically relational character of Christian theology, we should be wary of any system that dislocates humans from core relationships. As we revisit the creation care approaches of Barthian "environmental stewardship" and an alternative model of Franciscan "participatory spirituality," we follow signposts toward a biblical, theological, inclusive, canonical ecological spirituality.

In an earlier chapter, I was sharply critical of the stewardship ethic popular in evangelical Christian environmental discourse. Stewardship, I argued, is limited as an ethic because it places humans in a managerial position, administering to the world on behalf of God, who is something like an absentee landlord. This ethic both removes God from direct association with creation and removes humans from participation as creatures within creation. Moreover, this scheme reduces human motivation to performative fulfillment of duty rather than inspired love. However, here I wish to submit my criticism to correction through limited engagement with Karl Barth's eco-theology. Willis Jenkins, more generous to Barth and to the idea of environmental stewardship than many other eco-theology commentators, suggests that Barth represents the most theologically robust version of the popular stewardship ethic and, in turn, redeems stewardship from the blistering criticism often directed its way.

Karl Barth and Franciscan Contemplation

Karl Barth towered over twentieth-century theology, bursting "upon the Western theological world like a tidal wave from some distant, unknown geological upheaval."[12] Central to Barth's theological method is the "infinite qualitative difference" between God and the world, so we find only an indirect relation between Christian vocational responsibility and its earthly context. As a matter of ecological concern, Paul Santmire, among others, sharply criticizes Barth for his vision of "God and humanity alone," his subsequent failure to generate an ecologically alert theology, and his landless eschatology. Santmire writes,

> Barth depicts the scene of eternity, which for him is the alpha and omega of all things, the ontological principle of everything, as

essentially a *landless* event. "God and man" above—that is Barth's first and last word, as far as the keystone of his dogmatic thought is concerned. Barth formally begins this thought where Thomas and Bonaventure and Dante materially ended theirs, with the saints alone with God in eternity, far above the earth—so far above, indeed, that the earth does not even come into view.[13]

For Barth, creation is necessary only as a theater outside of God for the drama of salvation history to play out. Creation is essential in these terms, but it is purely instrumental and has no eternal determination. Consequently, creation maintains limited and indirect moral claim on our lives except insofar as we exercise responsible dominion over this creation. This is, in essence, a version of commonly held beliefs in the pews and pulpits of evangelical churches. Yet, Jenkins insists, if we see Barth's doctrine of creation through the lens of his Christocentric theology of redemption, we discover ways Barth mitigates his own reduction of creation to instrumentalism. Contra Santmire, Jenkins finds in Barth a robust version of environmental stewardship as human response to God's living Word.[14] This is critical because human dominion does not repeat God's sovereignty; it only points to it. In correction to some other contemporary stewardship theologies, Barth does not envision humans operating on God's behalf in the world's management. The point of stewardship is the obedient performance itself, testifying to God's blessing. Active companionship with God in obedient stewardship becomes the place of God's rest and blessing for creation, not deputized management.[15]

For Barth, environmental stewardship leads to the place of God's encounter with creation and, ultimately, Christ's redemption. Therefore, Jenkins's generous assessment of the stewardship ethic deserves serious attention if he is right that our responsibility to steward the Earth, when exercised rightly, is more than fulfillment of managerial duty—it is Trinitarian worship.

> Jesus Christ is not simply the exemplary steward, around whom the ethical imagination swirls, wondering what vehicle he would drive. He becomes himself the environment in which faithful stewardship arises, the habitat in which humanity flourishes. God's

> [incarnation] act makes a special place for creatures, only now the grove of Gethsemane is the garden of Christian stewardship. . . . Stewardship is not a form of management, but of invocation.[16]

Compared to a coldly managerial posture, does Barth's stewardship model take us a long way, farther than I anticipated, toward a robust creation-affirming spirituality? Jenkins certainly thinks so: "After Barth, Christian environmentalists may claim that conversion to the way of Jesus entails care for the earth, and that earth care bears comparable theological significance to practices like feeding the poor and preaching the good news."[17] However, rather than contemporary stewardship ethics successfully building on this insight, it is St. Francis and Franciscan spirituality that more fully embody the doxology enfolded within Barth's eco-theology. Saints Francis and Clare pick up at the horizon of Barth's affirmation of creation care,[18] especially if we are to take seriously Philip Sheldrake's assertion that an awareness of the current fragility of our planet and ecosystems makes urgent the development of ecologically alert spiritualities informed by a contemplative dimension that counter the irresponsibility of extreme consumerist lifestyles.[19] Francis and Clare offer a contemplative strategy for Barth's stewardship theology.

Contemplation of Creation

The prayer journey articulated by St. Clare, which begins with a penetrating gaze and thoughtful consideration, moves into its third phase with contemplation. Contemplation marks a definite shift in the journey. In the first two steps, *gaze* and *consider*, we read the text, icon, or other object of our attention with patience and humility. Having done so, we enter the third step, open to the mystery of God's presence with us. Niemier evocatively describes the experience: "Deep contemplative prayer is not so much learning how to contemplate God by some method or practice, as it is becoming aware that it is God who is contemplating us."[20] This "becoming aware" is the fruit of "paying attention" and "carefully considering." We become aware not just of the object of our inquiry but of ourselves. Some describe the experience as seeing yourself from God's point of view.

At the very least, the experience has a mystical dimension: I am not alone. God is with me here in this place: "Like Clare, *gaze* on Jesus, and you will become like the One you see. Like Clare, *consider* Jesus and you will be transformed. Like Clare, *contemplate* Jesus and you will see yourself with new eyes as you look at him looking back at you with delight and with love."[21]

For the Franciscan intellectual tradition, contemplation of God through creation is inherently relational and christological. Against the backdrop of medieval theology that reduced the purpose of the incarnation to satisfaction for human sin, the Franciscans developed the "primacy of Christ" drawing from patristic sources and from St. Paul's vision of Christ as "the image of the invisible God, the firstborn of all creation (Col 1:15)." Keith Warner explains how the Franciscan school, namely Scotus, questioned God's original intent for the incarnation:

> What kind of God would choose to become Incarnate among us? He asserted that God is absolutely free and loving; therefore, the Incarnation must be an expression of love and freedom. Arguing from this principle, God could not have been motivated to remedy sin; this motive would be an inferior rationale. The Incarnation was not an afterthought, a remedial strategy. Rather, the Incarnation was conceived before the creation of the world as a means to unite humanity with God through love; it was not a discrete historical event, nor merely a precondition for the Word to be preached to us; it was not necessitated by sin. Rather, the Incarnation is the highest expression of divine love. Scotus does not discount sin or disregard the need for human redemption, but he insists they are subordinate concerns relative to full communion with God through the Incarnation.[22]

Creation, therefore, is christoform, capable of bearing Christ and the incarnation as the fulfillment of God's cosmic purposes for creation: to bear Christ. Thus, Warner concludes,

> The Incarnation is a much better point of departure for Christian environmental ethics than the Creation stories of Genesis because

it begins with a positive affirmation of the religious significance of creation. . . . The primacy of Christ orients us toward the gift of Creation in bearing Christ, and thereby reflecting Christ to us. Therefore, gratitude for this gift becomes the central thrust in our understanding of the biophysic world.[23]

Our primary relationship with creation, then, is eucharistic gratitude and spiritual-incarnational communal participation. Barth's notion of stewardship as doxology comes to fulfillment through its embeddedness in the contemplative prayer of Clare.

Moses

In our reading of Moses, whom God *sees*, we are now prepared to ask how the text, especially in its contemplative orientation, speaks to us and our situation. As God is revealed in the material sphere, humans perceive God's transcendent power and presence in uneven understandings. Likewise, as this story develops, revealing implies concealing: "the more the narrator reduces the gap between the human and the divine, the more he has to emphasize the distance."[24] Once Moses became conscious of the divine presence, he hid his face, "for he was afraid to look at God" (Exod 3:6).[25] From this moment onward, the book and story of Exodus have a new narrative center in YHWH. It is at the bush where the divine name is established, "I AM who I AM. . . . Say this to the people of Israel: I AM has sent me to you" (Exod 3:14).

Few passages lend themselves so fully to a theological vision of Christian interpretation as Exodus 3. Most major Church Fathers left at least one treatise on the passage. For most patristic and medieval commentators, identification of the "angel of the Lord" in the burning bush with Jesus Christ was obvious and inescapable.[26] In standard iconography, Moses is depicted removing his sandals before a bush in whose flame appears the Theotokos holding the Christ child. Mary is thus dubbed the "Unburning Bush," the creature in whom God fully is manifest, yet she is not consumed. This passage, theologically coupled with the incarnation of Jesus Christ, reveals the sacramental potential of all creation. It is as if the icons pose the question: If God can use an anonymous shrub on the far side of nowhere to call Moses, where else might God be revealed? Is all ground "holy ground," and how would we live differently if it were? Formed by this passage, we are prepared to discover God's imminence in unexpected places, even those not considered beautiful.

A contemplative-incarnational lens enables us to see ourselves and our world through the text. This is an image of a more thoughtful, careful, sacred approach to non-human creation, not as a repository of resources but with sacramental possibility and a hopeful approach to our fellow human creatures—perhaps not endlessly, hopelessly enslaved in the tyranny of inhumane systems. Moreover, we are free to read the text incarnationally, with St. Clare and the early Orthodox Christian liturgists who read the story of the burning bush and through it saw Christ alive in the world.

Maximus

Maximus the Confessor is a figure in whom many strands of the Christian tradition coalesce. Diverse expressions of Christianity are rediscovering him as a source of theological clarity and spiritual vitality. Having engaged the evangelical Moos (twenty-first century), the Protestant Barth (twentieth century), and the Catholic Clare (thirteenth century), we move further upstream to the Orthodox theologian Maximus (seventh century). He is called "the last great theologian of Greek patristics"[27] and the greatest and most profound of Byzantine theologians."[28] Here I survey Maximus's life and examine the theological flowering of his spirituality in the Monothelete controversy. I conclude by considering contributions from *The Church's Mystagogy*, one of his finest spiritual works, for contemporary spirituality. This extended treatment of Maximus helps us more fully contemplate the mystery of the primacy of Christ.

The Life of Maximus the Confessor

Little is definitely known of Maximus's early life. He was born in 580 in Constantinople, a city, then and now, like Maximus, uniquely positioned between East and West, ancient and cosmopolitan, church and empire, pope and emperor. Due to his mastery of Aristotle, Neoplatonism, the early fathers of the Christian spirituality, and the Bible, scholars surmise that Maximus was provided the kind of broad humanistic education that characterized the "university" at Constantinople and, therefore, was likely born into a family among the intellectual elite. True or not, it suggests, along with his early political career, that Maximus's formative years were spent in and around the corridors of power in Constantinople.

A visitor to the bustling tourist district of modern Istanbul may readily imagine how the eyes of a young Maximus fourteen centuries ago gazed up toward the domed ceiling of the glittering Hagia Sophia Cathedral (ca. 537). Dedicated to the *Wisdom of God*, the *Logos*, the second person of the Trinity, Hagia Sophia was an engineering marvel and the largest building in the world. We may speculate how the enduring memory of Hagia Sophia influenced Maximus's interest in and defense of the *Logos* as fully divine and also fully human in nature, will, and energy. Hagia Sophia does not appear to float lightly above the ground. It does not soar to the heavens like a gothic Chartres. It does not "float upon ethereal tides" like St. Paul's. Rather, Hagia Sophia is a structure with heft. Its bulky walls and heavy dome were like a hymn in masonry to the material incarnation of Christ and the enduring strength of the church. If Hagia Sophia could speak, and it would in the person of Maximus the Confessor, it would say to the world that Christ's humanity cannot be lost in his divinity but completed by it. The materiality of the world has sacred meaning, fulfilled by participation with the divine in the glory of God. The great cathedral of Maximus's childhood surely must have inspired his theological and spiritual reflections on the relationship of transcendence to imminence, the divine and material worlds.

Like Hagia Sophia's masonry and mosaics, the architecture of Maximus's theological imagination is seen memorably in writings like *Mystagogy*, which draws on the symbolism of the church and the world as spiritual images. Like the city in which he and the great church resided, Maximus's theology was the meeting place of diverse influences synthesized together in manifestly new and exciting ways.

As a young man, Maximus was appointed as protosecretary in the emperor's court. Three years later, he abruptly resigned and left the court to become a monk at Chrysopolis, where he soon became abbot. In the spring of 626, as the Persian invaders were pressing on the city, Maximus departed from Constantinople. By 628, he had arrived in North Africa. We have little evidence that Maximus read Augustine while he was in North Africa, but his quarter-century of "western exile" anticipates a theologian in whom *synthesis* will characterize his life and work. During this early stage in his life, Maximus expressed his brilliance through the theological and cosmologically informed ascetic teachings in the group of his writings from around 626–630: *Ambigua, Four Centuries on Love*, and the *Mystagogy*, each of which offers practical guidance in the ascetic and spiritual life and demonstrates Maximus's spiritual theology fully developed except for precision, which matured in time, on the issue of Monotheletism. *Questionnes ad Thelassium*, considered his greatest work, was composed between 630 and 634.

The latter period of his life until his death was characterized in his writings, travels, and suffering by engagement in the raging theological debate of the era. In this period Maximus is established as a true theologian par excellence, the father of Byzantine spirituality, and the soul of the resistance to Monotheletism. In 645, Maximus defeated the Monothelite ex-patriarch Pyrrhus in a public debate. In 649, his participation in the Lateran Council implicated him on the western side of a showdown between the Vatican and the Imperial authorities in Constantinople. When he returned to his native city, he was put on a series of trials beginning in 655, after which he was publicly mutilated, exiled, and died in disgrace in 662 at the age of eighty-two on the eastern shore of the Black Sea.

Though it is accepted form to divide Maximus's writings into the two groups: (1) the ascetic and spiritual (until around 634) and (2) the philosophical and theological (640–662), the seeds of Maximus's later christological convictions were already budding in his works on spirituality. The syntheses that characterize his life exemplify his contributions from Christology to cosmology. He was a man of the empire and the monastery, East and West, Hagia Sophia and the

Lateran Basilica, Constantinople and Rome, Augustine and Gregory of Nyssa, Origen and Dionysius, Neoplatonism and biblical revelation. Maximus was perfectly prepared by his life's journey and intellectual breadth to offer a crowning theological achievement, arguing decisively for the preservation of christological synthesis.

In 681at the Sixth Ecumenical Council at Constantinople, twenty years after his suffering and death, Dyothelite orthodoxy, which Maximus grasped intuitively and intellectually and articulated enduringly—and for which died in agony—was adopted as the definitive Christian interpretation of Chalcedon. It was the final achievement of the great christological formulations of the Creedal centuries. Maximus was vindicated, assuring his role as one of the few genuinely ecumenical orthodox, catholic theologians of the patristic era.[29]

Theological Controversy, Spiritual Legacy

The Chalcedonian Confession of 451 accomplished a significant theological achievement, affirming dual natures of Christ, divine and human with no confusion, no change, no division, and no separation. Through the *communicatio idiomatum*, Chalcedon rejected the Monophysite impulse to affirm Christ's divine nature at the expense of his human nature: his humanity disappearing in his divinity like a drop of honey into the water of the sea. Yet Chalcedon left unanswered questions in its wake that would undermine its hope of unifying Christendom's Christology. Throughout the next century, christological disputes continued to divide the church. All Christians confess that in Christ the *Logos* is made flesh, but six hundred years into the Christian era theologians still grappled with how to give a full and reasonable account of the incarnational mystery. Matters left ambiguous at Chalcedon would reemerge as critically divisive for Christology and fatal for Maximus.

Monotheletism

By the late 630s, the looming theological issue over Christ's will(s) inherited the lingering controversies from Chalcedon. To modern ears, this might seem to be typical of the countless sets of controversies over abstractions and speculations, and it sounded that way to some seventh-century ears, too. The relative importance of this theological dispute appears to pale compared to monumental theological decisions that shaped Christian Orthodoxy through its battles over Arianism, Apollinarianism, Nestorianism, and Monophysitism. After the four great ecumenical councils, it may appear that the most important christological disputes had been sufficiently resolved for Orthodox confession of faith. Some leaders, weary of ecclesial infighting or incapable of understanding the significance of this issue, saw only the need for mutually advantageous political resolutions to what seemed to be a relatively minor skirmish among theologians.

The Monothelete controversy may have indeed been brushed aside through political resolution were it not for the monk Maximus, who publicly and forcefully resisted the Monothelete position in his writings and in public debates with those who advocated for its proposals. For Maximus, in even a seemingly minor point of Christology, everything was at stake from the integrity of the cosmos to the hope of salvation. Maximus's insistence about christological dogma "was not simply the rightness of a speculative construct of his own private philosophical theology (though it was certainly also that) but the validity of the spirituality of the entire orthodox and catholic Church, of which he believed himself to be a faithful exponent."[30] Beyond any other principal in the dispute, Maximus recognized what was at stake. As the latest Christological iteration of the philosophical tension between Creator and creation, Monotheletism was the argument that Christ only had a divine will. To proponents of Monotheletism, a human will in Christ would imply he deliberated (an activity inherent to the exercise of the human will). In their dualistic theological calculus, a human would render Jesus Christ less than fully divine. Thus, he has two *natures*, per Chalcedon, but only a divine *will*. But Maximus keenly understood that Christ must have exercised both a divine will and a human will. The absence of a preserved human will in Jesus Christ would have meant that the human will of sinful humanity would not have been redeemed based on the patristic principle that only what is assumed in the incarnation may be saved.[31]

If the Monothelete position had prevailed, by implication spiritual progression, even salvation, would require abandoning our nature into a disembodied spirituality. It fell to Maximus to preserve the "rights of nature against the rampages of an unchecked supernaturalism."[32] While Christian spirituality had strong tendencies toward dualism, the time had arrived for Christianity to decide which path it would follow—a dualistic Gnosticism or a sacramental ontology. When Maximus opposed proposed Christologies of "one nature" or "one will" or "one energy," he did so with the recognition that, "despite their attractiveness to a Christian spirituality based on a yearning for union with God, such theories would in fact undercut this spirituality by severing the bond between our humanity and the humanity of Jesus Christ."[33]

In a battle that can appear to be a footnote in Christology, Maximus understood the implication; "Maximus rescues human natures from the brink of extinction by rejecting the inverse proportionality principle between spirituality and materiality. Indeed, only when both natures are preserved are both radically revealed."[34] Arguing that Christ "did not come to undermine the nature that he himself, as God and Word, had created,"[35] Maximus preserved the potency of creation to participate with the divine Logos as Christology, and cosmology, and anthropology. This preservation, as the signature achievement of Maximus, "is realized," according to von Balthasar,

> through the unification of human nature, in the highest degree, with the God who produces and affirms it; by being divinized, the world is perfected as world. So the world is given to itself, each of us is given to ourselves, when God gives himself the world and to us in Christ. . . . One must not, then, any longer misunderstand the abiding distance between the natures, as if there were between them only an extrinsic relationship of parallel existence.[36]

Two negative statements can be made to clarify the relationship of the human and divine wills in Christ. First, in Christ, the divine and human wills do not exist in opposition such that to affirm the divine will of Christ would be to deny his human will participating in his activities. Second, the two wills are not in extrinsic relationship to one another, such that one will determine some actions and the other will determine other actions. In other words, the two wills are not moving against one another, which would end with divine will swallowing human will, and the two wills are not merely running in parallel, ultimately ending with a split between his two natures. Rather, according to Maximus, the wills, like the natures, perfect one another in him as Incarnate Word.

Theological Anthropology

Maximus collects and corrects his predecessors' theologies into a spiritual and theological synthesis of a type not seen again until Thomas Aquinas. For Maximus, Christology begets a sacramental cosmology, a theological anthropology, and a creation-affirming spirituality. As the fruit of an astute theological instinct and an expansive spiritual vision, Maximus not only preserves creation from extinction but also rescues orthodoxy from tipping over the Neoplatonic cliff with Dionysius, from evaporating into Originest gnosticism, reducing itself to Evagrian asceticism, or becoming merely intellectual doctrinal ascent all the while drawing from each of the masters what each can offer. The christological formulation of Chalcedon expands for Maximus into a "fundamental law of metaphysics. Illuminated by the highest level of theological synthesis—the union of God and the world in Christ—Maximus searches out the traces of the developmental principles, of the conditions of possibility of this synthesis and discovers the formal structure of all created being, even the formal structure of the relationship between the absolute and the contingent."[37] Maximus's contemplation of the Incarnate Word, the *Sophia* of God-made-flesh, gives him an enduring vision of Christ's humanity broken open for the world and an invitation for us to be broken open for one another in participation with him toward the redemption of the cosmos.

Does the journey into God entail a rejection of our creaturehood and material being, or is it a fulfillment of our creaturehood and an embrace of our material being as transformed by its participation in the divine life? For humanity to live fully is to live into the fullness and intended promise of our humanness. There can hardly be a more creation-affirming theological claim that at the same time offers the hope of divinization. As the fruit of the Confessor's personal reflection on the christological conviction of the Council of Chalcedon, Maximus's anthropology was motivated by "his vision of man as the center of God's creation and a particular object of His providence, man as both microcosm and mediator. Christian spirituality implies for him the restitution of this microcosm and the fulfilment of this mediating function."[38] Maximus's spirituality is never individualized but always the life of the community of faith in the sacred liturgy and in the liturgies of everyday life.

This is a critical point for appreciating the importance of Maximus's cosmic spiritual vision, expressed most fully in the first season of his writing and then sharpened and focused by the christological controversies in the second season of his writing. Maximus's unbending theological conviction on the relatively obscure issue of the human and divine wills in Christ is the outcome of a spirituality that broadly encompasses his account of the nature of all creation. Maximus offers to Christian life a profoundly affirmative view of creation: "A unity which does not violate the differences constitutes the mystery of this incarnation, but is it thereby also the mystery of man and of the world. Love alone as a unifying factor is for Maximus capable of combining these elements into one divine-human activity since it includes all and respects the freedom of all."[39] That unity, fully realized, is the hope of divinization, made possible through the church in participation with the Incarnate Word, drawing together creation and Creator as one. This exalted ecclesial role is most poetically explicit in *The Church's Mystagogy*.

The Church's *Mystagogy*

In *Mystagogy*, Maximus contemplates the symbolism of the church as an analogy of the work God does in making the many one with God's self without confusing what is distinctive about each. As the church does what God does, it is an image of God by its participation in

Christ's flesh; "The church is the image of God because it participates in God's translation of himself on the plane of creaturely material life."[40]

One way to interpret the *Mystagogy* is to read its twenty-four brief chapters as a working out of the church's ascetic and missional activity borne from Chalcedonian Christology. The first seven chapters examine the mutual indwelling and symbolic worlds of church, world, and man. Chapters 8 through 23 consider elements in the Divine Liturgy as symbolic of ways worshipers are "transformed into [Christ] himself . . . through sensible symbols here below."[41] Examples include the following:

- Chapter 9: What is the meaning of the entrance of the people into the holy church of God?
- Chapter 11: What do the divine chants symbolize?
- Chapter 12: What do the salutations of peace signify?

Chapter 24 concludes the treatise by putting ascetic feet on Maximus's spiritual theology through love of people experiencing poverty. For Maximus, the church's liturgical acts are performed on a cosmic stage as humanity, given vocational identity by the church, participating in Christ, mediates the world's redemption in God.

Here I highlight two important passages from the first part of the treatise. From Chapter 1, *How and in what manner holy Church is an image and figure of God*, I consider Maximus's vision of God as theological speculation and as archetype for the life of the church. And from Chapter 5, *How and in what manner still is the holy Church of God an image and figure of the soul considered in itself*, I sketch Maximus's fusion of mind and intellect in the pursuit of truth and goodness. Taken together, these chapters integrate ecclesiology, theology, and anthropology in a sacred cosmology of type and archetype in the soul's journey to God as creature through participation in the church. I highlight chapter 24 as the surprisingly creation-affirming *telos* of this spirituality.

The Church's diversity and unity is an image of God: *Mystagogy* 1
The Church's Mystagogy begins by taking in the vast scope of diversity within the Church: "numerous and of almost infinite number are the men, women, and children who are distinct from one another and vastly different by birth and appearance, by nationality and language, by customs and age, . . . and still again by reputation, fortune, characteristics, and connections."[42] Beginning with the diversity of the church, Maximus affirms the unity that is also present: "In accordance with faith [the Spirit] gives to all a single, simple, whole, and indivisible condition . . . . To be and to appear as one body formed of different members is really worthy of Christ himself, our true head."[43]

The church is almost infinitely diverse yet spiritually unified. To achieve an account of this unity in diversity, Maximus deftly pivots to a Christology in which all become one without forfeiting their unique creaturehood. Christ is identified as the "center of straight lines that radiate from him," who also "circumscribes their extension in a circle and brings back to himself the distinctive elements of beings which he himself brought into existence."[44] The world, like the church, is a centered and bounded set of which Christ is the center point and circumference, the alpha and omega of all that is. All beings originate and are enclosed in hgim. Maximus has put forward three important propositions through this image in which all creatures live and move and have their being. *First, all things participate in Christ.* Over against the Originest conception of the material world created as the result of evil, Maximus values the material world as the good creation of God. *Second, all beings are connected with one another in a kinship of love.* This is a paradox that unites creatures by preserving their uniqueness and preserves their uniqueness by uniting them. We live with hope in Christ through the church that we will not be strangers and enemies to one another but bound with one another. God's presence holds the individual parts of the whole together and allows them through their created unity to live more for each other than for themselves. *Third, no created being dissolves into non-being.* Maximus corrects the Neoplatonic diminishing chain of being by rehabilitating all creatures now encompassed by the Incarnate Christ, who brings back to himself the distinctive elements of being that he himself brought into existence. Finally, we discover that the church is an image of God as a microcosm of the world in its diversity and unity. As different as churches are by language, places, and customs, they are made one through faith.

Through the next five chapters, Maximus continues to explore the typologies of church, world, and man from various directions—how the church is an image of the world and how the church is an image of man, how Scripture is like a man, how the world is like a man and how man is a microcosm of the world. Demonstrating the interrelatedness of all reality as bound to one another as extensions of Christ and bounded by Christ, all things are held together in Christ (Col 1), visible and invisible. This section culminates in chapter 4 as Maximus explores how the architecture of the church (as sanctuary and nave) is like a man: "For the soul it has the sanctuary and for the mind the divine altar, and for body it has the nave."[45]

Body and Soul Joined Together: *Mystagogy* 5

In chapter 5, the human soul, divided into *mind* and *reason*, is contemplated in depth. This is the longest chapter in *Mystagogy*, its most complex, and arguably its most fruitful. The *mind* is the intellectual faculty of the soul, its contemplative source. When directed to God, it is the seat of wisdom. While this account of humanity's highest dimension is familiar to Neoplatonic anthropology, and while Evagrius would have offered the *nous* as the highest human faculty that ascends to God when freed from the weight of its material cocoon, instead of recapitulating Evagrius's severe asceticism or the Aeropogite's platonic ascent, Maximus puts forward an integral perspective that foreshadows his later christological dogmatism. Here, the active life, as represented by the *reason*, complements and fulfills the contemplative life, represented by the mind. The reason "bears the same divine image by virtue as does the mind . . . for it is not licit to think of either as deprived of life . . . . In both these things consists the true science of divine and human matters, the truly secure knowledge and term of all divine wisdom according to Christians."[46]

This spiritual insight will sharpen later into Maximus's christological Dyotheletism. It is the source of love that alone is sufficient to overcome the divisions within creation and between the creation and Creator. The implications are distributive far beyond Maximus's era and surely even his imagination. In considering Maximus's contribution to contemporary challenges of race and racism, J. Kameron Carter writes,

> Love is what causes the reality of the Creator and that of creation to fruitfully converge—the dissimilarity between them at the level of nature notwithstanding. Rather than the creature-Creator distinction between the violent division of a purely extrinsic or parallel relationship, love, rendered concrete in Christ, enacts the "closest union" between the creature's and the Creator's modalities of existence causing these two modalities to thoroughly "interpenetrate" each other while in no way "annulling" the distinction between the natures that the modalities enact.[47]

As we have seen, Divine Love, incarnate in Christ and manifest in the church, moves toward synthesis from division, mutual fulfillment arising from completion. This spirituality, explored here in speculative reflection on the architecture of spiritual formation, is distributed into Christology, anthropology, ecclesiology, cosmology, and soteriology. Likewise, contemporary readers of Maximus increasingly appreciate his invitation to contemplative ecology, by which the world is seen as infused with spirituality, and true spirituality, a participation with the world instead of rejection of it by dualism or its utilitarian use for self-interested purposes. "The world is a church," Maximus wrote, "since it possesses heaven corresponding to a sanctuary, and for a nave it has the adornment of the earth."[48]

In chapter 5, we encounter the lively synthesizing spirit of Maximus's spirituality. The two parts of the soul, the *mind* and *reason*, appear at first to move toward God on their own respective paths through two lists of virtues presented in parallel. Through the intelligent *mind*, the contemplative aspect, to the soul is given "wisdom, contemplation, knowledge, and enduring knowledge, all directed to Truth."[49] Truth is "simple, unique, one, identical, indivisible, immutable, impassible, all-seeing, and wholly eternal."[50]

Goodness, likewise, is the aim of the soul's *reason* and the path by which creatures return in Christ to God: "Through its rational reason, [to the soul] belong reasoning, prudence, action, virtue, and faith, all directed to the Good."[51] Goodness reveals God when it manifests God in God's manifold activities. Goodness is expressed in abundance, fecundity, diversity, and movement.

By this point, Maximus has exalted Truth and Goodness as dual aims of the respective contemplative and active dimensions of human spirituality. In doing so, he is more or less in accord with spiritualities that distinguished between earthly and heavenly life. But, as we have seen, Maximus is a synthesizer and, as we might anticipate, connects each stage of the mind's path to truth and the reason's path to goodness as five pairs in ascension toward their highest end in God:

Mind and Reason
Wisdom and Prudence
Contemplation and Action
Knowledge and Virtue
Enduring Knowledge and Faith
Truth and Goodness

These pairs move toward their *telos* in God as ultimate Truth and Goodness. Perhaps Maximus, having paired the progression of the mind and reason in parallel ascent to God, could have stopped at this point, or he could have set them in tension with one another, resolved as the contemplative life asserts its prominence over the active life, the divine over the human, the spiritual over the bodily. Yet, with a Christology unsatisfied with parallel tracks of being, Maximus continued to synthesize, demonstrating even more fully his integrated spirituality. These things, he says, are united and *woven* into each other: "reason with mind, prudence with wisdom, action with contemplation, virtue with knowledge, faith with enduring knowledge, without any of these things being inferior or superior to the other."[52] In the process, the ten become one, moving toward unity in similarity to God such that the soul has "a rational mind, a prudent wisdom, an active contemplation, a virtuous knowledge, and along with them an enduring knowledge which is both very faithful and unchangeable."[53] Through the remainder of the chapter, Maximus weaves the mind and reason closer and tighter as cause and effect, as movement and result, as potency and fulfillment until finally, "All of these things [the holy church of God] gathers together for the mystery accomplished on the divine altar."[54] In the image of a centered and bounded set, Truth is the center point from which everything radiates and to which everything returns. Truth is the ontological unity all things possess as creatures of God. Goodness is the outer bound that draws all things back to God. In Truth and Goodness, the church's liturgy comes to fulfillment.

The Completion of the Mysteries in the Faithful: *Mystagogy* 24
Chapter 24 concludes the *Mystagogy* with an ecclesiology, drawn from the incarnation, revealed through the liturgy and its symbolism, then fulfilled in divinization through caring for people experiencing poverty. How else could Orthodox doxology be made complete without a return into the world as is characteristic of Orthodox ecclesiology and mission? John Chrysostom pointed eucharistic celebrants to "the sacrament of the brother" in the service believers offer outside the place of worship, on the altar of their neighbors' hearts. This is the liturgy outside the Liturgy.[55]

Here, then, is the ultimate and perhaps surprising fruit of Maximus's spirituality flowering from the soil of Chalcedonian Christology, a deeply symbolic ecclesiology and divinely given anthropology. Turning not away from but deeply into creaturehood and community, spirituality is not only a vertical relationship of ascent to a transcendent deity but is also horizontally embedded as charity. Christ's humanity makes possible an opening of our humanity to one another and all creation:

> . . .the man who needs our help in any way becomes as much as possible our friend as God is and we do not leave him abandoned and forsaken but rather that with fitting zeal we show him

in action the disposition which is alive in us with respect to God and our neighbor. . . . Now nothing is either so fitting for justification or so apt for divinization, if I can speak thus, and nearness to God as mercy offered with pleasure and joy from the soul to those who stand in need.[56]

Finally, we see that the movement toward divinization is not an ascent beyond our materiality but a descent toward shared life with the impoverished. The path toward *theosis* is *kenosis*. Through it all, for Maximus, faith means "the complete surrender of man at his highest point of expression to God manifesting himself fully: the logos of the whole man being lit up by the divine *logos* made flesh."[57] In *Mystagogy*, liturgical symbolism connects with an expansive vision of the two natures of Christ, each remaining completely itself even at the summit of the union. The church is an image of God and, simultaneously, of the whole world, a cosmic synthesis in which spirit and matter are inseparably united as sanctuary and nave. Church and man are images of one another, with Christ present, uniting himself to Creator and creature. Truth and Goodness are encountered through contemplation and kenotic charity, participating with Christ, fully divine and fully human.

Conclusion

In this chapter, we have explored the imaginative christological implications suggested by the encounter at the burning bush and discovered that we have our hands on solid theological handles in doing so. Douglass Moo provides a biblical hermeneutical reading strategy for engaging the Scripture text with consciousness of our present context. While Karl Barth centers Christ as "qualitatively other" regarding creation, Barth teaches that our stewarding acts are not merely managerial but doxological. St. Clare and the Franciscan tradition offer a vision of all creation as christocentric through "the primacy of Christ" doctrine. Maximus the Confessor highlights the unique role of the church's life and physical presence as a witness to and a model of Christ's relationship with humanity and with all creation.

This engagement with some of the most creative, theologically rich figures in the Christian tradition helps us see that creation is not merely an inert backdrop to our salvation, nor are creation's travails merely problems to be solved. We can see now that "what should be happening" is a eucharistic participation as creatures within the gift of creation. Each local congregation has the opportunity and calling to embody this in their shared life on their grounds. How they can do this, as an imitation of Christ's ministry of redemption and reconciliation, is the subject of the next chapter. In dramatic fashion, through the revelation at the burning bush, God calls Moses to embrace his new identity as a servant of God, whose own identity is revealed as the God of Israel's fathers Abraham, Isaac, and Jacob. God tasks Moses to take on, with the promise of divine help, the insurmountable challenge of delivering God's suffering people from the social, political, and ecological degradations of Egyptian captivity. Neither Israel nor Moses is alone anymore nor at the center of the story, as they were in the beginning. God is now the central character of a story that, until now, seemed to be absent of divine presence and redemption. Although Moses is still in the wilderness by the end of the burning bush episode, the whole Earth does not seem as barren and hopeless as it did before his encounter with God. We find encouragement for the liberation of God's people and their relationship with creation from the hold of Egypt's pillaging of Earth's goodness and mocking of the Creator's intentions. If the task ahead of us seems insurmountable, the story offers encouragement to trust in God's call and God's provision for the way forward.

Chapter 5

Church Grounds as a Geography of Hope

When St. Clare used the term "imitate" as the fruit of contemplation, she meant to embody in herself the image of God: "What God has wanted me to be from all eternity, who I am to be in my inmost self, is imaged in God's Son hanging on a cross. When I gaze at the cross, I am looking into a mirror. I see my true self. . . . Imitation is transformation insofar as Christ comes alive in my life."[1] Rather than promoting a balance of work with prayer or contemplation with action, Clare's prayer envelops Christopraxis—our action in Christ—as the expression of a life of embodied prayer.[2] To imitate Christ is more than a "What Would Jesus Do?" notion—it is to become who *we* are called to be in Christ in and for *this* place and time. Franciscan Sister Clare D'Auria poses a series of reflective questions that draw on this kind of prayer of imitation:

> Do I see myself as I truly am—both flawed and graced?
> Do I see myself, not only as "the fairest one of all," but also as part of the human family, as one who is truly intrinsically poor and, therefore one with and at home with those who are poor? Does this vision impel me, like the One I contemplate, to imitate his choice for the downward mobility that led him to live poverty stretched to the extreme limits of love?
> How do I contemplate others in the light of this vision, especially my sisters and brothers in community (family)?

> How does my imitation look like washing feet, nourishing others from my table, healing the sick and the sick of heart, and preaching by example—all in mutual exchange?[3]

These are insightful questions. To press them a step further along the lines we have been following, how might we be shaped by the burning bush story to respond in similarly reflective ways in this context? One way is to look for Christ's imminent presence in creation, even in the wilderness of the Anthropocene or the relatively mundane geography of a church's grounds. A sacramental imagination enlivens our prayer and calls us to imitate Christ, lighting the way toward the liberation of God's people in a world still groaning in travail. The burning bush, offering meaning for our prayer and action as Christians in an era of ecological crises, encourages us to listen to the voice of creation. Resources for the ecumenical Season of Creation have drawn on this story:

> Moses was told to remove his sandals, for he was standing on holy ground in God's presence. May this symbol move us to remove the "sandals" of our unsustainable lifestyles that disconnect us from creation and our Creator, contemplate our connection to the holy ground where we live, and listen for the voice of creation.[4]

Similarly, Gordon Lathrop poses a series of insightful questions about congregational life deriving from this story:

> If the Christian assembly gathers in the presence of this same God, the God celebrated in this story, does that assembly similarly deal so gently with the earth as God does with the bush? Does the assembly carry itself so harmlessly to the location of its meeting? Do we take off our shoes? The question is deeper yet: does that assembly invite us to see the place on which we meet—and the earth all around the meeting—as holy ground?[5]

We rediscover along with Moses in the wilderness that humans "do not merely *have* relations; they *are* their relations. Their very selves are constituted by their transactions with the world."[6] God is one-in-three, a perichoretic eternal relation of Father, Son, and Spirit. Created in the image of God, humans understand themselves as distinct from the other creatures while sharing much in common with them. In an echo of divine relations, human beings also exist in relationship with one another within the community of creation, which the story of Moses at the burning bush and the redemption of God's people from enslavement makes clear. Through theological reflection on relationship, we are brought to lament and confess for the ways we break relationship with one another, with creation, and with God. This lens, this lament, and this hope give us a hermeneutic for reading Scripture and creation with receptivity to places where personal encounter with God active in the world brings the hope of reconciliation out of the dusty wilderness of our rifts. With hope, we are far more than stewards of the Earth's resources because, in Christ, we have been given the ministry of reconciliation. We know this is our hope, but where shall this hope be nurtured? We need actual places, especially to distinguish between optimism and hope.

The Landscape of Optimism

On a Sunday afternoon in 1960, the "Dean of Western Writers" Wallace Stegner sat down to his typewriter. Sitting at a typewriter was not unusual for Stegner. He won the Pulitzer Prize in 1972 and the National Book Award in 1977. From there, he initiated the Stanford University Creative Writing Program, where his students included Wendell Berry, Sandra Day O'Connor, and Larry McMurtry, near and dear to all Texans for *Lonesome Dove*. Stegner was friends with Robert Frost, who was a frequent guest in his home, and Ansel Adams, with whom he often corresponded.

In 1960, government bureaucrats were working on a report on recreational uses of wilderness areas: hiking, camping, fishing, and so forth. One of them asked for Stegner's input. The letter the official received in return was so extraordinary it came to be known simply as the "Wilderness Letter."[7] The Wilderness Letter went viral (if there were such a thing in 1960). It was reprinted in the *Washington Post*, read aloud before Congress, and significantly influenced the legislature to move on the Wilderness Act, which was passed in 1964. The

"Wilderness Letter" is among most influential American short reflections this side of the Gettysburg Address. "Not bad for an afternoon of two-finger typing on an old Remington manual," his daughter proudly boasted years later.

Stegner's letter would not promote hiking, camping, fishing, and other forms of recreation but an *idea* of wilderness as a spiritual resource, "tucked between the leaves of the report." Stegner famously concludes his letter, "we need to put into effect, for preservation, some other principle than the principles of exploitation or 'usefulness' or even recreation." At the time there were no US federally designated wilderness areas until, partly due to Stegner's advocacy, the Wilderness Act passed and was signed by President Johnson on September 3, 1964. Under the coordination of the National Wilderness Preservation System, the law established the official designation of wilderness as "an area where the earth and community of life are untrammeled by man, where man himself is a visitor who does not remain."[8] Once established, a wilderness area is restricted to non-motorized recreation, scientific research, and other noninvasive activities. Visitors are strongly encouraged to practice a "leave no trace" ethic. Today the US's 759 designated wilderness areas make up about 5 percent of the nation's land, much of it in Alaska. In the continental US, approximately 2.7 percent of acreage is set apart as federal wilderness across forty-four states.

Think of wilderness areas as a step more remote than state parks, beyond national monuments (like our own Waco Mammoth Site), and even beyond national parks such as Yellowstone, Big Bend, and Grand Canyon. Wilderness is to be what the name implies: wild, untamed, unaltered, uninhabited. It is open space. Wilderness areas may be beautiful, but they are not always meant for hordes of visitors, like Yosemite or Glacier National Parks. They are to be left alone: no four-wheelers, no motorized fishing boats, no trucks, no cabins or lodges, no paved roads. They are quiet places where silence and solitude are still possible.

Wallace Stegner recognized that the error of developers who saw land as a commodity was repeated by preservationists who argued that land's true value lay in research and recreation. While he was willing to marshal any available arguments in favor of preservation over development, it's the *idea* of wilderness he called upon that Sunday afternoon, admitting coyly that wilderness, "being an intangible and spiritual resource, will seem mystical to the practical minded—but then anything that cannot be moved by a bulldozer is likely to seem mystical to them." Stegner's indelible gift to American consciousness was the wilderness *idea* at a moment when everyone else argued about wilderness *uses*. Stegner's letter was profoundly American but not explicitly an expression of Christian spirituality. Christian reflection on creation exceeds even Stegner's epic vision. I submit that wilderness is not merely a nationalistic ideal by which we know our identity as Americans; creation is a sacrament by which we know and are renewed in our identity as creatures of God.[9] Stegner pointed in this direction by his closing crescendo of poetic prophecy in the letter: "We simply need that wild country available to us, even if we never do more than drive to its edge and look in. For it can be a means of reassuring ourselves of our sanity as creatures, a part of the geography of hope."

A Geography of Hope

One may ask, nevertheless, in just what way do wilderness areas function as a geography of hope? Stegner isn't clear on this point, but he recognizes that gazing on dramatic landscapes gives many people a touch of mystical experience. Those places must be preserved, Stegner argues, lest we destroy all the places that remind us that transcendent beauty and majesty exist in the world. Moreover, he envisions preserved wilderness spaces to enliven hope because their mere existence proves that Americans have the capacity and collective discipline to curtail their insatiable appetites for consumption by agreeing to designate some places off-limits to development. These places, wilderness areas, can endure and survive the desecrating onslaught brought about by unrelenting industrial and commercial expansion and the consequent metabolism of nature into consumer products.

As forward-looking and revolutionary as Stegner's vision was, it still falls short of what is needed now to account for our place in creation. For one thing, no place is truly off limits to human impact. In a changing climate, no geography—no matter how remote—is immune to the effects of human industrial activity. For another thing, while preserving some places is a good practice, Stegner's conservation ethic offers little guidance for how we are to treat the other 97 percent of the land on which we live and work (and go to church). In some respects, we are victims of the success of the national park and public lands initiatives. So dominant have been the narratives around "America's best idea" that we have neglected to consider, carefully and courageously, how we live where we move and have our being. So the Stegner ethic gives us a thoughtfully preserved 3 percent and little but an unsteady optimism for our relationship with the other 97 percent.

This conundrum is represented by fellow Texans not far from us in Waco. Ninety miles south of DaySpring's church campus, and contrary to just about everything that constitutes hope, are the headquarters of the Texas Public Policy Foundation (TPPF), which claims to offer "the moral case for fossil fuels." Emblematic of TPPF rhetoric, on Thanksgiving 2022, an executive with TPPF named Jason Isaac tweeted this: "Today, I'm thankful to live a high-carbon lifestyle and wish the rest of the world could too. Energy poverty=poverty. #decarbonization is dangerous and deadly."[10]

While his tweet could be dismissed as a dog whistle to liberal, tree-hugging social media interlocutors, TPPF is powerful, well-funded, and politically effective, committed to supporting fossil fuel industries in Texas and beyond, and likewise committed to defeating public support for renewable energy alternatives. Their "moral case for fossil fuels" defends fossil fuels as the vehicle for justice for the poor: "American prosperity is rooted in an economy based on oil, gas and coal and . . . poor communities and developing nations deserve the same opportunities to grow."[11]

Isaac is correct that fossil fuels have driven Western economies since the industrial revolution and literally fueled the prosperity they have offered many of their citizens. While that prosperity is undoubtedly unequally distributed, it would be almost impossible to argue against the correlation between the Western industrial economy and the material prosperity of its beneficiaries. Yet critics accuse Isaac of pushing a false dichotomy between being environmentally responsible and enjoying economic prosperity.[12] Advocates of renewable energy and environmental stewardship point to economic benefits accessible to a nation that cares for its land, water, and air. This contention, one of the intractable features of debates around transitioning to a "green economy," is based on the premise that, by neatly swapping renewable energy for fossil fuels, we can maintain our standard of living *and* protect the Earth. Seeking a win-win for consumers and the Earth, renewable energy advocates generally accept that maintaining our lifestyles (i.e., our *consumption*) is the goal and contend that a full commitment to renewable energies can maintain those lifestyles without the residual effects of saturating the atmosphere with greenhouse gases. Isaac is skeptical of those claims. I am as well, but for different reasons.

Isaac's celebrated "high-carbon lifestyle" rhetoric and the arguments against it both obfuscate efforts to cultivate a culture of care for creation because the issues we face as a culture go deeper than our technological challenges. To be fair to Isaac, a "high-carbon lifestyle" is the lifestyle most Americans live and enjoy and for which they also feel gratitude on Thanksgiving Day. Few people, however, recognize just how high-carbon their lifestyles are, and few want to think too much about it. For example, unlike Isaac, I do not *celebrate* my use of carbon-producing burnt fossil fuels but am happy to drive a vehicle to work and grateful when my home is air conditioned in August in Texas. I am thankful for the food I consume, much of which is trucked from somewhere in the world and grown in soil heavily amended with industrial fertilizers. I am utterly typical. Americans of all geographical locations, political persuasions, and theological confessions live high-carbon lifestyles relative to much of the rest of the world and certainly compared to the carbon-zero lifestyles we need to achieve if we are to mitigate climate change successfully. Even those among us who "care about creation" often have a difficult time reducing our carbon footprint because we are entangled in patterns of life—transportation, food sourcing, energy sourcing—that make change on a personal level difficult and costly, and even more so on the national and international scale. The insidious reality of the Anthropocene is that high-carbon lifestyles, which are an existential problem, become normalized.

Isaac's Thanksgiving tweet celebrates the culture of individualism, greed, and superficial optimism in which we are all captive. Christians may have the instinct to respond to this culture with winsome witness to the creation-affirming gospel of Jesus Christ that is also truly good news for the poor, but I am not sure we know where to begin either to deconstruct Isaac's arguments or how to offer an alternative. Through this book, I have sought to uncover the theological reasoning and practical wisdom necessary to see through the mistruths and false dichotomies that dominate contemporary environmental discourse in politically and theologically conservative communities so we may offer and model an alternative.

For his part, Isaac is not a climate change denier; he just claims to believe that the implications of climate change do not substantially matter: "Absolutely, man is having an impact," he said. "I just disagree with the argument that it's dangerous."[13] This opinion runs counter to the overwhelming scientific consensus that climate change is exceedingly dangerous for all life on Earth, in particular the most vulnerable ecosystems and the most vulnerable human populations. The TPPF argues that so-called climate change dangers are hypothetical while the jobs and relatively cheap electricity produced by coal, oil, and natural gas are the clear immediate concerns.[14] Pressing the point further, the foundation is currently suing the Environmental Protection Agency by challenging its designation of greenhouse gases as a danger to human health and welfare.[15] They claim the Paris Climate Agreement was a political stunt that "will push more people into poverty"[16] and push the false narrative that the blackouts suffered across Texas in the February 2021 winter storm were caused by frozen wind turbines.[17] Donations to TPPF increased from $4.7 million in 2010 to $25.6 million in 2021, so clearly the message of TPPF resonates with many Americans. Frankly, this is not surprising. TPPF's arguments and advocacy extend the interests of a self-interested, short-sighted, consumeristic culture, which is exactly the one we have developed.

In this context, we are faced with a more complex and insidious problem than can be solved with renewable energy technologies. Isaac manifests a deeper truth that his interlocutors ignore: we have a cultural and spiritual problem as much as a technological problem. The climate crisis is only one part a technology problem; the technology problem is entangled with a widespread cultural rift between modern human life and the Earth's life. As discussed in chapter 3, environmental sociology's biting critique of Western-style capitalism is pictured by the treadmill metaphor: twin treadmills of production and consumption keep us each doing what we are already doing because the ordinary person cannot find a way psychologically or financially to get off the treadmills of income-getting and material consumption. Indeed, we must run faster and faster simply to keep up.[18] There's a relentlessness of consumption to life on the treadmills because enough is never enough.

For the world's poorest nations, immediate needs for warmth, food, and transportation demand fossil fuels, as do developed nations in the "mid-transition."[19] But continued use of fossil fuels comes with generational costs. We know enough now about the consequences of burning fossil fuels, measured in CO_2 ppm in the atmosphere, to face the planetary existential crisis of this century with much more than self-indulgent thanksgiving for our high-carbon lives. We can see the climate crisis as a technology crisis and a spiritual crisis long in the making. The success of the TPPF to defend fossil fuels and promote high-carbon lifestyles is the very definition of a pyrrhic victory.

In the face of the crisis and seeming intractable path of planetary environmental trouble, individuals can feel that nothing they do makes a difference. Convinced that they have little agency and that major actors—governments and energy companies—will not act, ordinary people become apathetic or give in to despair. In his beautiful book on race and racism, Wendell Berry names humans's need for hope: "There is, I am sure, such a thing as a sense of guilt about historical wrongs, but I have the strongest doubts about the usefulness of a guilty conscience as a motivation; a man, I think, can be much more dependably motivated by a sense of what would be desirable than by a sense of what has been deplorable."[20] Recognizing this same truth as a psychology of climate action, atmospheric scientist Katharine Hayhoe tries to communicate reasons we can have hope and how individual actions can make a difference. She continually communicates a positive, forward-looking, encouraging message in the face of daunting challenges.[21] Yet we still need a place and a community to enact such individual hope, even if we adopt Hayhoe's outlook. This is precisely why church grounds are key: they offer an alternative to the dichotomies between public and private space—between "I'm too small to make a difference" and "They're too large and entrenched to change." Church grounds are spaces where communities of ordinary individuals can exercise agency with purpose and creativity. They can do more than "leave no trace" as they address global issues on a manageable scale. Congregations are doing this all around the country.[22]

Season of Creation

In the fall of 2021, DaySpring observed our first Season of Creation. Five focused weeks on ecology, spirituality, and practical care for the church grounds inspired changes in individual and collective ecological attitudes and behaviors. Moreover, the experience validated the insights of Richard Osmer, whose *Practical Theology* discusses how transformational leadership brings about deep change by "leading an organization through a process in which its identity, mission, culture, and operating procedures are fundamentally altered. . . . It involves projecting a vision of what the congregation might become and mobilizing followers who are committed to this vision."[23]

Osmer's description of deep change details our experience as though a connection between creation care and church grounds as core matters related to our identity, mission, and culture were at stake in amplifying the ecological dimension of our faith in and beyond the Season of Creation. Setting out to embrace a vision of the church grounds as more integral to our lives than as an aesthetic setting for church activities, I had to be open to an ecological and perhaps sacramental vision of material reality. This also involved engaging fields of knowledge beyond theology to understand soil science, tree care, and environmental crises, such as climate change, facing our grounds and habitats beyond our grounds. I set out to introduce a Franciscan-like, incarnational spirituality aligned holistically with ecological alertness and, in some unexpected ways, traditional Baptist sensibilities.[24] Moreover, I wanted to integrate a christological theology of creation with every aspect of church life and mission, communal and individual spirituality, and evangelical witness. It's not difficult in many places to empower a small group to organize some creation-care initiatives in a congregation, but a Christopraxis of creation care is the ultimate goal, a purpose that fuels and sustains practical implications such as carbon footprint reduction, habitat conservation, and food justice.

While DaySpring was a healthy congregation generally receptive to such transformations,[25] a wider transformation among Baptists and evangelicals requires courageous and transformational leadership from individual pastors, theologians, and congregations who demonstrate creativity and ecological alertness on their own grounds.[26] A congregation's grounds offer rich, underappreciated, and underleveraged habitat for a congregation who engages their grounds with transformative leadership. In the Season of Creation, and in the Anthropocene, church grounds, not wilderness areas, are the geographies of hope.

The Season of Creation has been observed in various ecumenical and environmental settings in congregations each year from September 1 to October 4 since 1989. Inspired by its observance, Christians around the world take initiatives in a wide variety of local and international, public, and private spheres of creation care action—from international fossil fuel public policy advocacy to local efforts to build community gardens and rainwater catchment systems. Prayer services devoted to creation care are typically scheduled from September 1 (World Day of Prayer for the Care of Creation) to October 4 (Feast Day of St. Francis of Assisi).

At DaySpring, we engaged the season in prayer, study, and action as an exploration and celebration of the ways creation care functions as a set of meaningful spiritual practices, sharpening instincts present in the congregation even before we first acquired property of our own in 2001.[27] To complement individual initiatives and the work of public advocacy and policy-making, it is critically important to identify arenas in which we can communally participate directly as creatures in creation. In theories of practical action embedded in much environmental advocacy concerning climate change or other environmental crises, attention to the places where ordinary human activity takes place is lacking.[28] The DaySpring church grounds, like those of many congregations, offer an alternative cultural geography between the duality of private property and publicly managed land. We can think of this from several angles.

First, ownership is held by a *congregation*. In contrast to a suburban home lot or a business, church grounds are not privately held by one family, individual, or corporation; church grounds in the Baptist tradition are owned by the local, autonomous congregation.[29] This ownership can promote personal connection and responsibility. Unlike other privately owned property, the church is typically not interested in monetizing the property or activities held on the property, so the grounds can occupy something like an alternative political economy than most other spaces in a capitalistic society.[30]

Second, *church members* have agency on the church grounds. In many cases, the church's grounds are available to the public, like a public park. Unlike a park, however, activity on the grounds is not restricted to recreation or contemplation. Plainly put, I cannot plant a garden or a tree at our local city park, but I can, presumably, take part in tree planting or garden keeping on the grounds of the church to which I belong. For church members who live in apartments or in university residence halls, the church's grounds may be the only place they can put their hands in the soil. Church grounds are a geography where communal participation in creation can take place.

Third, congregants have had *spiritual experiences* at the church. We are not merely discussing a community garden, preserved recreational areas, or an idea or ideal of wilderness, but sacred space. Church grounds are a place experienced by church members as sacred, or at least in the arena of the sacred, in some way or another. As Margaret Visser observes,

> A church is a recognition, in stone and wood and brick, of spiritual awakenings. It nods, to each individual person. . . . It constitutes a collective memory of spiritual insights, of thousands of mystical moments. A church reminds us of what we have known. And it tells us that the possibility of the door swinging open again remains.[31]

The grounds are not just human-centric but are dedicated, often formally, to God and God's redemptive purposes in the world. In this most important sense, people experience participation in creation on church grounds as spiritual participation with God's presence. "All Christian communities," writes Pope Francis, "have an important role to play in ecological education. It is my hope that our seminaries and houses of formation will provide an education in responsible simplicity of life, in grateful contemplation of God's world, and in concern for the needs of the poor and the protection of the environment."[32] Taken together, these three "educations"—responsible simplicity, grateful contemplation, and concern for the poor and protection of the environment—gesture to the wide, encompassing scope of an ecologically alert spirituality.

As a geography for a practical theology of creation care, church grounds occupy an unusually promising habitat for ecologically alert activity and spirituality to flourish. Yet the church's grounds are overlooked both in the literature on environmental issues and in the practices of church communities. I have found few resources among Baptists that specifically address the potential of church grounds for ecologically alert spirituality. This neglect has deep roots in the church's theological reflection. Maximus the Confessor, for example, offered enduring creation-affirming insights into the connection between the *Logos* and the *logoi*, a connection now at the heart of contemporary Orthodox ecological theology,[33] and Maximus devoted careful and creative attention to cosmic architectural typologies. In his *Ecclesiastical Mystagogy*, Maximus typologically linked the human being, the architecture of a church building, and the cosmos:

> The Church is a representation of the intelligible and sensible realms, because she possesses the sanctuary as a symbol of the intelligible realm and the nave as a symbol of the sensible realm. And,

she is also an image of man, because she portrays the soul through the sanctuary, and she presents the body through the nave. She is a representation and image of the soul considered on its own, because she bears the eminence of the contemplative part through the sanctuary, and she possesses the ornamentation of the principal part through the nave.[34]

Strikingly, however, nowhere in *Mystagogy* does Maximus contemplate the importance, symbolic or ecological, of the outside of the sanctuary or the fields, trees, or grounds around it. Maximus simply did not seem to *see* church grounds as holy spaces though, in the mystagogical imagination of North and East African Christians, such as in the forest churches of Ethiopia, the church's grounds are paramount.[35] Thus, we remember, before we act, the first spiritual challenge is to learn to *see* and be attentive to what is in front of our eyes. With St. Clare's approach to prayer as a guide, DaySpring set out in the Season of Creation to see, consider, contemplate, and imitate Christ on and through our relationship with our church's grounds. When asked their topics of interest, the congregation's top three responses were

- the connections between environmental issues, race, and poverty (64 percent);
- the lessons and legacy of St. Francis of Assisi (63 percent); and
- silence in a noisy world (55 percent).

A Season of Creation on Sacred Ground

Worship

The worship of God is the center of our life together as a congregation, so it is not surprising that the congregation reported the Sunday worship services held outdoors in the grove of oak trees as the most "meaningful" communal activity in the Season of Creation. For many Sundays in 2020 and 2021, DaySpring's worship was held outdoors in the Cathedral of the Oaks, prompted initially by Covid-19 pandemic concerns. We soon realized that worshiping outdoors was not just a popular alternative to online-only worship but was also embraced by the congregation as a meaningful habitat for worship regardless of pandemic concerns. During the Season of Creation, we continued meeting outdoors for pandemic-related caution and to embody the season's focus in our worship setting.

Teaching

We structured the church's teaching ministry during the Season of Creation to focus on our relationship with the church grounds by following the story of Moses and the burning bush in Exodus 3 as read through the lens of St. Clare's method of contemplative prayer. While this sounds complex, it was quite intuitive in practice. Each week of the series was oriented around a move in Clare's prayer and its echoes in the burning bush story, as I have been exploring throughout this book.

On Wednesdays, we welcomed guest presenters. Butch Tindell, a local farmer, spoke with us about the beauty and life of good soil and the spirituality of regenerative approaches to agriculture. Butch said we know more about the oceans and deep space than we do about the soil under our feet. Holding up a handful of soil, Butch discussed the presence of billions of microorganisms in the soil. Soil, Butch taught us, is alive and should be treated with love and care. The following week, Robert and Melinda Creech joined by Zoom from their hundred-acre farm in Floresville, Texas, which they are restoring with native Texas prairie grasses. The Creeches talked about the vast prairies of the American Midwest, which are 99 percent gone now. They explained how these "boring" grasses can plunge their roots twenty feet down, aerating the soil, storing rainwater, and sequestering carbon dioxide from the atmosphere. Through a deep look at soil and grass, Butch and the Creeches helped us learn to see and understand how these ordinary, overlooked features of the world give and sustain life.

In week four, we joined Moses as he was told, "You are standing on holy ground" (Exod 3:5). This revelation correlates with Clare's *contemplation*, a mystical seeing and being present to God, who is present with us. The week began with a Saturday silent retreat on our church grounds. Whereas other activities on the grounds were more active (composting, workdays, etc.), this day was set aside for contemplative prayer. Attendees were invited to find a quiet place among the trees and trails to be still and be present to God. One of the great gifts the church grounds can offer the community is a place to pray. The next morning, we followed the retreat by discussing the life and spirituality of St. Francis of Assisi and the poetry of Gerard Manly Hopkins, whose poem "God's Grandeur" prompted vibrant discussion.

In the poem, "The world is charged with the grandeur of God," but because "generations have trod, have trod, have trod," the poet laments that "the soil is bare now, nor can foot feel, being shod." Nevertheless, "for all this, nature is never spent," and the Holy Ghost still "over the bent World broods with warm breast and with ah! Bright wings."[36] This marvelous poem gave us a model for lament and praise. With "God's Grandeur" in mind, a few days later, we spent the evening with church members Scott and Andrea Moore at their Benedict Farm, where they taught us about the joys and trials of life with the animals on their small farm. The Moores offered us a window into some practical realities of having one's life oriented around care for creatures.

In week five, we followed Clare into *imitation*, the journey to become what we love. As Moses was called to return to Egypt to free enslaved Israelites (Exod 3:7-12), so God calls us to imitate Christ, in whom we are called to embody God's liberating love. Christ's ministry of reconciliation in a broken world gives birth to the church's ministry of reconciliation (2 Cor 5:18). One significant manifestation of the church's ministry can be about food—its sourcing, distribution, and availability. Norman Wirzba, for example, writes in *Food and Faith*,

> Food is about the relationships that join us to the earth, fellow creatures, loved ones and guests, and ultimately God. How we eat testifies to whether we value the creatures we live with and depend upon. To eat is to savor and struggle with the mystery of creatureliness. . . . Eating invites people to develop a deeper appreciation for where they are and who they are with so that their eating can be a sacramental rather than sacrilegious act. A thoughtful, theological

relation to food makes possible the discovery that eating is among the most intimate and pleasurable ways possible for us to enter into the memberships of creation and find there the God who daily blesses and feeds life.[37]

Food is not merely for our enjoyment or contemplation but a means by which we share our goods. To highlight the ministry of food availability in the face of hunger and poverty, Jeremy Everett, director of the Baylor Collaborative on Hunger and Poverty, spoke about his work and the convergence of environmental concerns and food justice.[38] Everett's mission with the Baylor Collaborate is to end food insecurity in Texas and beyond, believing everyone has a right to healthy local foods.

Celebration

Continuing the theme of food and community life, we celebrated our annual Covenant Day Retreat at the World Hunger Relief Farm outside of Waco, Texas, to conclude our Season of Creation. We reinforced our longstanding support for "The Farm's" mission in the community and worldwide.[39] As a counterpoint to industrial-scale food processing and distribution systems, the Farm exists to model regenerative agriculture and how the spirituality of a community is formed by commitment to the rhythms and practices of this approach to the land. This celebration in October was the final bookend to a season that began with an all-church workday on the grounds in late August. We began and ended with attention to our place on and with the land.

Composting

One of the surprising outcomes of the Season of Creation was our introduction to community composting. During the August workday at the beginning of the season, we constructed boxes for vegetable gardens and a three-bin community compost system. This system is the most enduring physical vestige of the 2021 Season of Creation.[40] Near the compost bin system, we constructed a large collection bin for "browns" (leaves and woodchips) to be mixed in with the "greens" (food scraps). At the beginning of the season, we distributed one hundred one-gallon buckets to church members and their families, asking them to use the buckets to collect food scraps and then return them to the church for processing. Volunteers weighed and recorded the amount of food scraps brought in by the congregation. Then, the volunteers emptied the buckets, chopped and combined the food scraps with leaves, and added the mixture to the compost bin.

Between September 5 and October 10, 2021, 896 pounds of food scraps were composted at the church. In the following year more than three thousand pounds of food scraps were brought to our community compost site and transformed into garden soil instead of garbage in the landfill. Americans discard 30–40 percent of our food as waste. More than half of the wasted food goes to landfills, making up 24 percent of landfill volume.[41] This compost project allowed us to see how even a small system like ours can make a meaningful difference in handling our food waste and healing the metabolic rift.[42]

Lessons from the Season of Creation

Overall, during the Season of Creation, we wove together the story of Moses and the burning bush, St. Francis's spirituality, and St. Clare's prayer. Members participated in an all-church workday, a silent retreat, and an ongoing community compost project on the grounds. We connected with a local regenerative farmer's attention to soil, church members' embrace of native grasses on their farm, church members' care for animals, and our mission partners' food relief and justice ministries worldwide.

One congregant reflected that the activities in the Season of Creation "made me more aware of how we all need to take better care of our world and how what we do affects everyone." Another said, "The spiritual formation meetings have been an eye-opening learning experience. It has been very meaningful to discuss and reflect on the topics of race and stewardship of the Earth so far." A third likewise wrote of what they learned as the classes tied together "issues of faith and care for God's creation in ways I had not previously considered."

Not everyone was new to the concepts of Christian care for creation. One wrote, "I found the naming of the way we have treated creation over the past half century as 'blasphemous' was like a valve being released. I was asked for initial thoughts after hearing that in the spiritual formation class. My thought was, 'Finally!!! Someone said it.'"

In October 2021, I closed our celebration of the Season of Creation by asking the congregation to consider the next five years as preparation for the celebration of the Feast of St. Francis on October 4, 2026, the eight-hundredth anniversary of his death. In the subsequent years, a number of things happened in and through the life of the DaySpring congregation. Here are some of the highlights:

Beyond Our Grounds

Three local congregations established community composting sites on their grounds. Coffee shop owners and employees are working with city leaders to expand community compost tenfold within the next five years. A DaySpring member who is part of the Waco Sustainability Network helped organize the Waco Green Communities Conference in September 2022. Three of us from the church spoke at the conference.[43]

Community Compost

In the first year of our community compost project, it is estimated that we processed more than three thousand pounds of food scraps that otherwise would have been added to the landfill. Since then, scraps have continued to pour in. The finished compost supplied our vegetable gardens at the church and has been distributed to church members for their home gardens.

Community Gardens

We designated a table in the narthex as our Community Table. Every week, we offer fresh produce from the church's and members' home gardens to anyone who would like to take it home to enjoy.

Eucharist

In March 2022, we began celebrating Communion each Sunday in worship.[44]

Franciscan Pilgrimage

In 2022 and again in 2024, sixteen church members undertook a pilgrimage to Assisi, Italy, to walk in the steps of St. Francis and St. Clare. The group visited with the proprietors of a 1,000-year-old, zero-kilometer agritourismo and drew inspiration for care for our church grounds by exploring the restored hillside forest, the Bosco di San Francesco, affectionately called "the other half of Assisi."[45]

Prayer Trails

The walking trails in the woods behind our sanctuary were connected through community workdays. Volunteers blazed and labeled them the St. Francis Trail, St. Theresa of Avila Trail, and St. Julian of Norwich Trail.

Support for Mission Partners

Our congregation voted unanimously to add mission partners World Hunger Relief Farm and the Baptist Texans on Mission Relief organizations to our annual budget. Texans on Mission responds to disasters, such as Hurricane Ike, which will become more common as the air and oceans warm.[46]

Sustainable Power

In April 2022, our Coordinating Council changed our electric provider to a 100 percent renewables plan, reducing our buildings' carbon footprint to near zero. We celebrated this change in October 2022 as an opportunity to give thanks for, in St. Francis's words, the gifts of Brother Sun and Sister Wind. Members are researching the viability of adding solar panels to the roofs of our buildings.

An Annual Season of Creation

Each fall, we celebrate Season of Creation with renewed emphasis and teaching on composting, presentations from environmental scientists on climate change, community meals on the grounds, adult spiritual formation classes based on St. Clare's prayer method, and a Covenant Day Retreat at a local farm.

Hospitality

In 2022, after much discernment and preparation, we opened the Naomi House, a hospitality home for asylum seekers, and received our first guests, a family from Honduras. The intersection of the Anthropocene, the plight of the people experiencing poverty in Central America, and the immigration crisis is evident. The Institute for Economics and Peace projects that up to 1.2 billion people could be displaced globally due to the effects of climate change.[47] At our Naomi House property in north Waco, about five miles from our church campus, our second community garden is being planted with the intent to feed the residents and be shared with neighbors. In the corner of the lot stands a large old live oak tree. In preparing the house, we cleared underbrush from the tree and hung a swing in its branches. The residents of the home dubbed that tree the St. Clare Tree. Together, she and the St. Francis Tree on the DaySpring campus anchor a five-mile-long axis of grace and hospitality that now runs through our city.

Conclusion

All of this gives me hope for what can happen through congregations who look closely at their relationship with their church grounds and begin to see that relationship as essential to their identity and mission. Church grounds invite us to exercise agency to care for creation communally, creatively, and generously. Because the modest steps, and so much more, are repeatable in congregations throughout the country, I have hope that the church's ecological awakening will lead to environmental repair and toward an enlivening of the church's witness to Christ, the Incarnate One. The ministry of reconciliation, as Fred Bahnson says, "has too often been discussed in Christian circles as if it took place in a vacuum, as if only people and not trees, rivers, mountains and farms are swept up in God's redemptive drama."[48] We learn to see, however, how the material world has always been an integral dimension of God's redemptive purposes. Moses's encounter at the burning bush changed his life and the trajectory of an enslaved nation. So may our participation in care for sacred spaces change our lives and the trajectory of a planet engulfed in environmental crises.

Chapter 6

Church Grounds as a Place of Conversion

> Stay away from anything
> that obscures the place it is in.
> There are no unsacred places;
> there are only sacred places
> and desecrated places.[1]

Climate change is the critical issue facing humanity in this century. Without significant reduction in the production of greenhouse gases pumped into the atmosphere, scientists project a rise of at least 2.7 degrees Fahrenheit in global temperatures, setting off a cascading series of environmental catastrophes as we cross global temperature thresholds. If Christians care about the environment, people experiencing poverty, or their own communities, this daunting reality will stir their attention. The changing climate, biodiversity loss, and environmental injustices that go with it collectively form the context of our care for creation in this generation and beyond. Climate change data such as the Keeling Curve reflect the consequences of our lives more clearly. In the mirror, we see that the typical structure and assumptions of modern life are not sustainable for the flourishing of life on Earth. As the Earth bears witness to the ways humans are not living sustainably, our response will reveal the character of our care for the Earth.

Christians can act, individually and congregationally, to respond in courageous, sacrificial, creative, and hopeful ways. In the Anthropocene, we are past the time for dualistic sociologies, geologies, or anthropologies, and, as Philip Sheldrake insists, we are past the time for romantic nature spiritualities.[2] We have come to the moment of conversion.

"Day to day pours forth speech" sings Psalm 19, "and night to night reveals knowledge. Yet there is no speech, nor are there words whose voice is not heard." Even still, "their voice goes out through all the earth; and their words to the end of the world."[3] The psalmist's "book of creation" encourages the reader to listen to the Earth, which "speaks" without words. To an earlier generation, this might have been received as romantic poetry on the enchantment of nature, but in the Anthropocene it is also a warning to heed the "words" of the Earth: pay attention to how the Earth is bearing witness to its life and ours.

We may, like St. Paul, hear the Earth's travail and become aware of the rifts that are tearing it apart. In the Theory of Metabolic Rift, the Earth system is a living organism; "creation" does not name something static. Therefore, to care for creation is not to try to preserve what currently exists as if it is frozen in time or as if humans are merely interlocutors. While conservation movement rhetoric can imply that humans have no redemptive place in pure nature, a Christian doctrine of creation sees all creation as a living organism of which humans are necessarily, intrinsically, and vocationally a vital part. To care for creation is to participate in thoughtful, intentional ways for all creatures with whom we share interrelated dependence for life on Earth and with whom we join our voices in praise of God (Psalm 148). This alone is a tremendous challenge. Perhaps in a pre-industrial culture, habits and practices that constitute caring participation in the life of creation could be part and parcel of the life of the human community. But in a culture enmeshed in industry and consumption, we have forgotten the ways of *shalom*, the ways to live in metabolic relationship with the world around us, so we need more than better technology. We need an ecological conversion. The good news is that such an ecological conversion is interwoven with a Christian vision of creaturely life. While Christian environmental ethics often turns to the opening chapters of Genesis for inspiration, the story in Exodus 3 of Moses at the burning bush shows us what ecological conversion entails as a spiritual encounter that leads to contemplation and redemptive mission. For Moses, the experience of the burning bush was a startlingly personal and transformative divine encounter.

Before the decisive divine encounter, Moses is an image of humanity in the Anthropocene, where core relations that make humans who we are—creatures of God within a story of divine provision and promised land—are severed. Like Moses, we are lost on the far side of a wilderness where we cannot return to who we once were nor redeem who we have become. There is not even a vision for what we would return to. John Markey demonstrates how Moses's own story, steeped in the abusive, desecrating privilege of Pharoah's (high carbon?) house, required a conversion on Moses's part for him to begin to become who God called him to be and to deliver his people who were suffering in their bondage. Such conversion enabled him to see Pharoah's palace as a prison for himself and an oppressive burden on the people whom he came to identify as his own. From this perspective, we could say that Moses, all but lost in the wilderness, has already experienced the first steps of his conversion. Alone in the wilderness, he is better positioned to meet the God of his fathers than he was when he was surrounded by Egypt's industrial power and privilege. To translate to our context, the first steps in ecological conversion can seem like being thrust into the wilderness of despair. Those who realize the enmeshment of ordinary modern life with what is destroying life often weep in despair. Thus, we do well to remember that the etymology of the word "care" includes lamentation. To care for creation now requires us to begin by lamenting all that is broken in our relationship with creation.

The materiality of the burning bush manifests divine disclosure to Moses, who *sees* the bush and then *considers* it carefully. Theologians and the church's poets have long seen a connection between the burning bush and the incarnation of Christ. In Orthodox liturgy, the Theotokos is referred to as the unburnt bush—she who brought forth the Word of God without herself being consumed. To Christian ecologists, it represents the potential of all creation to house and manifest divine transcendence. "Do we deal as gently with the earth as God deals with the bush?" asks liturgical theologian Gordon Lathrop. Does the assembly of gathered Christians "invite us to see the place on which we meet—and the earth all around the meeting—as holy ground?"[4] Lathrop brings this idea to the front door of gathered believers—the church on its church grounds. This, too, is where this book is located—on the church's grounds. I wanted to share what can happen within the hearts and minds of a congregation who care for the church grounds as a practice of caring for creation and fulfilling their ministry. Central Texas, as host to a massive oil and gas industry and organizations like TPPF that support it, is ground zero for the ecological rift in so many ways—social, political, and geological. Can Central Texas—through congregations like DaySpring—also become the habitat for ecological conversion? Yes! The answer is yes, when creation care is enfolded in contemplative love for God and understood as an expression of the gospel ministry of reconciliation with which all Christians are charged.

Climate change, as pressing and daunting as it is, is the context in which we find ourselves, but it is not the foundational reason we should care about our relationship with the Earth. Christian concern about the flourishing of creation arises from christological and ecclesiological conviction, extending the biblical trifold call to covenantal faithfulness: to land, to society, and to God. Our care for creation, then, is not primarily reactionary or problem-solving. Christian motivation to care for creation is not solely because an environmental crisis calls for an adequate response. Instead, our care for creation arises as a spiritual practice from our formation as Christians. I grant that this is not obvious for generations for whom the spirituality of our relationship with the land has been obscured, but that recognition belies the hermeneutical premise: just to the extent we are morally formed by modern Western life, practices that constitute participation as creatures in creation are not intuitive to us. Christian communities, therefore, must *intentionally* form and re-form the habits and practices constitutive of lives whose care for creation bears witness to the love of God and incarnation of Christ. Because this soil bears the fruit of ecological conversion, church grounds can be the place of ecological conversion.

A practical theology for church grounds for such purposes is inherently about learning to inhabit sacred space and meaningfully participate in the life of creation. A Christian ecological spirituality is predicated on learning to *see*, which entails learning *how to see* and *unsee* as we have been seeing. I contend that most congregants in most places will need to learn to unsee their grounds (and all creation) in the ways they have seen them until now. Church grounds have been merely the utilitarian and aesthetic backdrop to the congregation's real life and work within the sanctuary, classrooms, kitchens, and meeting rooms. As "nature" has been a source of fuel and resources to fuel the growth machine, as "creation" has served as the stage or backdrop for the drama of salvation, so church grounds have been the backdrop for the congregation's activity. Conversion will be a reintegration of location and vocation. For many who are formed within the evangelical Christian culture, this dualism between materiality and spirituality is so inherent to their understanding of salvation that it will be a challenge to overcome. For them, the grounds, such as they are, are on the profane side of the dualistic ledger, distinguishing what matters to them and what does not. But rather than arguing that the grounds should be transferred from the profane to the sacred side of the ledger, ecological conversion entails wholesale revision to pre-Christian divisions of the sacred and profane.

In an ecologically converted vision, categorial distinctions in space between sacred and profane are rejected or at least mingled.[5] Brian Walsh rightly suggests that if we employ the idea of sacred space at all, it must refer first and foremost to all creation. While acknowledging that some places may need to "function" as sacred space, Walsh rejects the ontological legitimacy of the distinction between sacred and profane. It is beyond this project's scope to resolve this argument metaphysically, but we can approach it as a matter of practical spirituality. My fellow Baptist Wendell Berry says, "there are no unsacred places; there are only sacred places and desecrated places."[6] If we are to understand all space as sacred while yet retaining substantive meaning to the idea of sacred space, and recognize a phenomenology of all creation as sacred space, we going to need somewhere to begin to recover such a vision.

Church grounds offer a generative space for the vital work of beginning to reconsecrate desecrated space. I invited Butch Tindell to walk the DaySpring church grounds with me. Butch grew up playing in the trees and fields that are now our church's grounds, and I wanted him to see how pretty everything is. So one afternoon we walked together. While he was delighted to reignite old memories—climbing the old oaks, exploring the creek—he also saw the place with considered sadness. He studied the thick stands of invasive Ligustrum bushes that try to take over the trees on the property. He knelt to feel the hard ground under a thin layer of weedy grass. Finally, Butch said quietly, "This land has been desecrated. It was not well-loved. It was neglected. You have hard, and holy work to do." We needed to care for the grounds as a site of active participation in the health of the land and as a site of hospitality for the biotic life of soil and animals who could call it home. Philip Sheldrake is to describe reconciliation in terms of hospitality, "A space of reconciliation invites all who inhabit it to make space for 'the other,' to move over socially and spiritually, to make room for those who are unlike, and in that process for everyone to be transformed into something new."[7] For church grounds to serve as the site of hospitality to other people and other creatures, we need to learn to unsee the grounds in a merely utilitarian way and see the grounds as a place of encounter with the triune life of God.

How shall we learn to *see* in such a way? Moses at the burning bush gives us a model as he gazes upon the bush, considers the sight, contemplates the God who is revealed, and enacts God's redemptive call through his liberative service to captive Israel. St. Clare's approach to prayer—which Moses models—teaches us that prayer begins by gazing intently on what is before us as the place of sacramental encounter with Christ. As modeled by Butch, this discipline of paying attention is, according to Simone Weil, the highest form of generosity.

In *Culture Care*, the artist Makoto Fujimora describes an experience in which he learned to see in a new way; it was a conversion enabling him to become able to pay fresh attention to God's grace. He calls it a "genesis moment" that came when his wife brought home a bouquet of flowers to their apartment when they were young and desperately poor. "How could you think of buying flowers if we can't even eat!" Fujimora complained. His wife replied, "We need to feed our souls, too." As a "genesis moment," this experience gave Fujimora a new perspective and "engendered many more genesis moments in the years that followed, contributing to decisions small and large that have redefined my life and provided inspiration for myself, my family, and my communities."[8] As Fujimora learned to see what was before him in a new way, so we can learn to see our grounds in new ways—as a place of generative hospitality and meaningful participation. This experience will have the force of spiritual conversion for most people, but we may learn to know them as "burning bush" moments rather than "genesis moments."

Toward Ecological Conversion

My intention has been to make clear the difference between a stewardship ethic and a spiritually vibrant ecological relationship through the lens of Moses's encounter with God at the burning bush. Though he is regarded as the great Lawgiver, Moses's vocation to free enslaved Israel did not come from obedience to a law but from an encounter with God. That specific encounter at the burning bush, as we have seen, echoes St. Clare of Assisi's four-fold model of prayer. For Moses, this was an encounter of prayer, even an incarnational prayer. We see this in the actions Moses takes: to remove his shoes, hide his face, and ultimately respond in faithfulness. From head to toe, Moses was physically transformed by this divine encounter. Importantly, this theophany was mediated through creation (the scrub bush, holy ground) and has been broadly treated as a Christophany in the Christian tradition. This story evokes a new perspective on the world and on the presence of the risen Christ in our midst. To care for the Earth is to care for an Earth in which Christ is present to us and is calling us to the ministry of reconciliation. A stewardship ethic, familiar to evangelical Christians, can open wider to the fuller, richer call of an ethic rooted in ecological relationship and reconciliation.

Howard Snyder, 2004

Consider the example of evangelical theologian Howard Snyder. In an ecology conference keynote address in 2004, Methodist Howard Snyder argued that creation care is to be understood and prioritized within the scope of the church's ministry of reconciliation.

> Human disobedience brought alienation between humans and God and as a result an internal alienation with each person (alienation from oneself), alienation between humans, and alienation from nature. These are spiritual, psychological, sociocultural, and ecological alienations that afflict the whole human family. All derive from sin; all distort God's good purpose in creation. These are the concerns, therefore of the gospel of reconciliation, and they clarify the church's mission agenda. Faithful Christian mission focuses on healing the four alienations or divisions that have resulted from the fall. Creation care, therefore—working for reconciliation between humans and the created order—is an indispensable element in Christian mission. It is part of the Gospel.[9]

Snyder was drawing something less familiar to his audience (the priority of creation care) into the orbit of something quite familiar to them (the New Testament metaphor of reconciliation). Though not regularly applied to environmental concerns, reconciliation is a familiar and key rhetorical device for evangelical Christians.[10] Snyder understood his audience. For them, *ecology* was a signifier of the state of the natural environment and therefore only tangentially related to the church's mission in the world, if at all. Evangelical Christians were committed to *spiritual* reconciliation as a ministry of the church to a world detached from faith in God. To call for "restored relationship with creation" could immediately raise suspicions among his evangelical audience that he was a green romantic, an Emersonian pantheist, or the like. So, by highlighting the New Testament metaphor of reconciliation, solidly within green evangelical rhetoric, Snyder established sure footing on rhetorical ground with his audience. He used language his evangelical audience would recognize as normative and then expanded the concepts of both reconciliation and ecology.

Due to human disobedience, Snyder explained, the world's spiritual alienation from God results in and is refracted into various other experiences of alienation: psychological (from oneself), sociocultural (between humans), and ecological (between humans and nature). These alienations—spiritual, psychological, sociocultural, and ecological—touch the whole human family. Snyder widened the diagnosis of humanity and creation's woes by framing the state of the world not as merely the backdrop for the drama of personal spiritual salvation but as a set of broken relationships—of which we are a part—all in need of healing. Redemption, he said, is experienced in the healing of all these wounds, including ecological wounds.

In the following decade, Snyder's thought developed beyond the point of including "ecology" as one wound that the Gospel heals, but before turning to that shift, I want to note the importance of what he said and to whom he said it. If his appeal to ecological reconciliation had been widely embraced in 2004, Snyder's address would have marked a major shift in perspective among evangelical Christians. The main thrust of evangelical eco-theology tended to talk about "stewardship" as a responsibility to be exercised by those with "dominion" over the Earth rather than as participation in the healing of relationships constitutive of life on Earth. Take, for example, the statement, considered radical by some, of the National Association of Evangelicals (NAE) in 2004, "An Evangelical Call to Civic Responsibility." One of its principles, "We labor to protect God's creation," reads in part, "We affirm that God-given dominion is a sacred responsibility to steward the Earth and not a license to abuse the creation of which we are a part. We are not the owners of creation, but its stewards, summoned by God to 'watch over and care for it.'"[11] A world of semantic force, ethical framework, and Christian spirituality occupies the space between the NAE's *duty to steward the Earth as Christian responsibility* and Howard Snyder's *participation in Christ's reconciliation* of fractured relationships. In the difference, I believe we can find a key to our creation-oriented spirituality.

I lean with Snyder toward a vocation of participation in Christ's reconciliation even though the alienations Snyder addressed are more insidious and less linear than he understood or underscored to his audience in 2004. Moreover, our response is more urgent and more theologically central to Christian spirituality than Snyder acknowledged, even when he pronounces, "Creation care . . . is *part of* the Gospel!"

What Snyder identified as "alienations" in 2004, I have called "fractures" or collectively "the Rift," drawing on the metaphor of metabolic rift developed by environmental sociologists. We examined the force of the Rift as the fracture of a system of relationships necessary to life, the scale and implication of which is understood as the Anthropocene. The Rift highlights the dynamic nature of cycles, such as the soil-food-compost-fertilizer cycle. So we are not merely alienated in our spiritual *experiences*. Our collective human ecological alienation has material implications for the cycles of life on Earth. In a paragraph on human responsibility, the NAE urges "Christians to shape their personal lives in creation-friendly ways: practicing effective recycling, conserving resources, and experiencing the joy of contact with nature."[12] This is a fine guidance up to a point: the joy of contact with nature is a pleasure to experience and celebrate. However, deeper questions immediately arise: What does such contact entail? What does "contact" mean when humans also are part of nature? Where is this "nature" with which we are to enjoy contact?

Perhaps human "contact with nature" begins with examining the countless ways we do *not* experience contact with nature through the quotidian conveniences of eating in globalized, industrialized food, waste, and transportation systems. ("Take off your shoes, Moses!") Seen from this view, we are not merely alienated from a nature placidly awaiting some human contact; rather, human activity in the modern era has opened wide a rift between humans and the rest of creation. The significance of relationship—metabolic, spiritual, fractured, and reconciled—is a semantic and theological key to Christian living. The stakes of reconciliation are much higher than the NAE statement or Snyder's speech in 2004 reflected.

Howard Snyder, 2011

In the years after his 2004 speech, Snyder's thought progressed toward a holistic vision. By 2011, Snyder demonstrated a broadly expanded understanding of the meaning of "ecological."[13] No longer does ecology serve for him as a synonym for "environment" or "nature" as it functioned in his 2004 speech. Now, ecology is, according to Snyder, "the most comprehensive conceptual frame we have for visualizing the complex interrelationships of factors that make up human life and life on our planet. In an ecological understanding, everything is related to everything else."[14] When Snyder makes the move that biblical reconciliation includes ecology, he is not rehearsing the idea that "Christians should be good stewards." He knows we no longer have the luxury of seeing ourselves as dutiful stewards over a world entrusted to our benign care. We failed. The rhetoric of stewardship, such as it was used, failed to move the human heart or marshal Christian motivation to integrate our lives with the world around us.

In the Anthropocene of our making, we need to do more than conserve *some* natural resources or preserve *some* wilderness, recycle *some* plastic bottles or enjoy *some* contact with nature. Our context prompts a wholesale reevaluation of every doctrine and dimension of Christian life in repentance and then in mission.[15] As those who are given the ministry of reconciliation, the church is concerned with all broken relationships in need of healing. We are not just looking for activities of good stewardship; we are looking for places of reconnection with God and with creation, places from which our conversion begins.

By 2011, Snyder was openly working to heal "the great divorce" that severed heaven and earth in evangelical discourse. His trajectory is a particularly interesting example of an alternative to the lifeless, tangential attention evangelical Christians give to creation care if they give any attention at all. "This is not a book about environmental ethics," Snyder insists of *Salvation Means Creation Healed*. "Ethics, environmental and otherwise, come up in due course, but as a *consequence*, not a cause."[16] If Snyder is a bellwether, the rhetorical frames of relationship and reconciliation have begun to supplant stewardship-duty in evangelical Christian spirituality.[17] This is a development I follow and extend by emphasizing that ecological alienation is not just naming an existential distance humans may *feel* from the natural world in a psycho-spiritual sense but is a material, metabolic alienation from the way we live as creatures in creation. In the Anthropocene, we no longer have the luxury of nineteenth-century Emerson to "reach through every concrete detail of the environment seeking metaphors of some spiritual fact."[18] Reconstituting our relationship with creation is now a matter of life and death for ourselves and for the world. As a diagnosis of relationship, ecological alienation names, in a wide sense, the material reality of the Rift of the Anthropocene. As we have seen through a description of life on DaySpring church grounds, reconciliation is needed in every relational direction: God, land, other people, ourselves, and social structures. If ecological alienation is the problem, then reconciliation toward healing of all relationships is the church's missional response. Snyder powerfully asks, "Can there be a healthy church on a sick planet?"[19] I ask, "Can there be a healthy church on sick church grounds?"

At the moment of conversion for Moses and the pivot point in the biblical narrative between human and divine centrality, God instructed Moses to take off his shoes. When he did, his feet touched holy ground.[20] Moses, we might say, was getting in touch with the ground of his being, the ground from which humans were made.[21] Those sandals cast aside become an icon of conversion from the insulated distance between humanity and our identity in the image of God, reconnected on the ground beneath our feet.

Church Grounds as a Site of Conscience

In the excerpt quoted at the beginning of this chapter, poet and farmer Wendell Berry exhorts us to "stay away from anything that obscures the place it is in." Unfortunately, the American tendency is to make all things reductively generic and universal. This cultural tendency is manifest in sprawling suburban neighborhoods whose names intend to evoke something of nature long lost: Timber Ridge

Estates (in the middle of flat grassland in central Texas), Deer Run (where the wildlife was displaced), Mountainview (where there are no mountains or views). American Protestant churches fall prey to the same tendencies, if not in the naming of churches then certainly in the way they occupy their spaces a-historically. Indeed, a lack of historicity is a feature of typical American Protestant spirituality.

Attention to church grounds gives us opportunity to both attend to the particularity of the place and to do justice to its history. Reckoning with the cultural and social history and context of our church's grounds is an important early step in recognizing that the current owners of the property were not the first to know the place. Knowing this, we can ask two interrelated questions: *What is the environmental history of this particular place?* and *What is the human history in this particular place?* For DaySpring, as I suspect is true of many places, uncovering answers to these two questions provokes lament for what has been and what has been lost and points the way toward what redemption looks like in, and from, the particular place.

An Environmental History

Land in central Texas, including DaySpring's, was defined for thousands of years by vast prairies crisscrossed by creeks, rivers, and riparian zones of live oaks, cedar elms, and other trees. Some of the ancient trees remain today, but the prairie grasses are all but gone across the central United States. Learning this history prompts us to learn about the role of prairie grasses transferring rainwater to underground aquifers, sequestering carbon from the atmosphere as an ally in mitigating climate change, and as a habitat for quail and other animals whose existence is threatened by its loss. For DaySpring to restore the place-ness of the place likely involves restoring prairie grasses to the land to care for the health of the trees and rehabilitate the habitat for local birds and animals. The environmental history of the land directly informs current and future priorities for its care.

A Cultural and Social History

As far as we can tell, records show that "ownership" of DaySpring's property dates to the early twentieth century when the Methodist

Children's Home acquired over a hundred acres (including what is now our property) for a working farm for the children. Before MCH's ownership, we believe the land was farmland. Prior to that, as far as we know, it was likely visited, if not inhabited, by the local Native American tribes, the Huaco and Tonkawa, though we have not yet discovered physical evidence of their presence on the property. The history of the land as a working farm for the Methodist Children's Home informs our priorities and practices by sparking our imagination for how this land can be used to grow food and to welcome children. Knowing that we are worshiping on land used as a farm foregrounds Scripture's agricultural imagery while helping us envision how food grown on our land may be shared as a mission of the congregation in the community.

The happy history of ministry to children is only one part of the whole story of our place. Admittedly, and thankfully, we have no physical or historical evidence that suggests some of the tragic events in central Texas history occurred directly on our land. There's nothing to suggest, for example, that our land was ever worked by enslaved people or owned by enslavers. And there's nothing to suggest that any of the live oak trees on our property were used for a lynching. However, the wider social history of central Texas includes these tragedies and indeed is, in many ways, defined by them.

Given the violence and injustices woven into human communities in landscapes such as ours, righteous lament is a critical part of creation care if we are to be anything more than nature romantics. We lament the ways humans have desecrated creation, especially in violence toward one another. This lament gives rise to a hunger for redemption of the torn social fabric and the desacralization of creation. In our place, then, caring for creation under the canopy of these live oaks also means working for racial justice in our community.

An Embodied History

A congregation living an embodied history is mindful that they are living a life storied by those who have come before and by the land itself. For DaySpring that story includes prairie grass and live oaks, racial violence and the hope of redemption, community farming and care for vulnerable children. Drawing on these stories, our ministry story enfolds what has come before with hope for all that can manifest in the future. Each church's grounds will have a different story, which is precisely the point of not "obscuring the place" as congregations embrace the invitation to be part of the story of redemption being told in, for, and from their place.

A splendid example of this has taken place in Assisi, Italy. The Bosco di San Francesco, a forested hillside known as the "other side of Assisi," has been cleaned up and restored by the FAI (Fund for the Italian Environment) after generations of neglect and trash dumping. Enhancing the experience of walking the main path through the restored parkland, information points tell the biological and geological history of the land and the history of human life in the forest. Most interestingly, they tell the story of Franciscan and Benedictine spiritualities each shaping approaches to the hillside and valley through the centuries. The alluring invitation to the park reads,

> This path, which enters into the Woods, can be travelled in 45 minutes, but your soul on the road with your body has got another step and another time, so we give advice: stow your clocks and your phones in your bags because in this landscape of other times the key words are slowness and contemplation.
>
> Among holm oak and dogwood, the route is well illustrated by sign, it descends in hairpin bends towards the Tescio river. It leads you to do beneficial stops to enjoy the wildlife around: if you are lucky you can admire the fast flight of a sparrow hawk or you can catch the flicker of a porcupine which hurries off to hide into the bush.
>
> Continue toward the Galli Bridge, a work in travertine dating back to 1356, renovated in the late 15th century and rebuilt by the Municipality between 1948 and 1949. So you reach the valley floor where you can admire the remains of a distant world, dwelt between 13th and 14th century by Benedictine nuns: the huge complex of Santa Croce. What remains of the religious building are the renovated hospital facilities, the . . . Romanesque church, the windmill and the tower, each one with its own history to remember and to tell. So take a break to listen to what these old stones have to say.[22]

This example of a story of redemption told in and from a place of embodied history offers a vision of hope to visitors who come from, and return to, places with their own stories and spiritual histories to embody and redeem.

Church Grounds as an Ecology of Grace

To recognize a church's grounds as an ecology is to acknowledge the complex, interdependent network of relationships between diverse members of the biotic community who dwell in or near the church grounds—soil, water flow, air, species habitats, etc. These straightforward observations remind us that all life is interconnected. In theological terms, we are all creatures among the creation of the triune God. We are a community of creatures.

To recognize the grounds as an ecology is not quite yet to participate in an ecology of *grace*, but it is a first step. An ecology of grace describes a network of relationships that is hospitable to life in its various forms, that embraces the community of the creatures. One tangible way to embody an ecology of grace is through direct participation in the soil-food cycle. Where a church's grounds have space for a vegetable garden, this can be a source of education and delight. Where such a garden is robust, it can serve the church's mission of sharing healthy, locally sourced food with the hungry.

If the church's grounds have space for a compost system, the compost process can be a living parable of redemption. A community compost bin system is arguably the simplest, most straightforward way for a congregation to reconcile our dislocation from the metabolic cycle of life so typical of Western, urban lifestyles. Following the model of the concentric circles of carbon neutrality, a church can cultivate a practice of composting all its food waste generated by meals on the church's grounds and then extend the project by inviting congregants to bring their home food waste to the church's community compost system. Congregants can invite their neighbors to do the same. Thus, the church's aspiration can be that no compostable food or yard waste from the whole congregation ever goes to the landfill but is always composted or otherwise given the opportunity to naturally decompose, bringing life to soil and garden beds. The church grounds become a practical embodiment of reconciliation between humans and the soil from which all our food comes.

For an example of a congregation's land put to service in a holistic ecology of grace, consider Eastern Star Church in Indianapolis, Indiana. Since 2017, the congregation has made significant investment in its impoverished neighborhood community through the ROCK initiative, which stands for Renewing Our Community for the Kingdom. Large sections of the church's one hundred acres donated to the ROCK initiative are now sites of a small neighborhood of homes, a mixed-use building of apartments and retails, a credit union, grocery store, hair salon, and social service providers. A fresh food market provides healthy food in an area that otherwise is a food desert. Setting this in motion was the congregation's decision to scrap plans for a church expansion and instead repurpose land on behalf of the surrounding community. In the most impoverished zip code in Indianapolis, Eastern Star is establishing a blueprint for others to follow.[23]

Church Grounds as Holy Ground

A church's grounds offer the possibility of meaningful individual participation in communal life in a way that few other types of places can provide. Unlike privately owned homes for which an individual has agency but not community, and unlike municipally owned parks that are communally owned but for which individuals have little agency, church grounds invite individuals to exercise agency within a community. In all these ways, then, church grounds offer an alternative space for communal agency.

Individual participation within communal life is at the heart of the Baptist ecclesiological vision. Drawing on anabaptist roots, modern Baptists still prioritize the local, autonomous congregation as the primary meaning of "Church."[24] The foundational unit of church life is the individual-in-Christ who is baptized into relationship with other Christians in the local congregation, which is then in missional partnership with other congregations. All ecclesiology is from the "ground up" in Baptist life, so, in other words, the church's life already holds within it an ecological vision of relation, location, and connection.

First, church is *relational*. At its root the meaning of ecology is the science of relationships. A Baptist eco-ecclesiology of church grounds celebrates the diversity of creaturehood represented on the grounds and pursues a generative life of blessing and flourishing for these creatures. Second, church is *local*, which involves an awareness of the *this-ness* of the particular place. Each church has a different context and therefore a unique expression of its ecological vision. There is no single expression of an eco-ecclesiology. The diversity is to be celebrated as a strength. Third, church is *connectional*. What we do in one place necessarily is affected by and affects what happens in other places. No place stands alone—in history or in space—in the material world. All is connected in the relational fabric of creation. The church grounds give us an opportunity—through communal agency—to transverse the ecological rift, but the grounds are not an exception to the rest of creation. A congregation's relationship with its grounds can serve as an exemplar of the relationship of humanity with the rest of creation; we see the grounds as sacred and thereby learn to see all creation as sacred. We learn habits and practices on the church grounds that enable us to exercise those same habits and practices in various ways elsewhere.

At the burning bush, the divine voice entangles the announcement "This is holy ground" with the instruction "Take off your shoes." With sandals cast aside, Moses's feet again touch the ground from which he had been alienated. It is as if *adam* encountered his God through contact with *adamah*. Sacred ground is not served only by the verbs of environmental stewardship: preserve, conserve, protect. Sacred ground is to be touched, even by the feet of one untrained in how to walk on holy ground. This icon of participation draws us into the place as a site of participation, encounter, and conversion. Then we go out with eyes to see all places as the sacred places of participation in the redemption of creation from its travail.

DaySpring's church campus plays this role in the life of the congregation. I first became conscious of this on Easter morning more than ten years ago when the ministry staff decided to offer a sunrise service under the St. Francis tree, one of the majestic live oaks on the property. We did not expect many to join us before dawn for the service, but we committed to one another that we would be there even if we were the only ones. That morning, somewhat to our surprise, people showed up. The shadowy outlines of men, women, and children silently and sleepily shuffled in the darkness toward the canopy of the oak. The service began in the darkness as we greeted the morning of our Lord's resurrection. Only toward the end of the service, the morning light made clear what seemed possible in the dark: over one hundred people had come to the service. More and more have come each year. Some say it is their favorite moment of worship in the whole year. From that experience, the St. Francis tree became the unofficial symbol and spiritual center of gravity of the church campus. Years later, when the pandemic began and we could not worship inside, we knew already what to do—go to the trees.

The story of Moses at the burning bush enlivens our imaginations of a God who reveals the divine presence through creation to unsuspecting wayfarers on the borderlands of life. Makoto Fujimora describes characters such as Moses as "border-stalkers." Fujimora suggests all artists are border-stalkers, those who have a role that "both addresses the reality of fragmentation and offers a fitting means to help people from our many and divided cultural tribes" as messengers of hope and reconciliation.[25] Extending this image, we see the church grounds as a kind of borderlands on which we stalk. The grounds are neither privately held nor public, neither designated for financial profit nor municipal parkland, neither cloistered nor profane.

The grounds represent a third space, but unlike other spaces similarly noted as third spaces in society—coffee shops, for example—the church grounds are dedicated, often formally, to the worship and glory of God and the flourishing of the Christian community in witness to the grace and goodness of God. From this perspective, the grounds are not presented a sacramental exception to the profane character of all other land, but the grounds of a church are a microcosm—or can be redeemed as such—of the potential of all creation to be experienced as sacred and, moreover, as an invitation for humans to rediscover their participation in sacred creation as creatures who embody the Divine image.

Church Grounds as a Geography of Hope

The church's grounds can become the experimental site, the metaphor, or the first step for the members of a congregation. Just as the University of Texas has a slogan, "What begins here changes the world," we too can see the church grounds with the same potential: the change that begins on the church's grounds changes the community and then the world. This is our hope.

A goal of being carbon neutral on church grounds can expand to other spaces as a set of concentric circles. The center of the circle is the energy usage of the sanctuary and other buildings of a local congregation. The congregation begins by seeking to become neutral in its carbon footprint for the use of buildings. For most congregations, this will entail changing to an electricity provider that uses 100 percent renewable energy. If 100 percent of a church's electricity is provided by wind, solar, or hydro power, the center circle has been accomplished, and the congregation is on its way to the next outer ring.

For the next ring in the set of circles, a congregation calculates and then offsets its aggregate transportation carbon footprint for a typical Sunday service. This will entail calculating the collective carbon emitted by the congregants as they travel to and from the church. To accomplish this circle, the congregation will need to zero its carbon footprint at the church and offset the carbon produced by non-electric automobiles driven by congregants through various other means. Some churches, for example, will be able to add solar panels to generate electricity from their rooftops; others can sequester carbon by trees and grasses on the church grounds. By reducing carbon production and increasing carbon sequestration, the congregation may be able to accomplish this second circle and then extend its reach to the next and so on.

I propose that each congregation aspire that their collective energy use and energy production, carbon release, and carbon sequestration be carbon neutral for each home and automobile in the congregation. Working together, a congregation can find ways to decrease carbon emissions, increase carbon sequestration, and so move collectively closer to the goal. There is little doubt that this aspiration seems out of reach in modern life, but through baby steps of accomplishing the goal represented by each circle, a congregation working together can accomplish the collective, communal goal.

This is practical hope. Hope is not quickly realized, but it is necessary to overcome despair and apathy. Too often, discourse around environmental care is intertwined with messages of guilt and lament. Lament can be a starting place, but we also need a constructive path not just to take part in doing less harm but to take part in cultivating the good. Mark Labberton is right in the foreword to Makoto Fujimura's *Culture Care* when he says, "Hope takes time to mature. On the whole, quick fixes are no match for protracted suffering. Instead, the story of hope is often a long one with unexpected twists and turns, steps forward and often back too." Labberton goes on to say, "Hope is disruptive, counter to dominant wind patterns, interrupting what is mapped—a crosscurrent pushing with creativity and truth . . . hope that is truly hope must be realistic, slow, disruptive, and limited."[26] For all these reasons, church grounds are a geography of true hope that is realistic, slow, disruptive, and limited only in the sense that it is attentive to the limits inherent to any particular place. Every geography is unique to its place. Wallace Stegner gives us the evocative phrase "geography of hope" when describing the vast open spaces of the western United States for which Stegner advocated wilderness designation and protection. I employ his phrase to describe less dramatic landscapes but nonetheless places that invite us in as more than visitors who leave no trace. I believe the places where we are redeemed can be the true geographies of hope, even hope for the climate crisis. We know the industrial revolution began in factories in England and America in the nineteenth century. It is now time for the church to spark the sustainability revolution that begins on church grounds all over the world, even here in central Texas.

As Wendell Berry insightfully writes,

> I believe that it is psychologically necessary that people develop, in addition to the forms by which to enact the duties prescribed by their relationships to each other and to the earth, the forms by which to enact their *consciousness* of these relationships . . . [such that] a person would not consider himself to be involved in a series of abstract relationships, as one of a number, but a conscious responsible participant in the life both of the land he lived from and of the universe, dependent upon the grater life but also its protector.[27]

Berry's expression of a "conscious responsible participant" is an excellent pithy description of what I believe can be the fruit of a Baptist ecclesiological vision of a theology of church grounds in the Anthropocene. Genuine conversion is a process. It would be shortsighted to believe that ecological conversion is beyond reach for modern, Western, capitalistic Texans, but it would also be naïve to think such conversion would be immediately triggered and evident by the events surrounding a single effort. John Markey observes the model of conversion in the story of Moses, whose conversion is presented

> as a literal journey that takes him from the security and privilege of living in the royal household in Egypt to a pastoral life in the far-off land of Midian, then back to Egypt with the mission of rescuing his people and bringing them into a new land "flowing with milk and honey." From his initial insight of kinship with the people of Israel to the dramatic moment of God's self-revelation in the burning bush on the mountain of Horeb, Moses moves from a vague and almost unconscious awareness that there is something wrong with the "way things are" to an urge to find his identity. This physical and psychological journey leads him to a clear and unmistakable encounter with the creator at the heart of all reality. . . . At Horeb, Moses discovers himself in a relationship with a God who expects much more of him than he ever expected of himself.[28]

Conversion is a complex phenomenon in an individual or a community. Markey suggests that conversion is generally sparked by "some event or series of events that challenges one's accepted way of life [and therefore] prompts a reevaluation of one's habits and interpretations."[29] It follows the pattern on display in the story of Moses at the burning bush: breakdown and breakthrough. Bit by bit, we *break down* our complicity in dualistic, earth-harming, incarnation-denying lifestyles and, by God's grace, *break through* to new ways of seeing and experiencing the world as God's good gift into which we are called to live with care.

According to Markey, the breakthrough is a necessary part of the initial step of conversion, which also includes fundamental reorienting from irresponsibility to responsibility, seeing/hearing/perceiving differently, and moving away from habitual ways of thinking and acting.[30] One church member's recent comment to me reflects several aspects of conversion: "Connecting with nature and having the realization we are all part of God's creation is more important now than ever. Due to man's recklessness of the past, we truly reap what we sow. Keeping this at the forefront I believe is key to better relationships both with nature and with other people." This insight is consistent with initial steps of conversion.

Well within the horizon of the church's ongoing life is the agenda to continue engaging church grounds as a habitat where conversion is possible in an ongoing process. Pope Francis describes the attitudes and changes that can result from undergoing the ecological conversion of a community. Conversion results in gratitude and graciousness in recognition that the world is God's loving gift that calls us to imitate Christ's generosity in self-sacrifice and good works. As we do, we grow in loving awareness that we are not disconnected from the rest of creatures but joined in "a splendid universal communion." St. Francis demonstrates this generous spirit of loving awareness in the "Canticle of the Creatures." Ultimately, we are inspired to greater creativity and enthusiasm in resolving the world's problems as an expression of the serious responsibility toward care for creation that stems directly from our faith.[31] I am convinced this conversion takes place on church's grounds, and so I continue to have hope—for the church and for the world.

Epilogue

Your Sacred Place

From reactions I hear when a conversation turns to environmental concerns, hope is not the normal first response. There's plenty of cynicism from some, abject climate despair from others, and, in some Christian circles, rejection of the premise. Almost all people brace for a scolding for all the things they know they should change about the way they live: using Styrofoam plates, driving a pickup truck, eating meat, not composting, insufficiently caring about the climate crisis, and on and on. Creation care should be important, they admit, but there are so many other pressing matters. When they do think about creation care, many people carry on an inner dialogue in which one voice says, "You should care more about these things." And the other voice asks, "But what difference would it make?" I don't hear hope; I hear despair.

The voices within us catch us in an emotional conundrum. Each of us should care more about the climate crisis and all manner of environmental devastation. At the same time, in quantifiable terms, none of us alone can make a measurable difference in carbon emissions or global plastic waste. A lot of people feel both guilty and helpless, and that usually leads either to apathy ("I can't do anything, so why does it matter what I do?") or to anxiety ("I can't do anything that makes a difference; when is someone else going to fix the problem?")

We feel this or something like it, don't we? This essential division within, a severing of mind and body, of spirit and action. And there is a long list of other issues that surface when the subject turns to creation care: the perceived, or real, financial cost of environmentally responsible actions, contentious partisan debates about the reality and cause of climate change, and, for some Christians, theological tension between caring for the Earth when supposedly our true home is in an otherworldly heaven. Let's admit that creation care is exhausting, even if we haven't done anything yet. But ironically, part of what makes it feel despairing is that we haven't yet embarked on the journey of integrating our relationship with creation into the life of our soul or the commitments of our faith.

Creation care is at least one part healing the divisions within and between us. Parker Palmer is a master healer of inner relationships that can bedevil or give life. In *A Hidden Wholeness*, Palmer diagnoses the predicament for the modern individual as "a divided life." In the modern era, we live with many things we don't want to give up, but we also live with divided lives within ourselves, with others, and with God. The key, core relationships that make human life good and beautiful, not to mention sustainable, are fractured. The rifts that run through our divided lives are also at the heart of this book. We may strongly identify with the biblical character of Moses, early in the book of Exodus, alone in his wilderness exile.

We're just not equipped for the scale or the depths of this situation. Baptist pastors, like I am, were trained to accept and insist on distinctions between things like body and soul, spirituality and material concerns, and God and creation. These divisions were essential to preserve the theological principle of distinction between Creator and creation and between secular and sacred lest we submerge the uniqueness of Christ into a bland therapeutic deism or pantheism (or something like it). But in the process, we made it easy to lose our hidden, and essential, wholeness by severing the material and the spiritual.

As an example, I learned that I was to teach my congregation that baptism was a symbol functioning as an outward physical sign of an inward spiritual reality. For Baptists, salvation is in the heart through a personal relationship with Jesus, so the water of baptism is merely a symbol or an outward sign, not the means of grace for our salvation. We baptize new believers because Jesus told us to make disciples and baptize (Matt 28:26) and because Jesus was baptized (Matt 3). But we were taught to be sure to emphasize that the water does not save us. Only Jesus saves. I had no problem with this. I don't believe any ritual saves us. I believe Jesus saves us. I believe baptism is an outward sign of the inward reality of our new life in Christ born of grace, embraced by faith. I believe that a person arising from the waters of immersion is like a newborn birthed into a new life.

But there something else started to happen within me as I performed baptisms on Sunday mornings. I couldn't shake the sense that there was more to this act than I'd understood. When I baptized new believers in the baptistry perched behind the choir loft, all I knew was that something different was going on in the baptismal act, something special in and through the water. Soon I began to appreciate the same spiritual phenomenon in the celebration of Communion. There was something special going on. We'd been taught to believe that God was present everywhere but that baptism and Communion were only symbols to prompt mental remembrance. The result, ironically, is that we could preach that God is everywhere but not in the water of baptism or in the bread of Communion. That seems somewhat strange, right? Once the theological barriers began to crumble and God was "allowed" to be present in the water and the bread, it wasn't long before God started showing up everywhere.

Lynn White Jr. famously, in the late 1960s, blamed Western Christian metaphysics for erecting a wall of separation between the church and creation. Doing so, White scolded, Christian theology paved the way for the modern abusees of nature and environmental destruction. White's premise has come under significant criticism methodologically and historically, yet he is putting his finger on something that feels familiar to me and to observers of the human heart like Parker Palmer. We've disenchanted the world and have lost some life-giving, beautiful things, including attentiveness to the presence of God in unlikely places and the invitation of God to reconstitute a connection with the Earth and with one another.

Into a similar isolation, Moses heard the first instruction that would change his life and change the world: take off your shoes and touch the ground again. Moses, as surprised by that possibility as anyone could be, stood amazed at the sight before him: a bush burning but not consumed and a voice speaking from within the bush beckoning him to take off his shoes because he was on holy ground. The voice, way out there in the wilderness, was God's. God sent Moses from the wilderness to liberate his own people trapped in slavery back in Egypt.

This is a mighty ecological story, but few Bible readers or environmentalists have received it as such. I suppose that makes sense. The story of the burning bush isn't about stewardship at all. Unlike the creation stories in Genesis 1 and 2, where humans appear to be given authority and responsibility over the other creatures and are given the task to "till" and "keep" the garden of creation, there's nothing in the Exodus story about the place or role for humans in creation. The story is more about the place of God in all creation—even in wilderness—and God's desire for justice and mercy for the enslaved. Those themes are central to the story of Israel and powerful Christian typologies for the gospel, but what do they have to do with the Earth?

Moreover, there is no scolding in this story, and we have come to expect that a lesson about ecology must include some scolding that makes us feel guilty about how we are living. Moses is told to take off his shoes, but the story, as an ecological story, doesn't include a lesson on all the bad things Moses is doing by clomping around in those shoes on pristine landscape. How can there be an ecological story without a good scolding?

Yet, I contend, even without a moralism of stewardship or a proper scolding, the story of Moses at the burning bush is quintessentially ecological because ecology is about the relationship of an organism to its environment. This story is all about a person (Moses) and a people (Israel) recovering their place in relationship with one another, with God, and with their place on the Earth. The journey is long and there are many problems along the way, but from the beginnings when Israel is held in Egyptian slavery and Moses is alone and adrift in the wild, there's the first flicker of hope for restoration.

Gerard Manly Hopkins makes this connection in the poem "God's Grandeur" in which he evokes the image of treading in heavy boots to evoke the heavy pollution characteristic of late nineteenth-century industrial English landscapes:

> Generations have trod, have trod, have trod;
>   And all is seared with trade; bleared, smeared with toil;
>   And wears man's smudge and shares man's smell: the soil
> Is bare now, nor can foot feel, being shod.[1]

In the face of environmental crises that threaten the places we love, we sometimes wonder, "Can anything I do make any difference?" "How is my faith in God related to my concern for the Earth?" "Is there any reason for hope?" These and many similar questions express a desire to live in a world where people and other creatures flourish but where great uncertainty and despair weigh heavily. That's why the story of Moses at the burning bush is a powerful ecological story. If you'll recall, when we meet Moses, great uncertainty and despair weigh heavily. In the wilderness, he is the embodiment of a divided life. Wilderness in Scripture is virtually a landscape of uncertainty and despair. Even there, Moses is given a purpose and identity in restored relationship with God and his people.

Like Moses, unwittingly standing on holy ground, we too need a place to stand where we can find and follow the first flickers of hope. We need a geography of hope. In this book I have explored what it means to care for creation by caring for any place that you already know well. The property of the church I pastor was my primary subject, though the approach shared here extends to other church grounds already experienced and loved as sacred and to other places that you know. I teach a seminary course called Creation Care as Spiritual Practice. In the course, students are given an assignment called "Your Sacred Place." Each is to write a reflection on a place that is special to them, describing the place of their choosing as fully as possible in a few pages. On our class retreat when we light a bonfire and they read their papers to the group, there have been many tears. For many of the students, it's the first time their personal connection to a particular place has been celebrated as a spiritually meaningful and hopeful relationship. Over the years, I've heard stories about a park in Ecuador, a backyard in the Philippines, a vista in Yosemite National Park, and the shoreline of the Outer Banks. Most of the Sacred Place stories, I've found, are about ordinary places like a backyard or a garden on the university campus or a small farm that's been in the family for generations. The places we love the most, and where we experience something mystical, are often the places where our memories extend through time and where we feel a sense of belonging and responsibility for their welfare. It's this kind of place I had in mind—my place and yours—as I wrote this book: the ordinary, sacred, and threatened.

Bibliography

Angus, Ian. *Facing the Anthropocene: Fossil Capitalism and the Crisis of the Earth System*. New York: Monthly Review Press, 2016.

Arbuckle, Matthew, and David Konisky. "The Role of Religion in Environmental Attitudes." *Social Science Quarterly* 96/5 (November 2015): 1244–263.

Barthes, Roland. "The Struggle with the Angel: Textual Analysis of Genesis 32:23-33." In *Structural Analysis and Biblical Exegesis: Interpretational Essays*, edited by Dikran Hadidian, 21–33. Pittsburgh: Pickwick Press, 1974.

Baucom, Ian. *History 4° Celsius: Search for a Method in the Age of the Anthropocene*. Durham: Duke University Press, 2020.

Bell, Michael. *An Invitation to Environmental Sociology*. Thousand Oaks, CA: Pine Forge Press, 1998.

Bernstein, Patricia. *The First Waco Horror: The Lynching of Jesse Washington and the Rise of the NAACP*. College Station: Texas A&M University Press, 2006.

Berry, Wendell. *The Hidden Wound*. New York: North Point Press, 1989.

Berthold, George, translator. "The Church's Mystagogy." In *Maximus the Confessor: Selected Writings, Classics of Western Spiritualty*, 181–225. New York: Paulist Press, 1985.

Bingaman, Brock. "Becoming a Spiritual World of God: The Theological Anthropology of Maximus the Confessor." In *The Philokalia:*

A Classic Text of Orthodox Spirituality, edited by Brock Bingaman and Bradley Nassif, New York: Oxford University Press, 2012.

Bingaman, Brock, and Bradley Nassif, editors. *The Philokalia: A Classic Text of Orthodox Spirituality.* New York: Oxford University Press, 2012.

Blowers, Paul, and Robert Wilken, trans. *On the Cosmic Mystery of Jesus Christ: Select Writings from St. Maximus the Confessor.* Crestwood, NY: St. Vladimir's Seminary Press, 2003.

Bordeianu, Radu. "Maximus and Ecology: The Relevance of Maximus the Confessor's Theology of Creation for the Present Ecological Crisis." *The Downside Review* 127 (2009): 103–26.

Bosch, David. *Transforming Mission: Paradigm Shifts in Theology of Mission.* Maryknoll, NY: Orbis, 2005.

Bouyer, Louis. *The Spirituality of the Middle Ages*, vol. 2 of A History of Christian Spirituality. London: Burns & Oates, 1968.

Carr, Wylie, et al. "The Faithful Skeptics: Evangelical Religious Beliefs and Perceptions of Climate Change." *Journal for the Study of Religion, Nature, and Culture* 613/276 (2012): 276–99.

Carrigan, William. *The Making of a Lynching Culture: Violence and Vigilantism in Central Teas 1836–1916.* Chicago: University of Illinois Press, 2006.

Carson, Rachel. *Silent Spring.* New York: First Mariner Books, 1962.

Carter, Erik. "The Hermeneutical Promise of Practical Theology." *Andrews University Seminary Studies* 56/2 (2018): 241–55.

Carter, J. Kameron, *Race: A Theological Account.* New York: Oxford University Press, 2008.

Childs, Brevard. *The Book of Exodus: A Critical, Theological Commentary.* Louisville: John Knox Press, 2004.

Christie, Douglass. "Nature Writing and Mysticism." In *The Routledge Handbook of Religion and Ecology*, edited by Willis Jenkins et al., 229–36. New York: Routledge, 2016.

Chryssavgis, John. "The Face of God in the World: Insights from the Orthodox Christian Tradition." In *The Wiley Blackwell Companion to Religion and Ecology*, edited by John Hart, 273–85. Oxford, UK: John Wiley and Sons, 2017.

Clare of Assisi. "The Second Letter to Agnes of Prague." In *The Lady: Clare of Assisi: Early Documents*, edited by Regis Armstrong, New York: New City Press, 2006.

Cone, James. *The Cross and the Lynching Tree*. Maryknoll, NY: Orbis Books, 2011.

———. "Whose Earth Is It, Anyway?" In *Earth Habitat: Eco-Injustice and the Church's Response*, edited by Dieter Hessel and Larry Rasmussen, 23–32. Minneapolis: Fortress Press, 2001.

Davis, Ellen, *Preaching the Luminous Word*. Grand Rapids: Eerdmans, 2016.

Dean-Drummond, Celia. "Performing the Beginning in the End: A Theological Anthropology for the Anthropocene." In *Religion in the Anthropocene*, edited by Celia Dean-Drummond, 173–87. Eugene, OR: Wipf and Stock Publishers, 2017.

Delio, Ilia. *Care for Creation: A Franciscan Spirituality of the Earth*. Cincinnati: Franciscan Media, 1999.

———. *Franciscan Prayer*. Cincinnati: Franciscan Media, 2004.

Dickens, Peter. "Beyond Sociology: Marxism and the Environment." In *The International Handbook of Environmental Sociology*, edited by Michael Redclift and Graham Woodgate, 179–92. Northampton, MA: Edward Elgar, 1997.

Du Bois, W. E. B. "Jesus Christ in Texas." In *Darkwater: Voices from Within the Veil*, 70–77. Mineola, NY: Dover Publications, 1999.

Foster, John Bellamy. *The Ecological Rift: Capitalism's War on the Earth*. New York: Monthly Review Press, 2010.

———. "Marx's Theory of Metabolic Rift: Classical Foundations for Environmental Sociology." *American Journal of Sociology* 105/2 (September 1999): 366–405.

Foster, Richard. *Streams of Living Water: Celebrating the Great Traditions of the Christian Faith*. San Francisco: HarperCollins, 1989.

Fujimora, Makoto. *Culture Care: Reconnecting with Beauty for our Common Life*. Downers Grove: IVP Books, 2017.

Hamilton, Clive. *Defiant Earth: The Fate of Humans in the Anthropocene*. Malden, MA: Polity Press, 2017.

Hayhoe, Kathryn. *Saving Us: A Climate Scientist's Case for Hope and Healing in a Divided World*. New York: One Signal, 2021.

Hinson, E. Glenn. *Baptist Spirituality: A Call for Renewed Attentiveness to God*. Macon: Nurturing Faith, Inc., 2013.

Hitzhusen, G. E. "Judeo-Christian Theology and the Environment: Moving Beyond Skepticism to New Sources for Environmental Education in the United States." *Environmental Education Research* 13/1 (2007): 55–74.

Horrell, David. *Ecological Hermeneutics: Biblical, Historical, and Theological Perspectives*. New York: T&T Clark, 2010.

Jenkins, Willis. *Ecologies of Grace*. Oxford: Oxford University Press, 2008.

Jeoyoung, Jeon. *The Call of Moses and the Exodus Story: A Redaction-Critical Study in Exodus 3-4 and 5-13*. Tübingen, Germany: Mohr Siebeck, 2013.

Kearns, Laurel. "Saving the Creation: Christian Environmentalism in the United States." *Sociology of Religion* 57/1 (Spring 1996): 55–70.

Lane, Belden. *The Solace of Fierce Landscapes*. New York: Oxford University Press, 1998.

Lathrop, Gordon. *Holy Ground*. Minneapolis: Fortress Press, 2003.

Latour, Bruno. "Agency at the Time of the Anthropocene." *New Literary History* 45 (2014): 1–18.

Louth, Andrew. "Man and Cosmos in St. Maximus the Confessor." In *Toward an Ecology of Transfiguration: Orthodox Christian Perspectives on Environment, Nature, and Creation*, edited by John Chryssavgis and Bruce Foltz, New York: Fordham University Press, 2013.

———. *Maximus the Confessor*. Routledge: New York, 1996.

Markey, John. *Moses in Pharaoh's House*. Manchester, NH: Anselm Academic, 2014.

Merton, Thomas. *Turning Toward the World*. San Francisco: HarperCollins, 1966.

Mize, Bryan, *Legacy of Hope: A History of Methodist Children's Home*. Waco: Development Department at Methodist Children's Home, 2017.

Moo, Douglas, and Jonathan Moo. *Creation Care: A Biblical Theology of the Natural World*. Grand Rapids: Zondervan, 2018.

Munteanu, D. "Cosmic Liturgy: The Theological Dignity of Creation as a Basis of an Orthodox Ecotheology." *International Journal of Public Theology* 4/3 (2010): 332–44.

Niemier, Roch. *In the Footsteps of Francis and Clare*. Cincinnati: Franciscan Media, 2006.

Ollinaho, Ossi. "Environmental destruction as (objectively) uneventful and (subjectively) irrelevant." *Environmental Sociology* 2/1 (2016): 53–63.

———, and V. P. J. Arponen. "Incomegetting and Environmental Degradation." *Sustainability* 12/10 (May 14, 2020). https://www.mdpi.com/2071-1050/12/10/4007.

Osmer, Richard. *Practical Theology: An Introduction*. Grand Rapids: Eerdmans, 2008.

———. *The Teaching Ministry of Congregations*. Louisville: Westminster John Knox Press, 2005.

Polak, Frank. "Theophany and Mediator: The Unfolding of a Theme in the Book of Exodus." In *Studies in the Book of Exodus: Redaction-Reception, Interpretation*, edited by Marc Vervenne, 113–47. Leuven, Belgium: Leuven University Press, 1996.

Pope Francis. *Laudato Si': On Care for our Common Home [Encyclical]*. 2015.

Root, Andrew. *Christopraxis: A Practical Theology of the Cross*. Minneapolis: Fortress Press, 2014.

Santmire, Paul. *The Travail of Nature: The Ambiguous Ecological Promise of Christian Theology*. Philadelphia: Fortress Press, 1985.

Sheldrake, Philip. *Spaces for the Sacred: Place, Memory and Identity*. London: SCM, 2001.

———. *Spirituality: A Brief History*. Oxford: Wiley-Blackwell, 2013.

Sherrard, Philip. *Christianity: Lineaments of a Sacred Tradition*. Brookline, MA: Holy Cross Orthodox Press, 1998.

Sittler, Joseph. "Ecological Commitment as Theological Responsibility." In *Evocations of Grace*, edited by Steven Bouma-Prediger and Peter Bakken, 76–86. Grand Rapids: Eerdmans, 2000.

Snyder, Howard. *Salvation Means Creation Healed: The Ecology of Sin and Grace*. Eugene, OR: Wipf and Stock Publishers, 2011.

Taylor, Charles. *A Secular Age*. London: Belknap Press, 2018.

Theokritoff, Elizabeth. "The Vision of St. Maximus the Confessor: That Creation May All Be One." In *The Wiley Blackwell Companion to Religion and Ecology*, edited by John Hart, 220–36. Oxford, UK: John Wiley and Sons, 2017.

Thunberg, Lars. *Microcosm and Mediator: The Theological Anthropology of Maximus the Confessor*. Chicago: Open Court Publishing, 1995.

Tollefsen, Torstein. *The Christological Cosmology of St. Maximus the Confessor*. New York: Oxford University Press, 2008.

Visser, Margaret. *The Geometry of Love: Space, Time, Mystery, and Meaning in an Ordinary Church*. New York: North Point Press, 2000.

von Balthasar, Hans Urs. *Cosmic Liturgy: The Universe According to Maximus the Confessor*. Ignatius Press: San Francisco, 1988.

Warner, Keith. "Franciscan Environmental Ethics: Imagining Creation as a Community of Care." *Journal of the Society of Christian Ethics* 31/1 (2011): 143–60.

Watchel, Paul. *The Poverty of Affluence: A Psychological Portrait of the American Way of Life*. New York: Free Press, 1983.

Weil, Simone. "Attention and Will." In *Gravity and Grace*, translated by Emma Crawford and Mario van der Ruhr, 116–22. London, England: Routledge, 2002.

White, Lynn Jr. "The Historical Roots of our Ecologic Crisis." *Science* 155/3767 (March 10, 1967): 1205–209.

Whitney, Elspeth. "Lynn White Jr.'s 'The Historical Roots of Our Ecologic Crisis' after 50 Years." *History Compass* 13/8 (2015): 396–410.

Wilkinson, Katharine. *Between God and Green*. New York: Oxford University Press, 2012.

———. "Climate's Salvation." *Environment Magazine* 52/2 (March/April 2010): 47–57.

Wirzba, Norman. *Food and Faith: A Theology of Eating*. New York: Cambridge University Press, 2011.

———. *This Sacred Life: Humanity's Place in a Wounded World*. Cambridge: Cambridge University Press, 2021.

Woodley, Randy. *Shalom and the Community of Creation: An Indigenous Vision*. Grand Rapids: Eerdmans, 2012.

York, Richard, and Riley Dunlap. "Environmental Sociology." In *The Wiley Blackwell Companion to Sociology*, edited by George Ritzer and Wendy Wiedenhoft Murphy, 283–300. Hoboken: John Wiley and Sons, 2002.

Notes

Preface

1. Wendell Berry, "A Prayer after Eating," *Poetry* 199/2 (November 1971): 9.

2. See Patricia Appelbaum, *St. Francis of America: How a Thirteenth-Century Friar Became America's Most Popular Saint* (Chapel Hill: University of North Carolina Press, 2015).

3. Lynn White Jr., "The Historical Roots of our Ecologic Crisis," *Science* 155/3767 (March 10, 1967): 1205–1209. White believed that the environmental crisis was the direct result of Western agriculture and industry that drew their internal logic directly from Christian dualistic metaphysics. What the world most needed, he believed, was for Christians to recover a pre-enlightenment "enchantment." White, for example, invoked St. Francis of Assisi not as a model of orthodox Christian ecological faithfulness but as an anti-witness, a rebel whose true panentheism, in White's reading, was neatly papered over by his official ecclesial hagiographers.

4. See Richard Osmer, *Practical Theology: An Introduction* (Grand Rapids: Eerdmans, 2008), 4–12.

Chapter 1

1. There are many references by Hayhoe to "global weirding," including "Katharine Hayhoe: Global Weirding," *Biologos*, podcast, March 12, 2020, https://biologos.org/podcast-episodes/katharine-hayhoe-global-weirding.

2. "Climate Change," *World Health Organization*, October 12, 2023, https://www.who.int/news-room/fact-sheets/detail/climate-change-and-health.

3. Marco Boscolo, "Why Carbon Dioxide Is Both Friend and Foe," *National Geographic*, December 2, 2022, https://www.nationalgeographic.com/environment/article/carbon-dioxide-friend-and-foe.

4. Parker Palmer, *A Hidden Wholeness: The Journey Toward an Undivided Life* (San Francisco: Jossey-Bass, 2004), 1.

5. Palmer, *Hidden Wholeness*, 2.

6. Along with Nondenominational, Pentecostal, Holiness, and several other religious groups, the Pew Forum identifies Baptists as a "largely evangelical denominational family." See "America's Changing Religious Landscape," *Pew Research Center*, May 12, 2015, www.pewforum.org/2015/05/12/chapter-1-the-changing-

religious-composition-of-the-u-s/. This identity is not universally true among Baptists, and DaySpring's diverse membership straddles characteristics of evangelical, mainline protestant, emergent, and Anglo-Catholic expressions of faith.

7. Robin Veldman et al., "Who are American evangelical Protestants and why do they matter for US climate policy?" *WIRES: Wiley Interdisciplinary Reviews*, November 30, 2020, https://doi.org/10.1002/wcc.693.

8. US Government, "United States Census: Quick Facts," *Quick Facts: California*, accessed February 12, 2024, https://www.census.gov/quickfacts/fact/table/CA/PST045223.

9. Laurel Kearns, "Saving the Creation: Christian Environmentalism in the United States," *Sociology of Religion* 57/1 (Spring 1996): 55–70.

10. Dietrich Bonhoeffer, *Life Together* (1939; repr., Harper Collins, 2009).

11. Elspeth Whitney, "Lynn White Jr.'s 'The Historical Roots of Our Ecologic Crisis' after 50 Years," *History Compass* 13/8 (2015): 400.

12. Paul Santmire, *The Travail of Nature: The Ambiguous Ecological Promise of Christian Theology* (Philadelphia: Fortress, 1985), 111.

13. Ibid., 113.

14. Ilia Delio, Keith Douglass Warner, Pamela Wood, *Creation Care: A Franciscan Spirituality of the Earth* (Cincinnati: Franciscan Media, 2008), 169.

15. Keith Warner, "Franciscan Environmental Ethics: Imagining Creation as a Community of Care," *Journal of the Society of Christian Ethics* 31/1 (2011): 149.

16. Ibid., 150.

17. Ibid.

18. Ilia Delio, *Care for Creation: A Franciscan Spirituality of the Earth* (Cincinnati: Franciscan Media, 1999).

19. Ibid., 77.

20. The liturgy of the Orthodox Church preserves this linkage between the burning bush and the Incarnation by describing Mary, the mother of Jesus, as one who, like the burning bush, bore God but was not consumed in doing so.

21. Gordon Lathrop is a notable exception, as he draws on this story to highlight the relationship between Eucharist and earth care. See Gordon Lathrop, *Holy Ground* (Minneapolis: Fortress, 2003), 125.

22. Contra Roy Scranton, who believes narrative is a dangerous seductress in an era fated to birth destruction of our planet, I put forward the subversive story of Moses's conversion and calling. See Roy Scranton, "Narrative in the Anthropocene is the Enemy," *Literary Hub*, September 18, 2019, https://lithub.com/roy-scranton-narrative-in-the-anthropocene-is-the-enemy/.

23. Clare of Assisi, "The Second Letter to Agnes of Prague," in *The Lady: Clare of Assisi: Early Documents*, ed. Regis Armstrong (New York: New City Press, 2006), 49.

24. See Ilia Delio, *Christ in Evolution* (Maryknoll, NY: Orbis Books, 2008). For a critical view of the same, see Hans Boersma, *Heavenly Participation: The Weaving of a Sacramental Tapestry* (Grand Rapids: Eerdmans, 2011).

25. Quoted in Roch Niemier, *In the Footsteps of Francis and Clare* (Cincinnati: Franciscan Media, 2006), 119.

26. Ilia Delio, *Franciscan Prayer* (Cincinnati: Franciscan Media, 2004), 9.

27. Philip Sheldrake, *Spirituality: A Brief History* (Oxford: Wiley-Blackwell, 2013), 219.

Chapter 2

1. Kearns, "Saving the Creation," 57.

2. I want to point out the willingness of some to cynically adopt and distort a "stewardship" ethic to support a consumptive, anthropocentric dominion theology. A prime example of this is the Cornwall Alliance (www.cornwallalliance.org).

3. USGS.gov defines a glacier as "a large, perennial accumulation of crystalline ice, snow, rock, sediment, and often liquid water that originates on land and moves downslope under the influence of its own weight and gravity." See USGS, "What Is a Glacier?" *USGS*, https://www.usgs.gov/faqs/what-a-glacier?qt-news_science_products=0#qt-news_science_products.

4. See James Willard Shultz, *Blackfeet Tales of Glacier National* Park (New York: Houghton Mifflin, 1916). Available at https://www.gutenberg.org/files/43399/43399-h/43399-h.htm.

5. David R. Craig, "'Blackfeet Belong to the Mountains': Blackfeet Relationships with the Glacier National Park Landscape and Institution," *Graduate Student Theses, Dissertations, & Professional Papers*, 2008. Available at https://scholarworks.umt.edu/etd/1.

6. Quinn Smith, Jr., "A Stolen History, Future Claims: The Blackfeet Nation and Glacier National Park," *Wellian Magazine*, October 14, 2020, https://sites.duke.edu/thewellianmag/2020/10/14/a-stolen-history-future-claims/.

7. Niemier, *In the Footsteps of Francis and Clare*, 116.

8. Simone Weil, "Attention and Will," in *Gravity and Grace*, trans. Emma Crawford and Mario van der Ruhr (London, England: Routledge, 1952), 116–22.

9. Maria Popova, "Simone Weil on Attention and Grace," *Marginalian*, August 18, 2018, https://www.themarginalian.org/2015/08/19/simone-weil-attention-gravity-and-grace/#:~:text=Attention%2C%20taken%20to%20its%20highest,thereto%20in%20spite%20of%20itself.

10. Richard Osmer, *Practical Theology: An Introduction* (Grand Rapids: Eerdmans, 2008), 33.

11. As I will demonstrate, Moses's actions at the burning bush can be mapped onto the Franciscan prayer journey (see, consider, contemplate, imitate) and onto the four tasks of practical theology as outlined by Osmer (What is happening? Why is this going on? What ought to be going on? How might we respond?)

12. This is similar to the first step of sacred reading in the classically monastic tradition, *lectio*. The difference is that *lectio* as part of *lectio divina* implies its function as a reading strategy. Clare's *gaze* is an attentiveness that I extend to reading Scripture. Clare almost surely was thinking of the icon of San Damiano when she wrote this guidance. Cloistered at San Damiano, Clare spent each day of her life for years deeply contemplating this unique icon of the cross of Christ. For more on the San Damiano cross, see Susan Saint Sing, *Francis and the San Damiano Cross* (Cincinnati: St. Anthony Messenger Press, 1989).

13. The one possible exception is Exodus 1:20 in which "God dealt well with the midwives."

14. Norman Wirzba, *This Sacred Life: Humanity's Place in a Wounded World* (Cambridge: Cambridge University Press, 2021), 22.

15. Environmental concern is not best understood within a theory-to-practice methodology though this has been tried over and over. We do not simply need a new cosmology per Lynn White, Jr. in 1969, nor a bold statement from religious leaders per the Evangelical Climate Initiative in 2004. It is better approached as a practice-theory-practice hermeneutical spiral. A new imaginary comes only through critical integration of our practices with our theology that births new practices and in turn reshapes our theology.

16. See Cindy Crosby, *The Tallgrass Prairie* (Evanston: Northwestern University Press, 2017).

17. "Live Oaks Are a Texas Landscape Mainstay," *AgriLife Today*, February 22, 2007, https://agrilifetoday.tamu.edu/2007/02/22/live-oaks-are-a-texas-landscape-mainstay/.

18. Damian Carrington, "'Cake' mentioned 10 times more than 'climate change' on UKTV—report," *Guardian*, September 15, 2001, https://www.theguardian.com/environment/2021/sep/15/cake-mentioned-10-times-more-than-climate-change-on-uk-tv-report.

19. "The Keeling Curve," *UC San Diego Scripps Institution of Oceanography*, accessed October 28, 2024, https://keelingcurve.ucsd.edu/ (this site is regularly updated, so it shows current information); See also Ralph F. Keeling and Charles D. Keeling, "Atmospheric Monthly In Situ CO_2 Data — Mauna Loa Observatory, Hawaii" (Archive 2024-01-08). In Scripps CO_2 Program Data, UC San Diego Library Digital Collections, https://doi.org/10.6075/J08W3BHW.

20. The graph is named for its creator Dr. Charles Keeling, who established a measurement station at Mauna Loa Observatory in 1958 to collect continuous

data demonstrating the natural cycles of carbon concentration through the seasons of the year. His work established a dramatic picture of the continuous rise of carbon in the atmosphere through the years.

21. See "AR6 Climate Change 2021: The Physical Science Basis," Intergovernmental Panel on Climate Change Sixth Assessment Report, pages 5–8, accessed November 5, 2021, https://www.ipcc.ch/report/ar6/wg1/downloads/report/IPCC_AR6_WGI_Chapter_05.pdf.

22. Dan Patterson, "Climate change conspiracies are spreading rapidly during UN's COP26 event," *CBS News*, November 9, 2021, https://www.cbsnews.com/news/climate-change-conspiracies-are-spreading-rapidly-during-uns-cop26-event/.

23. Climate science attracts its share of skeptics. For examples of Christian skepticism among evangelicals and Baptists, see Paul Braterman, "'God intended it as a disposable planet': meet the US pastor preaching climate change denial," *The Conversation*, October 12, 2020, https://theconversation.com/god-intended-it-as-a-disposable-planet-meet-the-us-pastor-preaching-climate-change-denial-147712; see also Albert Mohler, "When Ecology Replaces Theology," *Southern Baptist Theological Seminary*, October 3, 2007, https://albertmohler.com/2007/10/03/when-ecology-replaces-theology.

24. Kathryn Hayhoe, *Saving Us: A Climate Scientist's Case for Hope and Healing in a Divided World* (New York: One Signal Publishers, 2021), 39.

25. Ibid., 39–40.

26. For a brief history of climate science from 1820–current, see Hayhoe, *Saving Us*, 40–42.

27. In chapter 3, I introduce critiques from as early as 1840s concerning the outsized impacts of modern industrial life not only on pollution in major industrial centers but also on the health of the soil and food systems.

28. Intergovernmental Panel on Climate Change, "Climate Change 2021—The Physical Science Basis: Summary for Policymakers" (Switzerland: IPCC, October 2021), 4. Available at https://www.ipcc.ch/report/ar6/wg1/downloads/report/IPCC_AR6_WGI_SPM_final.pdf.

29. Ibid., 21.

30. For an extended assessment of nature and wilderness, see the classic by Roderick Nash, *Wilderness and the American Mind* (New Haven: Yale University Press, 1982).

31. Joseph Stromberg, "Thoreau Leaves Walden Pond," *Smithsonian*, September 6, 2011, smithsonianmag.com/smithsonian-institution/thoreau-leaves-walden-pond-69655863/.

32. See the bio "Wallace Stegner," *The Wilderness Society*, accessed September 10, 2017, https://wilderness.org/bios/former-council-members/wallace-stegner.

33. For a Native American feminist critique of Stegner, see Elizabeth Cook-Lynn, *Why I Can't Read Wallace Stegner and Other Essays: A Tribal Voice* (Madison: University of Wisconsin Press, 1996).

34. James Cone, "Whose Earth Is It, Anyway?" in *Earth Habitat: Eco-Injustice and the Church's Response*, ed. Dieter Hessel and Larry Rasmussen (Minneapolis: Fortress, 2001), 23.

35. Some environmental movements are directly fueled by white supremacy. See Sam Adler-Ball, "Why White Supremacists Are Hooked on Green Living," *New Republic*, September 24, 2019, https://newrepublic.com/article/154971/rise-ecofascism-history-white-nationalism-environmental-preservation-immigration.

36. Ian Baucom, *4° Celsius: Search for a Method in the Age of the Anthropocene* (Durham: Duke University Press, 2020), 6.

37. Patricia Bernstein critically examines the conditions, culture, and details of the charges against Washington, the mishandling of the trial, and the chaotic scene in which a mob attacked him and murdered him. See Patricia Bernstein, *The First Waco Horror: The Lynching of Jesse Washington and the Rise of the NAACP* (College Station: Texas A&M University Press, 2006).

38. James Cone, *The Cross and the Lynching Tree* (Maryknoll, NY: Orbis Books, 2011), 15.

39. Bernstein, *The First Waco Horror*, 5.

40. Andrew Belonsky, "How the NAACP fought lynching—by using the racists' own pictures against them," *Guardian*, April 27, 2018, https://www.theguardian.com/us-news/2018/apr/27/lynching-naacp-photographs-waco-texas-campaign.

41. Quoted in William Carrigan, *The Making of a Lynching Culture: Violence and Vigilantism in Central Texas 1836–1916* (Chicago: University of Illinois Press, 2006), 191.

42. W. E. B. Du Bois, "Jesus Christ in Texas," in Dubois, *Darkwater: Voices from Within the Veil* (Mineola, NY: Dover, 1999), 70–77.

43. The Equal Justice Initiative estimates that 4,000 Americans, mostly Black, were killed between 1887 and 1950. See "Lynching in America: Confronting the Legacy of Racial Terror," *Equal Justice Initiative*, accessed January 2, 2022, https://lynchinginamerica.eji.org/report/.

44. Carrigan, *Lynching Culture*, 7–8.

45. Ibid., 8.

46. Ibid.

47. Charles Taylor, *A Secular Age* (London: Belknap Press, 2018), 29.

48. Cone, "Whose Earth Is It, Anyway?" 23.

49. Delio et al., *Creation Care*, 169.

50. Taylor comments on thin places in a variety of settings in the interview posted at "This Place That Has Made Us Kin," *Flycatcher*, accessed March 25, 2024, https://www.flycatcherjournal.org/bbt-interview.php.

51. Jessica Merzdof, "NASA Data Aids Ozone Hole's Journey to Recovery," *NASA*, April 15, 2020, https://www.nasa.gov/feature/goddard/2020nasa-data-aids-ozone-hole-s-journey-to-recovery.

52. See "Global Climate Change," *NASA*, accessed April 7, 2018, https://climate.nasa.gov/. NASA reported, "Ninety-seven percent of climate scientists agree that climate-warming trends over the past century are very likely due to human activities, and most of the leading scientific organizations worldwide have issued public statements endorsing this position." (This site also posts current data, so the link will give you information for today.)

53. Aaron McCright [with Riley Dunlap], "The Polarization of U.S. Public Opinion on Climate Change," *Scholars Strategy Network*, January 1, 2013, scholars.org/brief/polarization-us-public-opinion-climate-change.

54. The ad announced, "The Evangelical Climate Initiative (ECI) is a group of over 300 senior evangelical leaders in the United States who are convinced it is time for our country to help solve the problem of global warming.... We seek to do so in a way that creates jobs, cleans up our environment, and enhances national security by reducing our dependence on foreign oil, thereby creating a safe and healthy future for our children according to an intuitive medium. Our deep commitment to Jesus Christ and his commands to love our neighbors, care for 'the least of these,' and be proper stewards of His creation compels us to act." See "Climate Change: An Evangelical Call to Action," *Christians and Climate*, accessed December 27, 2021, http://www.christiansandclimate.org/.

55. White, "Historical Roots," 1203–1207.

56. It is not much of an exaggeration to say that nearly every expression of Christian concern about the environment since 1967 has engaged White's thesis in one way or another, typically following White's theory-to-practice methodology.

57. "The Politics of Climate," *Pew Research Center*, October 4, 2016, https://www.pewresearch.org/science/2016/10/04/the-politics-of-climate/; Michael Lipka, "U.S. Religious Groups and Their Political Leanings," *Pew Research Center*, February 23, 2016, www.pewresearch.org/fact-tank/2016/02/23/u-s-religious-groups-and-their-political-leanings/.

58. "Statement of the Evangelical Climate Initiative," *Christians and Climate*, accessed April 7, 2018, http://www.christiansandclimate.org/statement/; Katharine Wilkinson, *Between God and Green: How Evangelicals Are Cultivating Middle Ground on Climate Change* (New York: Oxford University Press, 2012), discusses the ECI at length. Chapter 4 is an assessment of opposition among conservative leaders.

59. At stake is an interesting question of methodology: do public statements from denominational leaders at the "grasstops" make a difference to Christians at the grassroots?

60. For further research of Protestant responses to environmental concerns, see Wylie Carr et al., "The Faithful Skeptics: Evangelical Beliefs and Perceptions of Climate Change," *Journal for the Study of Religion, Nature, and Culture* 6/3 (2012): 276–99; Wilkinson, *Between God and Green*, 85–110. Contra G. E. Hitzhusen, "Judeo-Christian Theology and the Environment: Moving Beyond Skepticism to New Sources for Environmental Education in the United States," *Environmental Education Research* 13/1 (2007): 55–74.

61. Katharine Wilkinson, "Climate's Salvation," *Environment Magazine* 52/2 (March/April 2010): 53.

62. Matthew Arbuckle and David Konisky, "The Role of Religion in Environmental Attitudes," *Social Science Quarterly* 96/5 (November 2015): 1245: "Religiosity conditions the relationship between religious affiliation and environmental attitudes for individuals identifying with some religious traditions. In general, religiosity tends to push evangelical Protestants, Catholics, and mainline Protestants toward less environmental concern."

63. Konisky, "Greening of Christianity," 4.

64. Jarrod Longbons, "I Seen a Better World: Theology's Gift to Ecology," *BET* 4/2 (2017): 1–18.

65. "Interpretation of Sites of Memory," *International Coalition of Sites of Conscience*, January 31, 2018, 14, https://www.sitesofconscience.org/wp-content/uploads/2018/08/Final-report-SoM-180131-en-1.pdf.

66. "Interpretation of Sites of Memory," 15.

67. See "Slavery at Monticello," *Monticello.org*, https://www.monticello.org/slavery/?ref=homeblock, for an account of slavery at Monticello, which is referred to not just as an "estate" but as a "plantation."

68. "Site of Conscience," *Monticello.org*, https://www.monticello.org/thomas-jefferson-foundation/site-of-conscience/.

69. Some, predictably, wring their hands over this transformation. See, for example, Douglas MacKinnon, "Jefferson, Madison's homes become woke monuments attacking Founding Fathers' legacies," *Foxnews.com*, July 22, 2022, https://www.foxnews.com/opinionjefferson-madison-homes-woke-monuments-attacking-founding-fathers-legacies.

70. "Interpretation of Sites of Memory," 25.

71. See Will Bostick, "Inside the Decades-long Effort to Commemorate a Notorious Waco Lynching," *Texas Monthly*, February 23, 2023, https://www.texasmonthly.com/being-texan/waco-historical-marker-saga-jesse-washington-lynching/.

72. Holland Carter, "Turning Grief for a Hidden Past into a Healing Space," *New York Times*, August 16, 2020, www.nytimes.com/2020/08/16/arts/design/university-of-virginia-enslaved-laborers-memorial.html.

73. Jordan Davidson, "Glacier National Park Is Replacing Signs that Predicted Glaciers Would Disappear by 2020," *EcoWatch.com*, January 10, 2020, https://www.ecowatch.com/glacier-national-park-signs-replaced-2644665325.html.

74. Margaret Visser, *The Geometry of Love: Space, Time, Mystery, and Meaning in an Ordinary Church* (New York: North Point, 2001).

Chapter 3

1. Paul Brockelman, "With New Eyes: Seeing the Environment as a Spiritual Issue," in John Carroll, Paul Brockelman, Mary Westfall, eds., *The Greening of Faith: God, the Environment, and the Good Life* (London: University Press of New England, 1997), 30.

2. Quoted in Brockelman, "With New Eyes," 31.

3. For a charitable view, see Ilia Delio, *Christ in Evolution* (Maryknoll, NY: Orbis Books, 2008). For a critical view of the same, see Hans Boersma, *Heavenly Participation: The Weaving of a Sacramental Tapestry* (Grand Rapids: Eerdmans, 2011).

4. Osmer, *Practical Theology*, 24.

5. Donald Worster, *Passion for Nature: The Life of John Muir* (Oxford: Oxford University Press, 2008), 403.

6. See Prakash Kashwan, "American environmentalism's racist roots have shaped global thinking about conservation," *The Conversation*, September 2, 2020, https://theconversation.com/american-environmentalisms-racist-roots-have-shaped-global-thinking-about-conservation-143783.

7. Michael Brune, "Pulling Down Our Monuments," *Sierra Club*, July 22, 2020, https://www.sierraclub.org/michael-brune/2020/07/john-muir-early-history-sierra-club.

8. See Jeon Jeoyoung, *The Call of Moses and the Exodus Story: A Redaction-Critical Study in Exodus 3-4 and 5-13* (Tübingen, Germany: Mohr Siebeck, 2013). Source theorists like Jeon approached this challenge with increasingly complex solutions to this unusual textual situation. Typically, it was determined, the final text was in one way or another a weaving together of J and E sources, though no single proposal proved satisfactory to account for the various strands.

9. Frank Polak, "Theophany and Mediator: The Unfolding of a Theme in the Book of Exodus," in *Studies in the Book of Exodus: Redaction-Reception, Interpretation*, ed. Marc Vervenne (Leuven, Belgium: Leuven University Press, 1996), 119.

10. Brevard Childs, *The Book of Exodus: A Critical, Theological Commentary* (Louisville: John Knox, 2004), 73.

11. Roland Barthes, "The Struggle with the Angel: Textual Analysis of Genesis 32:23-33," in *Structural Analysis and Biblical Exegesis: Interpretational Essays*, ed. Dikran Hadidian (Pittsburgh: Pickwick Press, 1974), 31.

12. Clive Hamilton, *Defiant Earth: The Fate of Humans in the Anthropocene* (Malden, MA: Polity Press, 2017), 9–10. *Italics* mine.

13. Unofficially, so far. See Raymond Zhong, "Are We in the 'Anthropocene,' the Human Age? Nope, Scientists Say," *New York Times*, March 5, 2024, https://www.nytimes.com/2024/03/05/climate/anthropocene-epoch-vote-rejected.html?searchResultPosition=1.

14. Quoted in Baucom, *History 4º Celsius*, 9. For a brief discussion of debates about the beginning of the Anthropocene, see Celia Dean-Drummond, "Performing the Beginning in the End: A Theological Anthropology for the Anthropocene," *Religion in the Anthropocene*, ed. Celia Dean-Drummond (Eugene, OR: Wipf and Stock Publishers, 2017), 173–87. Wes Jackson, director of the Land Institute, for example, contends that humans have been changing the planet through agricultural practices for ten thousand years, but those affects have intensified since the industrial revolution.

15. Baucom, *History 4º Celsius*, 8.

16. Not every community, though, is equally affected by changing climate conditions. Advocates of climate justice acknowledge these inequities and advocate for mitigation strategies. See Daisy Simmons, "What Is Climate Justice?" *Yale Climate Connections*, July 29, 2020, https://yaleclimateconnections.org/2020/07/what-is-climate-justice/.

17. See Ossi Ollinaho and V. P. J. Arponen, "Incomegetting and Environmental Degradation," *Sustainability* 12/10 (May 14, 2020), https://www.mdpi.com/2071-1050/12/10/4007.

18. See Andrew Prior, "Easter in the Anthropocene," *One Man's Web*, April 12, 2015, https://www.onemansweb.org/theology/the-year-of-mark-2015/easter-in-the-anthropocene-john-20-19-29.html, for comments on the adaptability of humans to changing situations.

19. John Bellamy Foster, "Marx's Theory of Metabolic Rift: Classical Foundations for Environmental Sociology," *American Journal of Sociology* 105/2 (September 1999): 382.

20. Foster, "Marx's Theory of Metabolic Rift," 383.

21. While it is commonplace to hear someone bemoan, "my metabolism is slowing down as I get older," as a way to explain weight gain in middle age, recent studies debunk as myth the idea that our metabolisms naturally slow down. Weight gain in middle age is more closely correlated with decreased physical activity and increased food consumption. See Damian McNamara, "Not So Fast Blaming Slow Metabolism for Midlife Weight Gain," *WebMD*, August 13, 2021, https://www.webmd.com/diet/news/20210813/dont-blame-metabolism-for-weight-gain.

22. Foster, "Marx's Theory of Metabolic Rift," 382.

23. An average person may or may not have a solid grasp on metabolic processes within physiology, but the concept still works on a popular level with minimal explanation. On face value, the metabolism metaphor works on multiple levels for a wide audience. The concept strengthens further as its history comes to light.

24. "Manchester's Smoke Nuisance: Air Pollution in the Industrial City," *Science+Industry Museum*, February 12, 2021, www.scienceandindustrymuseum.org.uk/objects-and-stories/air-pollution.

25. For example, beginner gardeners learn that beans are "nitrogen fixers," while corn requires a lot of nitrogen. This gives rise to the "three sisters" planting method of corn, beans, and melons together or in proximity.

26. Currently, public attention is turning to post-pandemic increases in the price of oil as a contributor to significant inflationary pressures on food. It is readily obvious that shipping costs in the industrial food system contribute to the cost of food. The degree to which synthetic fertilizers also depend on mass inputs of oil for production is becoming clearer to the public.

27. Butch Tindell speaks regularly to groups locally and nationwide on the issues of sustainable agriculture based on his thirty-five years of experience as a gardener and farmer. As an instructor at The Ploughshare for the past twenty-one years, he has taught sustainable farming and ranching to hundreds of beginning and experienced farmers and gardeners. He has also developed numerous courses and published curriculum on these topics.

28. Immediately after the presentation, I wrote down what Butch said so I would remember his words rightly.

29. Richard York and Riley Dunlap, "Environmental Sociology," in *The Wiley Blackwell Companion to Sociology*, ed. George Ritzer and Wendy Wiedenhoft Murphy (Hoboken: John Wiley and Sons, 2002), 284.

30. Bruno Latour, "Agency at the Time of the Anthropocene," *New Literary History* 45 (2014): 1.

31. York and Dunlap, "Environmental Sociology," 287.

32. Ibid.

33. Ibid.

34. Earth Day, as one example, was founded in 1969 by John McConnell, a Pentecostal Christian. A decade later, the Au Sable Institute was established in Michigan with Calvin DeWitt as its first executive director. See "About," *Au Sable Institute*, accessed May 16, 2022, www.ausable.org.

35. Evangelicals in the West are deeply entrenched in democratic and capitalistic assumptions, as I will demonstrate. So while I will argue that the appropriation of Marx within environmental sociology leads eventually to an important convergence with serious Christian ecologically alert spirituality, I recognize the path has

inherent challenges to the Western evangelical mindset, and ultimately wisdom will suggest jettisoning the sharpest of Marxist critique while engaging seriously the theory that arose from his insights.

36. York and Dunlap, "Environmental Sociology," 287. Also see Allan Schnaiberg and Kenneth Alan Gould, *Environment and Society: The Enduring Conflict* (New York: Oxford University Press, 1980).

37. Quoted in Michael Bell, *An Invitation to Environmental Sociology* (Thousand Oaks: Pine Forge Press, 1998), 56; see Paul Watchel, *The Poverty of Affluence: A Psychological Portrait of the American Way of Life* (New York: Free Press, 1983), 62.

38. Bell, Environmental Sociology, 64.

39. Ibid., 73.

40. John Bellamy Foster, *The Ecological Rift: Capitalism's War on the Earth* (New York: Monthly Review Press, 2010), 194.

41. Ibid.

42. The fundamentally unsustainable nature of economic growth is emphasized by the problems inherent to the escalation of production. Natural resources used to fuel sites of production are initially extracted from sites closest to production, but as these are depleted, production turns to lower-quality resources and/or resources farther from the sites of production. See York and Dunlap, "Environmental Sociology," 288. Also see J. O'Conner, "On Two Contradictions of Capitalism," *Capitalism, Nature, Socialism* 2/3 (1991): 107–109.

43. All quotes from Matt Kyle, "Woodway City Council Rejects Drought-Related Building Moratorium," *Waco-Tribune Herald*, September 26, 2023, https://wacotrib.com/news/local/government-politics/woodway-city-council-rejects-drought-related-building-moratorium/article_49370ee6-5c0c-11ee-93d8-8f416933c867.html.

44. O. I. Ollinaho, "Environmental destruction as (objectively) uneventful and (subjectively) irrelevant," *Environmental Sociology* 2/1 (2016): 53.

45. This important insight provides ecological grounding in the cultural-environmental context of the Anthropocene for Catholic theologian John Markey's critique of North American spirituality. To fully appreciate Markey's critique of our contemporary situation, and to more fully anticipate the holistic renewal needed to embody his solutions, we need to go a step beyond political economy. We need to go to the heart of the condition of human life in this culture in this time.

46. Foster, *Ecological Rift*, 373.

47. Ibid., 377.

48. Ibid., 379.

49. Ibid.

50. Ibid., 381.

51. Ibid., 378.

52. Ibid., 381.

53. The Theory of Metabolic Rift is not the sole contribution of environmental sociology, and appealing to a theory inspired by Karl Marx is not an obvious path to success for inspiring the environmental consciousness of Westerners. If evangelicals are "skeptical" of climate change, they are thoroughly hostile to Marxism, whatever they think Marxism is. Not surprisingly, nowhere in Prelli and Winter's "Rhetorical Features of Green Evangelicalism" is found "Marx" or "Marxism" within the fields of evangelical ecological rhetoric. See Lawrence Prelli and Terri Winters, "Rhetorical Features of Green Evangelicalism," *Environmental Communication* 3/2 (July 2009): 224–43. Undoubtedly, a move away from reference to Marxism will be necessary as a practical matter in most congregational settings, as Karl Marx is hardly an obvious choice as a source or interlocutor for any field concerning Protestant evangelicals in the United States. For a sample of the popular account of "cultural Marxism" within Christian discourse, consider Carl Trueman, "We All Live in Marx's World Now," *The Gospel Coalition*, March 19, 2019, https://www.thegospelcoalition.org/reviews/live-marxs-world-now/. To be sure, invoking Marx as a key source in a practical theology for Baptists in Texas is likely to spell the quick end of the initiative.

Sage wisdom in this case would appeal to other sources besides Marx to have any traction with a largely conservative, evangelical audience. Though rooted in nineteenth-century Marxist critique, the force of the idea of metabolic rift can be extracted from direct reference to Karl Marx. However, before dismissing Marx, we do well to heed the intersection of social justice with environmental justice that he helped bring to light. As an early critic of industrial agriculture and the industrial revolution as rift-making between humans and nature, Marx proved to be prescient. The concerns he raised were only intensified by developments through the twentieth century.

54. Peter Dickens, "Beyond Sociology: Marxism and the Environment," in *The International Handbook of Environmental Sociology*, ed. Michael Redclift and Graham Woodgate (Northampton, MA: Edward Elgar, 1997), 179.

55. The anonymous author of *Meditations on the Tarot* includes a sharp critique of Marx in a chapter on "The Devil" written in 1963. The Devil is not Marx himself, nor the ideals of communism necessarily, but the *egregore* of communism as class-hatred, atheism, and material interest unleashed upon the world. I quote a lengthy section here because the author's distinction between the "sober" Marx and the Marx of "intoxicated imagination" is helpful for those of us finding Marx's critiques salient while his solutions fall short:

> "If Marx and Engels had simply defended the interests of the industrial workers without having let themselves be carried away by their intoxicated imagination to make statements of universal historical significance, and even cosmic significance, such as the statement that God does not exist, that all religion is the 'opium of the people', that all ideology is only

a superstructure on the basis of material interests (and that this has always been so, everywhere), they would have been contributors to the tradition. Because care for the rights and well-being of the poor is an integral part of the very essence of tradition—Christian, Jewish, Islamic, Buddhist, Hindu and humanist. Carried away by indignation . . . they cast in the same mould God, the bourgeoise, the Gospels, capitalism, mendicant orders, industrial monopolists, idealistic philosophers, and bankers . . . and they declared all this, without a second thought, as riff-raff of the history of the human race."

See Robert Powell, trans., *Meditation on the Tarot: A Journey into Christian Hermeticism* (New York: Jeremy P. Tarcher/Putnam, 2002), 410.

56. Prelli and Winters, "Rhetorical Features," 225.

57. Ibid., 232. Through a framework of discourse screens, patterns of green evangelical discourse emerge, including several key metaphors and rhetorical devices: designer, healing, garden, stewardship, reconciliation, creation care, moral witnessing, appeals to scientific authority, appeals to biblical authority.

58. Ibid., 225.

59. Ibid., 229.

60. Willis Jenkins, *Ecologies of Grace* (New York: Oxford University Press, 2008), 7.

61. George Kehm, "The New Story: Redemption as Fulfillment of Creation," in *After Nature's Revolt: Eco-Justice and Theology*, ed. Dieter Hessel (Minneapolis: Augsburg Fortress Press, 1992), 91.

62. Jenkins, *Ecologies of Grace*, 17.

63. John Markey, *Moses in Pharoah's House: A Liberation Spirituality for North America* (Winona, MN: Anselm Academic, 2014), 28.

64. Ibid., 22.

65. I say this knowing that radical individualism pervades the spirituality of American evangelicalism as well. Evangelical soteriology is focused on individual, personal response in faith to God's grace in Christ. Ethics, as a result, are principally discussed as an individual's responsibility for righteousness, not social matters of justice. With all this, however, Baptists have a strong ecclesiological emphasis on the local community. See James Wm. McClendon Jr., *Ethics* (Nashville: Abingdon Press, 2002) for an account of Baptist ecclesiology.

66. Samuel Davidson's forthcoming dissertation invites us to expand our ecclesiology to include the "critters" who make the church's ground their home.

67. Quoted in Ian Angus, *Facing the Anthropocene: Fossil Capitalism and the Crisis of the Earth System* (New York: Monthly Review Press, 2016), 28.

68. A typical prayer in eucharistic liturgies follows this pattern: *Most merciful God, we confess that we have sinned against you in thought, word, and deed, by what we have done and by what we have left undone. We have not loved you with our whole*

heart. We have not loved our neighbors as ourselves. We are truly sorry and we humbly repent. Amen.

69. Wylie Carr et al., "The Faithful Skeptics," 288.

70. The Cornwall Alliance, for example, claims to promote "Christian stewardship" of the environment, but it promotes a cynical dominion theology, based, ostensibly, on God's election of humankind to rule over nature. For an assessment of the Cornwall Alliance agenda see Leo Hickman, "The US Evangelicals Who Believe Environmentalism is a 'Native Evil,'" *Guardian*, May 5, 2011, www.theguardian.com/environment/blog/2011/may/05/evangelical-christian-environmentalism-green-dragon.

71. Markey, *Moses*, 48.

72. James Cone, "Whose Earth Is It, Anyway?" in *Earth Habitat: Eco-Injustice and the Church's Response*, ed. Dieter Hessel and Larry Rasmussen (Minneapolis: Fortress, 2001), 23.

73. Norman Wirzba, *This Sacred Life: Humanity's Place in a Wounded World* (Cambridge: Cambridge University Press, 2021), 10.

74. Jason Moore, "The Rise of Cheap Nature," in *Anthropocene or Capitalocene? Nature, History, and the Crisis of Capitalism*, ed. Jason Moore (Oakland: PM Press, 2016), 79. Quoted in Wirzba, *Sacred Life*, 10.

75. Randy Woodley, *Shalom and the Community of Creation: An Indigenous Vision* (Grand Rapids: Eerdmans, 2012), 40.

76. Rebecca Randall, "Churches to Play Key Role in Spending $1 Billion Toward Climate Change," *Sojourners*, March 7, 2024, https://sojo.net/articles/churches-play-key-role-spending-1-billion-toward-climate-change.

77. The vision of 2 Corinthians 5, for example, points Christians to participate and promote the hope of the gospel in the world as ambassadors of God and ministers of reconciliation.

78. Understanding that the rift is both in the metabolism of earth processes and in the hermeneutical horizons of Scripture reading helps explain why the theory-to-practice method of much contemporary Christian-ecological discourse falls so flat on the human heart. As out-of-place "moderns," it's understandable that we read Scripture as if it has little to say to us about creation care or our place in creation. Even attempts to recapitulate the Scripture's original setting or intent seem out of emotional reach. And so it will be most helpful to find a bridge to a creation-affirming spirituality informed and inspired by the witness to Christ.

Chapter 4

1. The Barthian stewardship ethic, as a faithful response to the divine ordinance to exercise human dominion, is the dominant rhetoric of environmental concern among evangelicals. Yet, in light of the severe disconnections within the

Anthropocene, we need more than a duty to fulfill. We need ecological conversion of our theology and spirituality and a path to participation in ecological relationships. Stewardship is the most common framework for protestant ecology ethics but does not bite deep enough to spark the conversion we need. In search of conversion, I offer Franciscan kinship ethics as a spirituality of participatory love.

2. This echoes the methodology of Andrew Root, who defines the work of practical theology as Christopraxis, the "continuing ministry of Christ in the world." See Andrew Root, *Christopraxis: A Practical Theology of the Cross* (Minneapolis: Fortress Press, 2014), 90. Ministry, Root says, "is joining in God's contemporaneous becoming, in God's own ministry; it is doing God's work with God but doing so for the sake of being ontologically joined to God. This makes the text of practical theological reflection the present ministry of God as it is discerned and participated in by human forms of ministry done in concrete and lived experiences" (99).

3. Santmire, *Travail of Nature*. Santmire engages a wide range of leaders and theologians from Origen and Irenaeus to Reformers Luther and Calvin to twentieth-century luminaries Karl Barth and Teilhard de Chardin.

4. Jenkins, *Ecologies of Grace*.

5. Among many fine examples, I commend Douglas Moo and Jonathan Moo, *Creation Care: A Biblical Theology of the Natural World* (Grand Rapids: Zondervan, 2018); Richard Baukham, *The Bible and Ecology: Rediscovering the Community of Creation* (Waco: Baylor University Press, 2010); Richard Baukham, *Living with Other Creatures: Green Exegesis and Theology* (Waco: Baylor University Press, 2011); Daniel Brunner, Jennifer Butler, and A. J. Swoboda, *Introducing Evangelical Ecotheology: Foundations in Scripture, Theology, History, and Praxis* (Grand Rapids: Baker Academic, 2014).

6. Moo and Moo, *Creation Care*, 37–42.

7. See Moo and Moo, *Creation Care*, 35–36.

8. Delio says, "Only action that flows from a converted heart—informed by contemplation, fueled by love and sustained in community—has the holding power to cocreate with God a new world that is just and sustainable for all, including all of God's creatures and future generations to come" (Delio, *Care for Creation*, 185).

9. Ibid., 39–40.

10. Joseph Sittler makes this distinction:

> "I have been asked to speak about a theology of ecology or a theology for ecology, and I want to make a distinction. A theology *for* ecology is obviously demanded by the facts of the case. But it is rather a theology *of* ecology that I want to talk about. For if we start talking about a theology *for* ecology, we will try to manufacture out of uncriticized theological categories consequent moralistic efforts stretched to enclose new and crucial facts. Such an effort will not be a redoing of theology in view of ecology but only an extension of traditional ethics in the presence of

crisis. If that should happen, and if uncriticized fundamental categories are simply reassessed and extended, we will get ecology in the textbooks on systematic theology probably as one part of eschatology!"

See Joseph Sittler, "Ecological Commitment as Theological Responsibility," in *Evocations of Grace*, ed. Steven Bouma-Prediger and Peter Bakken (Grand Rapids: Eerdmans, 2000), 35.

11. See Douglas Christie, "Nature Writing and Mysticism," in *The Routledge Handbook of Religion and Ecology*, ed. Willis Jenkins et al. (New York: Routledge, 2016), 233.

12. Santmire, *Travail of Nature*, 146.

13. Ibid., 151.

14. Jenkins, *Ecologies of Grace*, 161–62. According to Jenkins, Santmire "missed the place Barth's theology had already made for nature: the way the Reconciler restores nature to theology and humans to the earth." However, Santmire is not the only sharp critic of Barth's ecology. Jenkins points out that Catherine Keller in *Face of the Deep* sharply critiques Barth, who "rejects all things aqueous, fecund, fluid, material, and chaotic." Keller suggests that Barth so desperately conceals co-creative energies in the biblical text that his account of stewardship as provisional witness is unsustainable. Keller further suggests that in affirming the biblical language of dominion, Barth ironically brought humans into the very sort of partnership that he wanted to exclude. While Jenkins casts doubt on Keller's reading of Barth, I suspect Barth would reject Osmer's methodological claim that the prophetic word of God is always an interplay between divine disclosure and creaturely participation. I wonder, as a practical matter, if Jenkins is overly optimistic about how Christians practice stewardship compared to Barth's nuanced ecologically infused doxology. Missing from Barth's account and Jenkins's apology is something fundamental to human life: our experience with Christ alive and active in the world. I hardly mean to suggest here that one's personal experience can stand toe to toe with Barthian stewardship ethic, but something important is missing when care for creation is not fully invested in the meaning of the word *care*, which involves love and sorrow, relationship and active attention.

15. Ibid., 160.

16. Ibid., 172.

17. Ibid., 187.

18. This is not intended as criticism per se of Barth or of redeemed stewardship, but it is to say that if we are still in a primarily stewardship discourse, we have not yet gone far enough given our context. To be clear, I do not want to use Barth or a Barthian-infused stewardship ethic as a foil for a romantic, bland Franciscanism. Rather, I hope to demonstrate how the fullest, richest, most generous account of Barth's stewardship is a Christian spirituality that begins to look a lot like St. Francis of Assisi.

19. Sheldrake, *Spirituality*, 219.

20. Niemier, *In the Steps of Francis and Clare*, 117.

21. Clare D'Auria, O.S.F., "Stirrings of the Spirit: The Incarnation Prayer of Clare of Assisi," *The Cord* 56/6 (2006): 12.

22. Warner, "Franciscan Environmental Ethics,"150.

23. Ibid.

24. Polak, "Theophany and Mediator," 121.

25. The dialectic nature of the narrative weaves throughout its major themes. Brevard Childs notes that this story has been viewed as a stereotypical call story, which then collapses its meaning into etiology and finally phenomenology. Childs protests, "The subtle dialectic of the chapter is certainly missed by commentators who would subsume the divine element within the category of the psychological. Moses' call then becomes the internal brooding of a man over the problems of his people and the mounting religious conviction that God wanted him to aid." See Childs, *The Book of Exodus*, 73.

26. For a famous example, see Gregory of Nyssa, The Life of Moses, 2.17-26 (SC 1:36-39). For a summary of other commentaries, see David Adamo, "The Burning Bush (Ex 3:1-6): A study of natural phenomena as manifestation of divine presence in the Old Testament and in African context," *HTS Theological Studies* 73/3 (2017): 1–8, https://dx.doi.org/10.4102/hts.v73i3.4576.

27. Louis Bouyer, *The Spirituality of the Middle Ages*, vol. 2 of A History of Christian Spirituality (London: Burns & Oates, 1968), 433.

28. Elizabeth Theokritoff, "The Vision of St. Maximus the Confessor: That Creation May All Be One," in *The Wiley Blackwell Companion to Religion and Ecology*, ed. John Hart (Hoboken: John Wiley and Sons, 2017), 220.

29. Andrew Louth, *Maximus the Confessor* (Routledge: New York, 1996), 16.

30. Jaroslav Pelikan, "Introduction," in *Maximus the Confessor: Selected Writings*, Classics of Western Spiritualty (New York: Paulist Press, 1985), 4.

31. Pelikan, "Introduction," 4.

32. Hans Urs von Balthasar, *Cosmic Liturgy: The Universe According to Maximus the Confessor* (San Francisco: Ignatius Press, 1988), 71.

33. Pelikan, "Introduction," 7.

34. von Balthasar, *Cosmic Liturgy*, 257.

35. Maximus, *Opuscula*, PG 91, 77C, quoted in von Balthasar, *Cosmic Liturgy*, 257.

36. von Balthasar, *Cosmic Liturgy*, 257–58.

37. Ibid., 70.

38. Lars Thunberg, *Microcosm and Mediator* (Chicago: Open Court Pub Co, 1995), 19.

39. Thunberg, *Microcosm and Mediator*, 19.

40. J. Kameron Carter, *Race: A Theological Account* (New York: Oxford University Press), 364.

41. Maximus, *The Church's Mystagogy*, 24, Classics of Western Spirituality (CWS), 208.

42. Maximus, *CM 1*, CWS 187.

43. Ibid.

44. Ibid.

45. Maximus, *CM 4*, CWS 190.

46. Maximus, *CM 5*, CWS 190–91.

47. Carter, *Race: A Theological Account*, 349.

48. Maximus, *CM 3*, CWS 189.

49. Maximus, *CM 5*, CWS 191.

50. Ibid.

51. Ibid.

52. Maximus, *CM 5*, CWS 193.

53. Ibid.

54. Maximus, *CM 5*, CWS 195.

55. David Bosch, *Transforming Mission: Paradigm Shifts in Theology of Mission* (Maryknoll, NY: Orbis, 2005), 210.

56. Maximus, *CM 24*, CWS 211.

57. Bouyer, *Spirituality of Middle Ages*, vol. 2 of History of Christian Spirituality, 553.

Chapter 5

1. Niemier, *In the Steps of Francis and Clare*, 119. It is this transformation and vocation of transformation finally that suggests Clare's model can be fruitful for Baptist life as it recovers its contemplative orientation.

2. I believe Clare and the Franciscan tradition stand in the spiritual stream that flows through Baptist life even if that stream has almost run dry. Arguing that recovery of the contemplative spirit among Baptists is necessary for spiritual renewal, Baptist historian Glenn Hinson describes early Baptist forms of communal life as an inheritance of the contemplative monastic traditions of medieval Europe. I believe Hinson's claim would be stronger if it highlighted the Incarnation-focused spirituality of the Franciscans. Perhaps we Baptists have wandered quite far from this stream in our spirituality, and surely the contemplative tradition through four centuries of Baptist life has "taken some heavy hits." But recovery is still possible.

Hinson draws out the connections: "We had best hitch up our britches and wade back down our Baptist stream to where it meets the Puritan stream, then down the Puritan stream to where it meets the Anglican stream, then down the Anglican stream to where it meets the Catholic mainstream, and then down the Catholic mainstream to where it flows out of the Jewish spring we have come to know in and through Jesus of Nazareth." See E. Glenn Hinson, *Baptist Spirituality: A Call for Renewed Attentiveness to God* (Macon: Nurturing Faith, Inc., 2013), 62–63.

3. Clare D'Auria, "Stirrings of the Spirit," 13.

4. "Season of Creation Celebration Guide 2022," *Season of Creation*, https://seasonofcreation.org/wp-content/uploads/2022/06/SOC-2022-Celebration-Guide-Final-English.pdf.

5. Lathrop, *Holy Ground*, 125.

6. Richard Osmer, *The Teaching Ministry of Congregations* (Louisville: Westminster John Knox, 2005), 231.

7. Wallace Stegner, "Wilderness Letter," December 3, 1960, https://psych.utah.edu/_resources/documents/psych4130/Stenger_W.pdf.

8. "The Wilderness Act of 1964," https://winapps.umt.edu/winapps/media2/wilderness/NWPS/documents/publiclaws/The_Wilderness_Act.pdf.

9. Drawing on Stegner's insights about the idea of wilderness, Christopher Thompson offers a robust case for recovery of a Thomistic account of the natural world. Such recovery would be anchored in the tri-fold vocations of contemplation, conservation, and cultivation. See Christopher Thompson, "The Place of Faith in the Geography of Hope," in *On Earth as It Is in Heaven*, ed. David Vincent Meconi, SJ (Grand Rapids: Eerdmans, 2016), 27–36. My suspicion is that Thompson stretches Stegner's argument so far beyond Stegner's spiritual sensibility that Stegner would have balked. Consider Thompson's exalted comparison of Cyrus's rebuilding of Jerusalem to the Johnson Administration's passage of the Wilderness Act: "The foundations were laid for the building of a new Jerusalem, a Catholic culture that can be built only upon the pillars of the earth, can be built only from the ground up" (28). I think it is better to receive Stegner on his own terms: as the "Dean of Western writers" offering the very best of a distinctly, and perhaps uniquely, American spirituality of wilderness. And let Christians applaud the Johnson Administration without beatifying it.

10. See David Gelles, "The Texas Group Waging a National Crusade against Climate Action," *New York Times*, December 4, 2022, https://www.nytimes.com/2022/12/04/climate/texas-public-policy-foundation-climate-change.html.

11. Ibid.

12. Ibid.

13. Ibid.

14. In one example, the TPPF produced a video to try to stop the closure of the Navajo Generating Station near Page, Arizona. The plant burned coal from

Peabody Energy, a donor to TPPF. In the video, TPPF argues that the coal plant not only has practical benefits for the Navajo people but is also an integral part of their culture: "Coal-based energy provides the Navajo Nation with jobs, dignity, and hope. Out of state billionaires and environmental extremists want to shut it all down." Notable is the framing of the coal-burning power plant in terms of the cultural and spiritual heritage of the Navajo. TPPF understands that energy is a cultural touchstone as much as a practical means to an end. To see the video, "Life: Powered—Navajo Nation," *Texas Public Policy Foundation*, go to https://www.youtube.com/watch?v=E5GaHpMvCNY&t=9s.

15. "TPPF Sues Biden Administration to Rescind Endangerment Finding," *Texas Public Policy Foundation*, April 22, 2021, www.texaspolicy.com/press/tppf-sues-biden-administration-to-rescind-endangerment-finding.

16. Gelles, "Texas Group."

17. Frozen natural gas pipes, not frozen wind turbines, contributed the most to the disastrous electric-grid failure. See Dionne Searcey, "No, Wind Farms Aren't the Main Cause of the Texas Blackouts," *New York Times*, May 3, 2021, https://www.nytimes.com/2021/02/17/climate/texas-blackouts-disinformation.html.

18. The TPPF's argument for fossil fuels is interwoven with the John Bellamy Foster's image of the Capitalistic Growth Machine and fulfills the elements of its logic: (1) increasing accumulation of wealth by a relatively small section of the population, (2) long-term movement of workers away from self-employment into wage jobs contingent on the continual expansion of production, (3) expansion of technologies for businesses to avoid extinction, (4) wants manufactured to create hunger for more, and (5) government policy designed to promote national economic development. Then there is the sixth element: "The dominant means of communication and education are part of the treadmill, serving to reinforce its priorities and values." The mission of TPPF serves this sixth element most directly.

19. See Emily Grubert, "Designing the mid-transition: A review of medium-term challenges for coordinated decarbonization in the United States," *Wires Climate Change* 13/3 (May/June 2022).

20. Wendell Berry, *The Hidden Wound* (New York: North Point Press, 1989), 62.

21. See Hayhoe, *Saving Us*.

22. The organization Interfaith Power and Light, for example, tells stories of congregations taking creative steps to reduce their carbon footprint. See the Cool Congregations website: https://interfaithpowerandlight.org/coolcongregations/.

23. Osmer, *Practical Theology*, 177. In many leadership theories, congregational leadership is expressed through the basic task competence of the leader (teaching, preaching, running committees, etc.) and through transactional leadership, in which various interests represented in a congregation are navigated and managed. Beyond these, the highest form of leadership involves "deep change."

24. I am drawing here on the chapter "The Incarnational Tradition: Discovering the Sacramental Life" in Richard Foster, *Streams of Living Water: Celebrating the*

Great Traditions of the Christian Faith (San Francisco: Harper Collins, 1989), 235–72. Paul Santmire describes this as the shift from a Metaphor of Ascent to a Metaphor of Migration to a Good Land (Santmire, *Travail of Nature*, 25–31).

25. The impact of the Covid-19 pandemic on congregational spirituality deserves attention here. From March 2020 to September 2022, our congregation almost totally abandoned our indoor sanctuary for worship. Many Sundays offered online-only worship services. However, soon into the pandemic, we also began meeting in person on our grounds, under the shade in a grove of live oak trees. Dubbed "The Cathedral of the Oaks," that space manifested our dependence on the grounds for our church's life. When the weather was not too hot or too cold, we met under the oaks. Meanwhile, in concert with pandemic caution, we paused celebrating Communion. Returning to weekly celebration of Communion became, for many, the enduring gift of post-pandemic life.

26. The hope of this project, and the issues addressed in our observance of the Season of Creation, extend beyond the boundaries of the property we own. In a different congregation with a different history or a politics suspicious of ecological concerns, the challenges could be significantly more daunting and would need to be addressed in ways appropriate to the challenges of local contexts. With an eye toward a potentially wider audience of Baptist and evangelical Christians, for whom an embrace of creation care may require a more significant change in priorities and attitudes, I recognize that fully forming a strategy for tackling hyper-resistant congregations is somewhat beyond the scope of this project.

27. We may be concerned about the diminishing polar bear habitat in the Antarctic, melting glaciers in Glacier National Park, or the future of the Everglades, but by and large, direct involvement by ordinary people in these renowned geographies is minimal and transitory. This is by design. Parks are designated lands in which humans have no permanent residence and for which governmental agencies bear direct managerial authority. Besides all of this, in practical terms, Central Texans are a long distance from any national parks, but we have churches on every corner. There we discover a habitat for our habitus.

28. This dichotomy particularly plagues conservation movements. I echo conservationists in the desire to set aside more land as federally designated wilderness. Wallace Stegner's "Wilderness Letter" powerfully embraces the notion of wilderness, even if we "only drive to its edge and look in" (see Stegner, "Wilderness Letter"). However, if our only strategy is to set aside land free of human intrusion, left unanswered is the obvious question: how are humans to live on the land where they actually reside? Ultimately, it cannot be sufficient either to our spirituality or our creation care to set aside some portion of land where humans have no lasting presence without reforming how we operate on the land and in the spaces where we live and incrementally destroy the environment. See O. I. Ollinaho, "Environmental Destruction as (objectively) uneventful and (subjectively) irrelevant," *Environmental Sociology* 2/1 (2016): 53–63.

29. In Baptist polity, the grounds are the sole property of the local congregation. In other denominational traditions, proprietorship of the grounds may belong to a governing body beyond the local congregation. Baptist polity emphasizes the autonomy of the local church.

30. I regard this feature of church grounds both as a strength and a potential weakness as an "ordinary" place. It is a strength insofar as the grounds are exempted from profit-generating pressures and therefore more readily available for experimentation and patience over against other private sector pressures. It is a weakness, however, insofar as collective care for the grounds may become yet another way to avoid critical analysis of and transformative practices in the ordinary "income-getting" activities of individual church members. See Ossi Ollinaho and V. P. J. Arponen, "Income Getting and Environmental Degradation," Sustainability 12/10 (2020). See https://doi.org/10.3390/su12104007.

31. Margaret Visser, *The Geometry of Love: Space, Time, Mystery, and Meaning in an Ordinary Church* (New York: North Point Press, 2000), 11–12.

32. Francis, *Laudato Si'*, 139.

33. See Radu Bordeianu, "Maximus and Ecology: The Relevance of Maximus the Confessor's Theology of Creation for the Present Ecological Crisis," *The Downside Review* 127 (2009): 103–26.

34. George Berthold, trans., "The Church's Mystagogy," in *Maximus the Confessor: Selected Writings*, Classics of Western Spiritualty (New York: Paulist Press, 1985), 181–22.

35. The witness of the historic church forests of Ethiopia supports the argument that the area around the church has intense theological significance, a mystagogy integrating the outside and inside worlds. Jeremy Seifert writes, "In Egyptian Orthodox teaching, a church, to be a church, should be enveloped by a forest. It should resemble the Garden of Eden. . . . the church is inside the forest; the forest is inside the church" ("The Church Forests of Ethiopia," *Emergence Magazine*, February 7, 2020, https://www.youtube.com/watch?v=8fGe-CPWZlE). See also the essay by Fred Bahnson, "The Church Forests of Ethiopia: A Mystical Geography," *Emergence Magazine*, January 11, 2020, https://emergencemagazine.org/feature/the-church-forests-of-ethiopia/.

36. Gerard Manly Hopkins, "God's Grandeur," *Poetry Foundation*, https://www.poetryfoundation.org/poems/44395/gods-grandeur.

37. Norman Wirzba, *Food and Faith: A Theology of Eating* (New York: Cambridge University Press, 2011), 4.

38. See Baylor Collaborative on Hunger and Poverty, "A Brief History," https://hungerandpoverty.web.baylor.edu/about/our-approach.

39. See World Hunger Relief Institute, www.worldhungerrelief.org.

40. Following plans made available to us by local organization Urban Reap, each bin is redwood framed, with mesh wire, 3 ft. x 3 ft. x 3 ft. To learn more about Urban Reap, see https://missionwaco.org/urban-reap/.

41. US Environmental Protection Agency, "Food: Material-Specific Data," https://www.epa.gov/facts-and-figures-about-materials-waste-and-recycling/food-material-specific-data.

42. See Clare Toeniskoetter, "Food Waste Solutions," *New York Times Climate Forward Newsletter*, October 14, 2022, https://www.nytimes.com/2022/10/14/climate/food-waste-solutions.html.

43. Balaji Aglave, Rachel Caldwell Hill, Eric Howell, Jenny Howell, and Matthew Whelan, "Growing Green Communities," *Green Communities Conference*, Waco, TX, September 14, 2022, https://greencommunities2022.sched.com/.

44. Connections between Communion and a community's care for creation are demonstrated in Gordon Lathrop's chapter, "Eucharist and Earth Care," in *Holy Ground*, 125–52.

45. See more at Bosco di San Francesco, https://fondoambiente.it/luoghi/bosco-di-san-francesco.

46. See Texans on Mission, https://www.tbmtx.org/disaster-relief.

47. "Ecological Threat Register," *Institute for Economics and Peace*, September 9, 2020, https://www.economicsandpeace.org/wp-content/uploads/2020/09/Ecological-Threat-Register-Press-Release-27.08-FINAL.pdf.

48. Fred Bahnson, "Field, Table, Communion: The Abundant Kingdom versus the Abundant Mirage," in *Making Peace with the Land: God's Call to Reconcile with Creation*, ed. Fred Bahnson and Norman Wirzba (Downer's Grove, IL: IVP, 2012), 91.

Chapter 6

1. Wendell Berry, "How to Be a Poet (to remind myself)," *Poetry Foundation*, https://www.poetryfoundation.org/poetrymagazine/poems/41087/how-to-be-a-poet.

2. See Kathryn Yussoff, *A Billion Black Anthropocenes or None* (Minneapolis: University of Minnesota Press, 2018). Also see Baucom, *History 4° Celsius*.

3. Psalm 19:3-4. Psalm 19 has often been interpreted as presenting two books of revelation: creation and Scripture.

4. Lathrop, *Holy Ground*, 125.

5. Brian Walsh, "Sacred Space, Desecration, and Reconciliation: A Story and Some Theses," *The Other Journal* 33, https://theotherjournal.com/2022/03/sacred-space-theses/#easy-footnote-5-12419.

6. Wendell Berry, "How to Be a Poet."

7. Philip Sheldrake, *Spaces for the Sacred: Place, Memory, and Identity* (London: SCM, 2001), 168.

8. Makoto Fujimora, *Culture Care* (Downers Grove, IL: IVP Books, 2017), 15–17. In this book, Fujimura's argument flows the other direction, drawing on the principles of creation care to develop a framework of culture care.

9. Howard A. Snyder, "Creation Care and the Mission of God" (Biblical-theological keynote presentation, CT-NAE-EEN Conference on Creation-Care, 2004), quoted by Lawrence Prelli and Terri Winters, "Rhetorical Features of Green Evangelicalism," *Environmental Communication* 3/2 (July 2009): 236.

10. Prelli and Winters, "Rhetorical Features of Green Evangelicalism," 232.

11. Quoted in Wilkinson, *Between God and Green*, 150.

12. Wilkinson, *Between God and Green*, 151.

13. Howard Snyder, *Salvation Means Creation Healed: The Ecology of Sin and Grace* (Eugene, OR: Wipf and Stock Publishers, 2011).

14. Snyder, *Salvation*, xvi.

15. To be sure, such a systematic endeavor is far beyond the scope of this project. Yet, when church members begin engaging their church grounds, they begin seeing God and themselves in God's world in new ways.

16. Snyder, *Salvation*, xiii. Emphasis original.

17. As a foremost example, in *Laudato Si*, Pope Francis's 2016 encyclical "on care for our common home," integral ecology drew on the same wide concept of ecology as the name for the web relationships between all things—our relationship with God, sociocultural relationships, and relationship with the other creatures and the metabolic processes that regulate those relationships.

18. Belden Lane, *The Solace of Fierce Landscapes* (New York: Oxford University Press, 1998), 17.

19. Snyder, *Salvation*, xiii.

20. Recent eco-psychology studies show the health benefits that come from touching dirt. See Carrie Dennett, "Could Walking Barefoot on Grass Improve Your Health? Some Research Suggests It Can," *Washington Post*, July 10, 2018, https://www.washingtonpost.com/lifestyle/wellness/could-walking-barefoot-on-the-grass-improve-your-health-the-science-behind-grounding/2018/07/05/12d-e5d64-7be2-11e8-aeee-4d04c8ac6158_story.html. Also see Georgia Kinch, "Body-Earthing," *The Psychology of Extraordinary Beliefs*, April 18, 2018, https://u.osu.edu/vanzandt/2018/04/18/body-earthing/. I must emphasize here that while the psychological benefits point to a deep wisdom about human connection with the earth, I am not merely advocating reconnection for mental health benefits. Rather, I am asking how a recovered connection with the earth makes more likely a holistic ecological conversion.

21. In many cultures, removing shoes is a sign of respect, though there is no other biblical precedent or antecedent for this sign.

22. "The Woods of San Francesco, a paradise on earth," *Cuore verde d'Italia*, accessed January 30, 2023, https://www.umbriatourism.it/en/-/il-bosco-di-san-francesco-en.

23. Shari Finnell, "Church's Money Management Lessons Lead to Transformation in an Impoverished Neighborhood," *Faith and Leadership*, October 15, 2019, https://faithandleadership.com/churchs-money-management-lessons-lead-transformation-impoverished-neighborhood.

24. Article VI of the 1963 Baptist Faith and Message addresses the meaning of church: "A New Testament church of the Lord Jesus Christ is a local body of baptized believers who are associated by covenant in the faith and fellowship of the gospel, observing the two ordinances of Christ, committed to His teachings, exercising the gifts, rights, and privileges invested in them by His Word, and seeking to extend the gospel to the ends of the earth. This church is an autonomous body, operating through democratic processes under the Lordship of Jesus Christ. In such a congregation, members are equally responsible. Its Scriptural officers are pastors and deacons. The New Testament speaks also of the church as the body of Christ which includes all of the redeemed of all the ages." See "The Baptist Faith and Message (1963)," accessed December 19, 2022, http://www.midwaybc.net/wp-content/uploads/2020/01/baptist-faith-message-1963.pdf.

25. Fujimora, *Culture Care*, 58.

26. Mark Labberton, foreword to Makoto Fujimora, *Culture Care*, 9–11.

27. Berry, *The Hidden Wound*, 89.

28. Markey, *Moses*, 77.

29. Ibid., 84. Changes encompassed in such conversion would include integration of the new orientation into the whole person or community, reshaping and reforming of other aspects of the personality, development of new habits, virtues, and values, and eventually a conflict with the culture's dominant/conventional ethos.

30. Ibid., 85.

31. Francis, *Laudato Si*, 142–43.

Epilogue

1. Gerard Manly Hopkins, "God's Grandeur," *Poetry Foundation*, https://www.poetryfoundation.org/poems/44395/gods-grandeur.

www.ingramcontent.com/pod-product-compliance
Lightning Source LLC
Chambersburg PA
CBHW071002160426
43193CB00012B/1889